EX LIBRIS
UNIVERSITATIS SANCTI JOANNIS

Directory of Orthodox Parishes & Institutions
1994 Edition

This 1994 edition is dedicated to the Mission to Alaska in September, 1794, exactly 200 years ago, which presented the Holy *Orthodox* Catholic and Apostolic Church to the North American Continent.

DIRECTORY OF ORTHODOX PARISHES & INSTITUTIONS IN NORTH AMERICA
1994 EDITION

ORTHODOX PEOPLE TOGETHER

Directory Offices:
P.O. Box 1128
Torrance, California 90505-0128
(310) 378-9245

Further Dedicated to All Those Persons,
Hierarchs, Clergy & Friends, Who
Cooperated in the Publication of
This Bicentennial-Year Edition
MANY YEARS!! (The Editor)

Published by: Oakwood Publications
for
ORTHODOX PEOPLE TOGETHER
ISBN No. 1-879038-16-1

Editor: Philip Tamoush
Directory Layout: David Wright
Advertisers Layout: Philip Tamoush
Distributors: Oakwood Publications
Graphics: Orthodox Information Data Associates
IconoGraphics Electronic Byzantine Art Collection
by TheoLogic Systems

Contents

Introduction

With the publication of this 1994 edition, ORTHODOX PEOPLE TOGETHER, a network of Orthodox Christians dedicated to United Witness in North America, continues its themes of assisting in the "discovering, communicating, and connecting the needs, resources, projects, and services of Orthodox faithful and their communities" (from the descriptive brochure of OPT).

OPT Projects

Ongoing projects which OPT supports or assists include: Paper Icon Project; Orthodox Christian Prayer Network; International Orthodox Christian Charities (IOCC); OPT Newsletter; United Lay Ministries; Local Inter-Orthodox Groups; A.C.O.R.N. (Orthodox Radio Network); Prison Ministries; Local Social Service groups; OCCNET (Computer Bulletin Board); other activities. Contact OPT National Offices for a descriptive brochure or more detailed information.

OPT Officers

North American Coordinator
Rhea Ballas
10124 Oxford Dr. N.W.
Pickerington, OH 43147
USA
614-863-9900 Voice/FAX

Assistant Coordinator
Fr. John Tkachuk
4381 Harvard Ave.
Montreal, PQ H4A 2W9
Canada
514-481-5093 Voice/FAX

Secretary/Treasurer
Fr. Dn. Brian Nassar
8 Cunningham Rd.
Dedham, MA 02026
USA
617-329-0009

Spiritual Adviser
Bishop MAXIMOS
5201 Ellsworth Ave.
Pittsburgh, PA 15232
USA
412-621-5529

Introduction - Jurisdictions and Canonicity

OPT News Editor
George Bedrin
Box 35
Grand Isle, VT 05458 USA
802-372-4361 Voice
802-372-5986 FAX

As Orthodoxy continues forward as a vitalized and significant movement in North America, suggestions for additional reference documents include:

- Orthodox White Pages & Yellow Pages (listing ALL Orthodox Christians and Advertisers)
- Register of Orthodox Shrines and Important Sites
- Directory of Oriental Orthodox Jurisdictions and Parishes
- Directory of Orthodox Publishers
- Directory of Orthodox Entertainers

Ideas about other related projects are welcome.

Jurisdictions

The Directory is generally current through mid-1994. Since there are so many groups identifying themselves as "Orthodox" or "Eastern Orthodox" today, it was felt that it would be more practical and make the Directory more useable and valuable if those jurisdictions whose hierarchs are members of the STANDING CONFERENCE OF CANONICAL ORTHODOX BISHOPS IN THE AMERICAS (SCOBA) were separated out. SCOBA is a Federation of Eastern Orthodox hierarchs who recognize one another's canonical status. By no means does this separation indicate any attempt on the part of OPT to indicate the 'canonicity' or 'non-canonicity' of any hierarch or jurisdiction listed herein. Rather, this directory includes all those jurisdictions which lay claim to or are known by the designation 'Eastern Orthodox' and generally conform to the norms of the Orthodox Church.

Jurisdictions regarded as part of the 'Oriental' Orthodox churches (e.g. the Armenian, Coptic, Ethiopian, Indian, and Syrian churches) are not included, since the significant unity discussions and dialogue of recent years have yet to produce a clear and definitive statement regarding the restoration of communion between these two groups.

Neither does inclusion in this directory mean that all the jurisdictions listed are in communion with one another, or that members of one are free to receive the Sacraments in all others. Should the reader happen to visit another parish, it is strongly urged, especially as a matter of courtesy, to contact the local priest about the desire to receive Sacraments, especially Holy Communion.

Calendar

Many jurisdictions and individual parishes included here worship according to the Julian (Old) Calendar). In the section entitled "Jurisdictions included in this Directory", these are indicated by the designation "J" following the jurisdictional code, whereas those which have adopted the Gregorian (New) Calendar are indicated by "G". In addition, some jurisdictions permit the use of both calendars - these are indicated by "J/G" or "G/J", the first letter indicating which calendar is used by the majority of parishes within that jurisdiction. In the event of questions concerning the calendar usage in any particular parish, contact the local priest.

Because many readers will be using this directory in their travels and will wish to know what day is being commemorated or to attend special services in any particular parish, one should note the simple way to translate between the two calendars. The basic difference is that the Gregorian (New) Calendar is thirteen days ahead of the Julian (Old). Thus, to determine the Julian date one must subtract thirteen days from the Gregorian date. Conversely, if the Julian date is known, add thirteen days to find the Gregorian date.

For example, Old Calendar Christmas is celebrated on January 7 (December 25 plus 13 days). Subtracting 13 days from January 14 on the New Calendar would get January 1, St. Basil's day, January 1 on the Old Calendar.

Jurisdictions affiliated with the Standing Conference of Canonical Orthodox Bishops in the Americas

SCOBA Headquarters
10 E. 79th St.
New York, NY 10022 USA

Officers

Archbishop IAKOVOS - Chairman
Metropolitan PHILIP - Vice Chairman
Metropolitan JOSEPH - General Secretary
Bishop NICHOLAS - Treasurer
Archbishop PETER - Canonical Advisor
Father Milton Efthimiou - Coordinator

Member Jurisdictions

Albanian Orthodox Diocese of America ADA G
6455 Silver Dawn Ln.
Las Vegas, NV 89118 USA
702-221-8245
Fr. Ilia Katre

American Carpatho-Russian Orthodox Greek Catholic Diocese of the U.S.A. CRC G/J
312 Garfield St.
Johnstown, PA 15906 USA
814-539-9143
Bishop Nicholas

Antiochian Orthodox Archdiocese of North America ANT G
358 Mountain Rd.
Englewood, NJ 07631 USA
201-871-1355
Metropolitan Philip

Jurisdictions included in this Directory

Bulgarian Eastern Orthodox Church BEC G

550A W. 50th St.
New York City, NY 10019 USA
212-581-3756

Greek Orthodox Archdiocese of North and South America GOA G/J

10 E. 79th St.
New York City, NY 10021 USA
212-570-3500
Archbishop Iakovos

Orthodox Church in America OCA G/J

P.O. Box 675
Syosset, NY 11791 USA
516-922-0550
Metropolitan Theodosius

Romanian Orthodox Archdiocese in America RMA G

19959 Riopelle St.
Detroit, MI 48203 USA
718-784-4453, 313-893-8390
Archbishop Victorin

Serbian Orthodox Church in the United States and Canada SOC J

P.O. Box 519
Libertyville, IL 60048 USA
312-362-2440
Metropolitan Christopher

Serbian Orthodox New Gracanica Metropolitanate, Diocese of America & Canada NGM J

P.O. Box 371
Grayslake, IL 60030-0371 USA
708-223-4300, FAX 708-223-4312
Metropolitan Ireney

- Since the restoration of communion between the New Gracanica Metropolitanate and the Patriarchate of Serbia, this jurisdiction is represented on SCOBA by the Serbian Orthodox Church in the United States and Canada.

Ukrainian Orthodox Church of America & Canada UOA G/J

90-34 139th St.
Jamaica, NY 11435 USA
718-297-2407
Bishop Vsevolod

Ukrainian Orthodox Church of Canada UOC J

5 St. John's Ave.
Winnipeg, MB R2W 1G8 CANADA
Metropolitan Vasily

Jurisdictions which are not affiliated with SCOBA

Antiochian Orthodox Patriarchal Vicariate of Mexico & the Carribean Islands AMC G

Pirules 110, Jardinas del Pedregal de San Andres
Mexico City, ZP 01900 MEXICO
525-652-7772
Bishop Antonio

Byelorussian Autocephalic Orthodox Church (Archbishop Iziaslav) BAI J

401 Atlantic Ave.
Brooklyn, NY 11217-1702 USA
908-560-0058
Archbishop Iziaslav

Byelorussian Autocephalic Orthodox Church (Archbishop Mikalay) BAM J

524 St. Clarens Ave.
Toronto, ON M6H 3W7 CANADA
Archbishop Mikalay

Byelorussian Council of Orthodox Churches in North America BYC J

P.O. Box 26
South River, NJ 08882 USA
908-254-6267
Fr. Sviatoslaw Kous

Chasnoverian Union of Old Orthodox CHU J

Jurisdictions included in this Directory

Eastern Orthodox Diocese of Houston & All Texas HUS J

3011 Roe Dr.
Houston, TX 77087-2409 USA
713-645-0843
Bishop Makarios

Greek Orthodox Metropolis of Canada GOC J

1474 Jarry St.
Chamedy, PQ H2E 1A7 CANADA
Metropolitan Akakios

Greek Orthodox Metropolis of North & South America GMA J

36-07 23rd Ave.
Astoria, NY 11105 USA
Bishop Paisios

Hellenic Orthodox Traditionalist Church of America CHR J

22-68 26th St.
Astoria, NY 11105 USA
718-932-1592, 718-274-5579
Bishop Petros

Holy Orthodox Archdiocese of Vasiloupolis & Missionary Eparchy of America VAS G/J

44-02 48th Ave.
Woodside, NY 11377-6344 USA
718-786-4495, FAX 718-786-7887
Metropolitan Pangratios

Holy Orthodox Church in North America (Metropolitan Auxentios) AUX J

850 South St.
Roslindale, MA 02130 USA
Bishop Ephraim

Holy Orthodox Church, American Jursidiction HOC G

355 Tusculum Rd.
Nashville, TN 37211 USA
615-834-1938, 615-833-9564
Metropolitan Francis

Jurisdictions included in this Directory

Holy Orthodox Synod for Diaspora & Hellas, Eparchy of Lincoln DHE J

740 S. 11th St., P.O. Box 22237
Lincoln, NE 68542-2237 USA
402-475-6492
Bishop Melchizedek

Macedonian Orthodox Church of North America MOC J

Ft. Wayne, IN USA
Bishop Stefan

Old Ritualist Metropolia of Moscow & All Russia MAR J

Moscow, Russia
Metropolitan Alympy

Orthodox Church in the Carribean (under AMC) OCC G

LYNX Air, P.O. Box 407139
Ft. Lauderdale, FL 33340
USA
509-57-48-05, FAX 509-57-06-72

Orthodox Fellowship of St. Germanus of Paris (St. Germaine) SGP G

P.O. Box 704
Baraboo, WI 53913-0704 USA
608-356-2808

Orthodox Old Ritualists of the Metropolia of Romania (Metropolitan Timofei) MOR J

Archbishop Iosif

Patriarchal Parishes of the Russian Orthodox Church in Canada PCN J

10812 108th St.
Edmonton, AB T5H 3A6 Canada
Bishop George

Patriarchal Parishes of the Russian Orthodox Church in the United States PER J/G

15 E. 97th St.
New York City, NY 10029 USA
212-289-1915, 212-831-6294, FAX 212-427-5003
Bishop Paul

Jurisdictions included in this Directory

Russian Orthodox Church (Moscow Patriarchate) PRC J

Cistyj Pereulok 5
Moskva 119034 Russia
7-095-201-3416, 7-095-201-2504
Patriarch Alexey II

Russian Orthodox Church Outside of Russia ROR J

75 E. 93rd St.
New York City, NY 10028 USA
212-534-1601
Metropolitan Vitaly

True (Old Calendar) Orthodox Church of Greece (Archbishop Andreas) MAT J

60 Mott St.
New Bedford, MA 02744 USA
Archbishop Andreas

True (Old Calendar) Orthodox Church of Greece (Metropolitan Cyprian) CYP J

P.O. Box 398
Etna, CA 96027-0398 USA
Bishop Chrysostomos

Ukrainian Autocephalous Orthodox Church in the U.S.A. UIU J/G

3107 Bailey Ave.
Bronx, NY 10463 USA
Metropolitan Alexis

Ukrainian Autocephalous Orthodox Church of the U.S.A. UOD J

5130 Prescott St.
Detroit, MI 48212 USA
Archbishop Isiaslav

Ukrainian Orthodox Church of the U.S.A. UCU J

P.O. Box 495
South Bound Brook, NJ 08880 USA
908-356-0090, FAX 908-356-5556
Metropolitan Constantine

Parishes and Missions

Parishes and Missions in SCOBA Jurisdictions

Parishes and Missions in the United States of America

Alabama

Birmingham AL 35233-1951
Holy Trinity / Holy Cross Cathedral GOA
307 19th St. S.
205-716-3080
FAX 205-716-3085

Birmingham AL 35205
St. Symeon the New Theologian OCA
3101 Clairmont Ave.
205-930-9681

Daleville AL
Orthodox Christian Mission ANT

Daphne AL 36526-8568
Presentation of the Virgin Mary GOA
9865 Hwy. 90

Huntsville AL 35816-3133
Holy Cross-Ss. Constantine & Helen GOA
3021 University Dr.
205-534-4221
FAX 205-534-4206

Mobile AL 36604-2131
Annunciation GOA
50 S. Ann St.
205-438-9888
FAX 205-438-9889

Montgomery AL 36107
Annunciation GOA
1721 Mt. Meigs Rd.
205-263-1366

Tuscaloosa AL
St. Gregory the Theologian OCA
205-674-8644

Alaska

Akhiok AK 99615
Protection of the Theotokos OCA
General Delivery

Akutan AK 99553
St. Alexander Nevsky OCA
General Delivery

Aleknagik AK 99555
Holy Resurrection OCA
General Delivery

Anchorage AK 99516
Holy Transfiguration GOA
2800 O'Malley Rd.
907-344-0190

Anchorage AK 99503-2055
Holy Trinity Chapel/ Patriarch Tikhon Diocesan Center OCA
513 E. 24th St. #6
907-272-6468

Anchorage AK 99504
St. Innocent Cathedral OCA
6724 E. 4th Ave.
907-333-7116, FAX 907-338-3910

Angoon AK 99820
St. John the Baptist OCA
P.O. Box 132
907-586-1179

Aniak AK 99557-0201
Protection of the Theotokos OCA
P.O. Box 201

Atka AK 99502
St. Nicholas OCA
General Delivery
907-839-2204

Atmartluaq AK 99557
St. Herman of Alaska OCA
General Delivery

Belkofsky AK 99559
Holy Resurrection OCA
General Delivery

Bethel AK 99621
St. Sophia OCA
P.O. Box 56
907-543-5919

Branch River AK 99625
St. Innocent of Irkutsk OCA
General Delivery

Chenega Bay AK 99574
Nativity of the Theotokos OCA
General Delivery

Chignik Lake AK 99548
St. Nicholas OCA
General Delivery
907-845-2222

Chignik Village AK 99565
Chignik Lagoon Mission OCA
General Delivery
907-845-2222

Choathbaluk via Aniak AK 99557
St. Sergius OCA

Clarks Point AK 99569
Orthodox Community OCA
General Delivery

Cordova AK 99574
St. Michael the Archangel OCA
General Delivery
907-424-7450

Crooked Creek AK 99575
St. Nicholas OCA
General Delivery

Dillingham AK 99576 MAIL
St. Nicholas OCA
<Ekuk AK>
P.O. Box 533

Dillingham AK 99576
St. Seraphim of Sarov OCA
P.O. Box 190
907-842-5470

Eagle River AK 99577
St. John Cathedral ANT
18936 Monastery Dr.
P.O. Box 771108
907-696-2002, FAX 907-696-5555

Eek AK 99578
St. Michael the Archangel OCA
General Delivery
907-543-2004

Egegik AK 99579
Transfiguration of Our Lord OCA
General Delivery

Eklutna-Chugiak AK 99567-1035
St. Nicholas OCA
P.O. Box 671035
907-522-2397

Ekuk AK 99576
St. Nicholas OCA

Ekwok AK 99580
St. John OCA
General Delivery

English Bay AK 99603
Ss. Sergius & Herman of Valaam OCA
General Delivery
907-235-8292

Fairbanks AK 99708
St. Herman OCA
2180 Goldstream Rd.
P.O. Box 80971
907-455-6099

False Pass AK 99583
St. Nicholas OCA
General Delivery

Hoonah AK 99829-0453
St. Nicholas OCA
P.O. Box 453

Iglugig AK 99613
St. Nicholas OCA
General Delivery
907-571-1209

Juneau AK 99802
St. Nicholas OCA
326 N. 5th St.
P.O. Box 20130
907-586-1023

Kakhonak AK 99695
Ss. Peter & Paul OCA
General Delivery
907-571-1209

Karluk AK 99608
Ascension of Our Lord OCA
General Delivery

Kasigluk AK 99609
Holy Trinity OCA
General Delivery
907-477-6528

Kenai AK 99611
Holy Assumption OCA
1106 Mission Ave.
P.O. Box 1227
907-283-4122

Ketchikan AK 99901-2015
Ketchikan Orthodox Community OCA
437 Langor Rd.
P.O. Box 7015
907-225-6802, FAX 907-225-8850

King Cove AK 99612
St. Herman OCA
General Delivery

Kodiak AK 99615
Ascension of Our Lord OCA
414 Mission Rd.

Kodiak AK 99615
Holy Resurrection OCA
410 Mission Road
P.O. Box 55
907-486-3854

Koliganek AK 99576
St. Michael the Archangel OCA
Box 5051
907-596-3446

Kongiganak AK 99559
St. Gabriel OCA
General Delivery

Kwethluk AK 99621
St. Nicholas OCA
P.O. Box 56
907-757-6514

Kwethluk AK 99621 MAIL
St. Sophia OCA
<Bethel AK>
P.O. Box 56
907-757-6514

Kwigillingok AK 99622
St. Michael OCA
General Delivery

Larsen Bay AK 99624
St. Herman OCA
General Delivery

Levelock AK 99625
Protection of the Virgin Mary OCA
General Delivery

Lime Village AK 99668
Ss. Constantine & Helen OCA
General Delivery

Lower Kalskag AK 99626
St. Seraphim OCA
General Delivery

Marshall AK 99585
St. Michael OCA
General Delivery
907-549-3827

Mountain Village AK 99632
St. Peter the Aleut OCA
P.O. Box 139

Naknek AK 99633
St. John the Baptist OCA
P.O. Box 285

Napaskiak AK 99559
St. Jacob OCA
General Delivery
907-737-7615

New Halen AK 99606
Transfiguration of Our Lord OCA
P.O. Box 225
907-571-1209

New Stuyahok AK 99636
St. Sergius OCA
General Delivery
907-693-3161

Nikolai AK 99691
St. Nicholas OCA
General Delivery

Nikolski AK 99638
St. Nicholas OCA
Box 100
907-576-2206

Ninilchik AK 99369
Transfiguration of Our Lord OCA
P.O. Box 53

Nondalton AK 99640
St. Nicholas OCA
General Delivery
907-294-2202

Nunapitchuk AK 99641
Holy Trinity OCA
P.O. Box 57

Old Harbor AK 99643
Three Saints OCA
Box 149
907-286-2294

Ouzinkie AK 99644
Nativity of Our Lord OCA
P.O. Box 62
907-486-5800 (Village Phone)

Pedro Bay AK 99647
St. Nicholas OCA
General Delivery

Perryville AK 99648
St. John the Theologian
OCA
P.O. Box 98
907-845-2222

Pilot Point AK 99649
St. Nicholas OCA
General Delivery
907-845-2222

Pilot Station AK 99650 MAIL
Ss. Peter & Paul OCA
<Pitka's Point AK>
P.O. Box 10

Pilot Station AK 99650
Transfiguration of Our Lord
OCA
P.O. Box 10
907-549-3827

Pitka's Point AK
Ss. Peter & Paul OCA
907-438-2647

Port Graham AK 99603-8998
St. Herman of Alaska OCA
General Delivery
907-235-8088

Port Heiden AK 99549
St. Agaphia OCA
General Delivery
907-845-2222

Port Lions AK 99550
Nativity of the Theotokos
OCA
General Delivery

Portage Creek AK 99576
St. Basil OCA
General Delivery

Russian Mission AK 99657 MAIL
Stony River Orthodox
Community OCA
<Stony River AK>
P.O. Box 70

Russian Mission - Yukon River AK 99657
Elevation of the Holy Cross
OCA
P.O. Box 70
907-584-5113

Sand Point AK 99661
St. Nicholas OCA
P.O. Box 149

Seldovia AK 99663
St. Nicholas OCA
General Delivery

Sitka AK 99835
Annunciation to the
Theotokos OCA
503 Lincoln St.
P.O. Box 697

Sitka AK 99835
St. Michael Cathedral OCA
503 Lincoln St.
P.O. Box 697
907-747-3340

Sleetmute AK 99668
Ss. Peter & Paul OCA
General Delivery

South Naknek AK 99670
Elevation of the Holy Cross
OCA
General Delivery

St. George Island AK 99660
St. George OCA
General Delivery
907-546-2324

St. Michael AK 99659
Orthodox Community OCA
General Delivery

St. Paul Island AK 99660
Ss. Peter & Paul OCA
P.O. Box 46
907-546-2324

Stony River AK
Stony River Orthodox
Community OCA

Tatitlek AK 99677
St. Nicholas OCA
General Delivery

Telida AK 99691
St. Basil OCA
General Delivery

Tuntutuliak AK 99680
St. Agaphia OCA
General Delivery

Tyonek AK 99682
St. Nicholas OCA
P.O. Box 82044

Unalaska AK 99685
Holy Ascension of Our Lord Cathedral OCA
P.O. Box 145
907-581-1667

Valdez AK 99686
St. Nicholas Community OCA
General Delivery

Wasilla AK 99687
St. Lazarus OCA
P.O. Box 873826

Arizona

Bisbee AZ 85603 MAIL
St. Stephen Nemanja SOC
<Warren AZ>
P.O. Box 3666
602-997-0232

Chandler AZ 85224
St. Katherine GOA
2716 N. Dobson Rd.
602-899-3330

Glendale AZ 85308
St. John the Baptist OCA
3749 W. Behrend Dr.
602-582-3156

Lake Havesu City AZ 86403-2248
St. Peter the Aleut Mission OCA
P.O. Box 2248
818-996-7013

Peoria AZ 85380-1286
St. Haralambos GOA
10320 N. 84th Ave.
P.O. Box 1057
602-486-8665

Phoenix AZ 85014
Holy Archangels Michael & Gabriel OCA
801 E. Camelback Rd.
602-582-3150

Phoenix AZ 85016
Holy Trinity Cathedral GOA
1973 E. Maryland Ave.
602-264-7863

Phoenix AZ 85069-9625
Ss. Peter & Paul OCA
1614 E. Monte Vista Rd.
P.O. Box 39625
602-253-9515

Phoenix AZ 85028
St. George ANT
4530 E. Gold Dust Ave.
602-953-1921, FAX 602-953-2460

Phoenix AZ 85068
St. Nikola NGM
11640 N. 16th Pl.
P.O. Box 9935
602-943-3459

Phoenix AZ 85008
St. Sava SOC
4436 E. McKinley St.
602-275-7360

Scottsdale AZ 85260
Assumption GOA
8202 E. Cactus
602-991-3009

Tucson AZ 85705-4137
Holy Resurrection ANT
715 W. Vanover Rd.
602-622-2265

Tuscon AZ 85719
St. Demetrios GOA
1145 E. Fort Lowell Rd.
602-888-0505

Warren AZ
St. Stephen Nemanja SOC
216 Park Ave.
602-997-0232

Arkansas

Ft. Smith AR 72901
St. George GOA
220 N. 7th St.

Hot Springs AR 71901
St. Archangel Michael NGM
P.O. Box 1523
501-525-8847

Hot Springs AR 71901
St. George SOC
108 Donnie Ct.
501-525-4285

Hot Springs AR 71901
Zoodochos Peghe GOA
502 Morrison Ave.
501-623-4646

Little Rock AR 72211
Annunciation GOA
1100 Napa Valley Dr.
501-225-6726

Rogers AR
St. James of Jerusalem OCA

California

Alhambra CA 91803
St. Steven's Cathedral SOC
1621 W. Garvey Ave.
818-284-9100

Altaville CA 95521 MAIL
St. Basil of Ostrog SOC
<Angels Camp CA>
P.O. Box 673
209-736-2340

Anaheim CA 92801
St. John the Baptist GOA
405 N. Dale St.
714-827-0181

Angels Camp CA 95222
St. Basil of Ostrog SOC
930 N. Main St.
209-736-2340

Apple Valley CA
St. Demetrios GOA
619-243-5025

Arcadia CA 91006
Christ the Savior NGM
1424 S. Baldwin Ave.

Atwater CA
Holy Virgin Mary OCA
@Roman Church; 2998 S. Buhach Rd.

Bakersfield CA 93301
St. George GOA
401 Truxtun Ave.
805-325-8602, 805-325-8694

Belmont CA 94002
Holy Cross GOA
900 Alameda de las Pulgas
415-591-4447

Ben Lomond CA 95005-0458
Ss. Peter & Paul ANT
9980 Hwy. 9
P.O. Box 458
408-336-2228, FAX 408-336-1748

Berkeley CA 94701 MAIL
Ss. Kyrill & Methodius OCA
<Oakland CA>
P.O. Box 11672
510-215-0301, FAX 510-531-3711

Berkeley CA 94703
St. John the Baptist OCA
1900 Essex St.
510-540-0617

Camarillo CA 93010
St. Demetrios GOA
400 Skyway Dr.
805-482-1273

Cardiff-By-The-Sea CA 92007
Ss. Constantine & Helen GOA
3459 Manchester Ave. #32
619-942-0920

Castro Valley CA 94546
Resurrection GOA
20104 Center St.
510-581-8950

Cayucos CA 93430
San Luis Obispo Parish GOA
10820 Santa Rita Rd.
805-434-2813

Claremont CA 91711
St. John the Evangelist OCA
@Chapel of McAlister Center; Claremont College Campus
966 Maryhurst
714-624-6811

Concord CA
Holy Cross ANT

Concord CA 94521
St. Demetrios GOA
1955 Kirker Pass Rd.
510-676-6967

Covina CA 91724
St. Nectarios GOA
20340 Covina Blvd.
818-967-5524

Cupertino CA 95014
St. Sava SOC
7811 Orion Ln.
408-257-6652

Danville CA 94526-1505
St. Michael the Archangel OCA
6 Donna Ln.
510-820-3861, 707-451-8447

Downey CA 90242
St. George GOA
12147 Lakewood Blvd.
310-862-6461

Dunlap CA 93621-0400
St. Nicholas GOA
38526 Dunlap Rd.
P.O. Box 400
209-338-2103

East Los Angeles CA 90022
St. Sava SOC
4355 2nd St.
818-288-1977

El Cajon CA 92029
St. Gregory of Nyssa GOA
311 Highland St.
619-258-2758

Elk Grove CA 95624
St. Katherine GOA
9734-A Dino Dr.
916-685-1322

Fair Oaks CA 95628
Holy Assumption SOC
7777 Sunset Ave.
916-966-5438

Fremont CA
St. Innocent OCA
415-647-1054

Fresno CA 93703
St. George GOA
2219 N. Orchard Ave.
209-233-0397

Fresno CA 93726
St. Peter SOC
3502 N. 1st St.
209-227-5565

Garden Grove CA 92640-6199
St. Luke ANT
13261 Dunklee Ave.
714-971-2244

Goleta CA 93117-4620
St. Athanasius ANT
976 Embarcadero del Mar
777 Camino Pascadero
805-968-4014, FAX 805-968-3767

Hesperia CA 92345
St. George the Great Martyr OCA
@Hesperia Medical Ctr; Main and 'I' Ave.
Box 504
619-245-7608

Huntington Beach CA 92646
St. Barnabas ANT
8011 Taylor Dr.
714-842-6282

Ignacio CA 94949
Nativity of Christ GOA
1110 Dickson Dr.
415-883-1998

Irvine CA 92714
St. Mark ANT
17840 Skypark Cir.
714-851-8933

Irvine CA 92714-7599
St. Paul GOA
4949 Alton Pkwy.
714-733-2366, FAX 714-753-0962

Jackson CA 95642
St. Sava SOC
724 N. Main St.
P.O. Box 1243
209-223-4320

La Verne CA 91750
St. George ANT
P.O. Box 7157
818-852-0377

Lancaster CA 93536 MAIL
Holy Cross ANT
<Palmdale CA>
2763 W. Ave. L, Suite 107
805-245-3571, FAX 805-245-0710

Lancaster CA 93539
Ss. Constantine & Helen GOA
4304 30th St. W.
P.O. Box 4404
818-345-4724

Lompoc CA 93436
St. Timothy ANT
403 N. J St.
P.O. Box 795
805-735-1821

Long Beach CA 90814
Assumption of the Blessed Virgin Mary GOA
5761 E. Colorodo St.
310-493-8929

Los Altos Hills CA 94022
Redeemer ANT
380 Magdalena Ave.
415-941-1570, FAX 415-253-7916

Los Angeles CA
Epiphany BEC
1530 N. Vermont

Los Angeles CA 90065
Holy Trinity OCA
3315 Verdugo Rd.
213-256-9180

Los Angeles CA 90026-3597
Holy Virgin Mary Cathedral OCA
650 Micheltorena St.
213-666-4977

Los Angeles CA 90048
St. John the Baptist OCA
6301 W. Olympic Blvd.

Los Angeles CA 90038
St. Klement Ohridsky OCA
5861 Virginia Ave.
213-467-2711

Los Angeles CA 90057
St. Nicholas Cathedral ANT
2300 W. 3rd St.
213-382-6269, FAX 213-382-0175

Los Angeles CA 90006
St. Sophia Cathedral GOA
1324 S. Normandie Ave.
213-737-2424

Menlo Park CA 94025
Nativity of the Holy Virgin OCA
1220 Crane St.
415-326-5622

Merced CA 95344 MAIL
Holy Virgin Mary OCA
<Atwater CA>
P.O. Box 3704

Modesto CA 95353
Annunciation GOA
313 Tokay Ave.
P.O. Box 707
209-522-7694, FAX 209-522-3926

Moraga CA 94556
Holy Trinity SOC
1700 School St.
510-376-5982

Northridge CA 91325
St. Nicholas GOA
9501 Balboa Blvd.
818-886-4040, FAX 818-886-3933

Oakland CA 94602
Ascension Cathedral GOA
4700 Lincoln Ave.
510-531-3400

Oakland CA 94610
Holy Resurrection OCA
124 Montecito
408-281-7013

Oakland CA 94602
Ss. Kyrill & Methodius OCA
@Ascension Greek Orthodox Cathedral, 4700 Lincoln Ave.
510-216-0301, FAX 510-531-3711

Oakland CA 94607
St. George NGM
94-9th St.
510-836-0591

Orinda CA 94563
St. John the Evangelist ANT
501 Moraga Way
510-939-4255

Oxnard CA 93030
St. Herman OCA
142 W. Wooley Rd.
805-486-5793

Palm Desert CA 92261
St. George GOA
74-109 Larrea
P.O. Box 4755
619-568-9901

Palm Springs CA 92263
Holy Archangels Michael and Gabriel OCA
@Palm Springs Senior Ctr.; 550 N. Palm Canyon Dr.
P.O. Box 9197
619-778-6098

Palmdale CA 93590-0310
Holy Cross ANT
@Christ the King Episcopal Church; 38658 N. 22nd St. E.

Pasadena CA 91107
St. Anthony GOA
778 S. Rosemead Blvd.
818-449-6943

Pittsburg CA 94565
Holy Cross ANT
344 Egret Pl.
510-437-8150

Pittsburg CA 94565
St. Dionysios GOA
1105 Harbor St.
510-432-3336

Pleasant Hills CA 94523 MAIL
Holy Cross ANT
<Concord CA>
2110 Hoover Ct.

Pomona CA
St. Anne OCA
@First Christian Church of Pomona; Artesia St & Park Ave.
714-779-2681

Poway CA 92064
St. John of Damascus OCA
16903 Espola Rd.
619-485-8433, 619-674-1931

Pt. Reyes Station CA 94956-0563
St. Sergius of Radonezh OCA
135 Balboa Ave.
P.O. Box 563
415-663-1705

Redding CA 96049-2584
Chapel GOA
1959 Eureka Way
P.O. Box 492584
916-241-1575

Redondo Beach CA 90277-4397
St. Katherine GOA
722 Knob Hill
310-540-2434, FAX 310-316-4655

Riverside CA 92503
St. Andrew ANT
10120 Indiana Ave.
909-352-9678

Rohnert Park CA 94928
All Saints ANT
1500 E. Cotati
5930 Commerce Blvd.
707-795-8093

Sacramento CA 95816-3895
Annunciation GOA
600 Alhambra Blvd.
3022 F Street
916-443-2033, FAX 916-443-2743

Sacramento CA 95821
Elevation of Holy Cross OCA
4415 El Camino Ave.
916-489-7230

Sacramento CA 95828
St. Athanasius ANT
7921 Cottonwood Ln.
916-689-9074

Salinas CA 93901
St. John the Baptist GOA
326 Park St.
408-424-4434

San Anselmo CA 94979
St. Nicholas OCA
102 Ross Ave.
P.O. Box 1936
415-454-0982

San Bernardino CA 92402
Prophet Elias GOA
1035 Inland Center Dr.
P.O. Box 296
909-885-6213

San Diego CA 92105-5955
St. George ANT
4175 Poplar St.
P.O. Box 5955
619-282-2417

San Diego CA 92117
St. George SOC
3025 Denver St.
619-275-4476

San Diego CA 92198-0291 MAIL
St. John of Damascus OCA
<Poway CA>
P.O. Box 28291
619-485-8433, 619-674-1931

San Diego CA 92104
St. Nicholas OCA
3873 Cherokee Ave.
619-284-9476

San Diego CA 92103
St. Spyridon GOA
3655 Park Blvd.
619-297-4165

San Diego CA 92115
Venerable Mother Angelina NGM
4808 Trojan Ave.
619-286-4438, 619-583-0122

San Francisco CA 94103
Annunciation Cathedral GOA
245 Valencia St.
415-861-0057

San Francisco CA 94118
Christ the Savior OCA
490 12th Ave.
2040 Anza St.
415-752-1347

San Francisco CA 94132
Holy Trinity GOA
999 Brotherhood Way
415-584-4747

San Francisco CA 94123-5102
Holy Trinity Cathedral OCA
1520 Green St. @ Van Ness
415-673-8565

San Francisco CA 94115
St. John the Baptist NGM
900 Baker St.
415-567-5869

San Francisco CA 94131
St. Nicholas ANT
5200 Diamond Hts. Blvd.
415-648-5200, FAX 415-647-0610

San Gabriel CA 91776
St. Sava SOC
1700 S. San Gabriel Blvd.
818-288-8811

San Jose CA
Ss. Michael & Gabriel OCA

San Jose CA 95120
St. Basil GOA
6430 Bose Ln.
408-268-3214

San Jose CA 95126
St. Nicholas GOA
1260 Davis St.
408-246-2770

San Jose CA 95123 MAIL
St. Nicholas OCA
<Saratoga CA>
155 Manton Ave.
408-867-0628

San Jose CA 95160
St. Stephen ANT
1570 Branham Ln.
P.O. Box 41310
408-266-6477

San Luis Obispo CA 93403-4945 MAIL
San Luis Obispo Parish GOA
<Cayucos CA>
P.O. Box 4945
805-434-2813

San Marcos CA 92069
St. Petka SOC
1854 Knob Hill Rd.
P.O. Box 1496
619-743-2178

Santa Barbara CA 93101
St. Barbara GOA
1205 San Antonio Creek Rd.
805-683-4492

Santa Barbara CA 93101
St. Luke ANT
331 W. Cota St.
805-899-3007

Santa Barbara CA 93101
St. Vladimir OCA
1328 Castillo St.
818-996-7013

Santa Cruz CA 95060
Prophet Elias GOA
223 Church St.
408-429-6500

Santa Maria CA 93456
Annunciation OCA
124 S. College Dr.
P.O. Box 5032
805-928-7386

Santa Rosa CA 95407
Protection of the Holy Virgin OCA
95 Mountain View Ave.
707-584-9491

Saratoga CA 95070
St. Archangel Michael NGM
18870 Allendale Ave.
408-867-4876

Saratoga CA
St. Nicholas OCA
14220 Elva Ave.
408-867-0628

Simi Valley CA 93065 MAIL
St. Peter of Cetinje NGM
<Sylmar CA>
1064 Stanford Dr.
805-527-4561, FAX 805-522-3161

Stockton CA 95207
St. Basil GOA
920 March Ln.
209-478-7564

Sylmar CA 91342
St. Peter of Cetinje NGM
13211 Hubbard St.
805-527-4561, FAX 805-522-3161

Tarzana CA 91356
St. Innocent OCA
5657 Lindley Ave.
818-881-1123

Temecula CA 92592
Greek Orthodox Mission of Temecula Valley GOA
37645 Via de Los Arboles
909-676-6067, 909-699-6912

Torrance CA
Ss. Archangels RMA
Alpine Village Chapel; 833 W. Torrance Blvd.
310-644-9802

Torrance CA 90510
St. Matthew ANT
4102 Hickman Dr.
P.O. Box 3531
310-371-2120

Tustin CA 92680
Falling Asleep of the Virgin Mary OCA
1221 Wass St.
714-730-6674

Upland CA 91786
St. Spyridon GOA
1391 Chaffee St.
P.O. Box 1327
909-985-4411

Vacaville CA
St. Timothy ANT

Vallejo CA 94590
Ss. Constantine & Helen GOA
1224 Alabama St.
707-642-6916

Van Nuys CA 91406
St. Michael ANT
16643 Vanowen St.
818-994-2313

Victorville CA 92393-0332 MAIL
St. Demetrios GOA
<Apple Valley CA>
P.O. Box 332
619-243-5025

Walnut Creek CA 94596-5026 MAIL
St. John the Evangelist ANT
<Orinda CA>
1878 Olympic Blvd.
510-939-4255

West Sacramento CA 95605
Holy Myrrhbearing Women OCA
833 Water St.
916-371-1041

West Sacramento CA 95691
Virgin Mary ANT
3060 Jefferson Blvd.
P.O. Box 2183
916-372-7776

Whittier CA 90601
St. Michael ANT
3333 Workman Mill Rd.
213-692-6121

Colorado

Aurora CO 80015 MAIL
St. Elias ANT
<Denver CO>
14336 'A' E. Temple Pl.
303-690-6045

Boulder CO 80301
Ss. Peter & Paul GOA
3101 Jay Rd.
303-443-0501

Boulder CO 80303 MAIL
St. Columba ANT
<Longmont CO>
536 Countughn
303-499-0476

Boulder CO 80301
St. Luke ANT
8212 Kincross Dr.
303-530-5680

Calhan CO 80808
St. Mary (Holy Dormition) OCA
28780 W. Ranan Rd.
719-347-2526

Colorado Springs CO 80907
Ss. Constantine & Helen OCA
2770 N. Chestnut St.
719-471-2239

Craig CO 81626
St. John the Baptist GOA
691 Green St.
P.O. Box 848
303-824-6664

Delta CO 81416
St. Andrew the Apostle OCA
298 Bert St.
303-874-5225

Denver CO 80222
Assumption Cathedral GOA
4610 E. Alameda Ave.
303-388-9314, FAX 303-329-6337

Denver CO 80209-0913
St. Augustine ANT
55 W. 3rd Ave.
P.O. Box 9913
303-698-2433

Denver CO
St. Elias ANT
303-690-6045

Denver CO 80210
St. Mark ANT
1405 S. Vine St.
303-722-0707

Denver CO 80216
Transfiguration of Christ Cathedral OCA
349 E. 47th Ave.
303-294-0938, 303-295-2811

Grand Junction CO 81506
St. Nicholas GOA
3585 N. 12th St.
P.O. Box 1122
303-242-9590

Greenwood Village CO 80111-3319
St. Catherine GOA
5555 S. Yosemite St.
303-773-3411, FAX 303-773-0343

Hot Sulphur Springs CO
Prophet Elias GOA

Littleton CO 80120
St. Herman of Alaska OCA
991 W. Prentice Ave.
303-798-7306

Longmont CO
St. Columba ANT
10656 Parkridge Ave.
303-499-0476

Pueblo CO 81004
St. John the Baptist GOA
1010 Spruce St.
P.O. Box 3011
303-544-8554

Pueblo CO 81004
St. Michael OCA
801 Summit Ave.
719-544-8423

Connecticut

Ansonia CT 06401
Holy Trinity GOA
Hubbell Ave.
P.O. Box 145
203-735-1919, 203-372-1976

Ansonia CT 06401-2233
Three Saints OCA
26 Howard Ave.
203-734-3988

Bridgeport CT 06608
Holy Ghost OCA
1520 E. Main St.
203-334-5700

Bridgeport CT 06604
Holy Trinity GOA
4070 Park Ave.
203-374-5561

Bridgeport CT 06605
St. Dimitrie OCA
579 Clinton Ave.
203-334-5649

Bridgeport CT 06610
St. John the Baptist CRC
384 Mill Hill Ave.
203-335-6170

Bridgeport CT 06606
St. Mary's Protection UOA
10 Oakwood St.
203-372-4883

Bridgeport CT 06604
St. Nicholas ANT
5458 Park Ave.
203-372-9767

Bristol CT 06010
St. Demetrios GOA
31 Brightwood Rd.
203-583-3476

Danbury CT 06810
Assumption GOA
30 Clapboard Ridge Rd.
203-748-2992

Danbury CT 06810
Holy Trinity CRC
17 Roberts Ave.
203-748-0671

Danbury CT 06811
St. George ANT
125 Kohanza St.
203-798-1771, 203-743-1921

Danielson CT 06239
Holy Trinity GOA
80 Water Street
P.O. Box 236
203-774-6245

Enfield CT 06082
St. Nicholas GOA
Church & Chapel Sts.
P.O. Box 1155
203-745-3880

Hartford CT 06105-1108
All Saints OCA
205 Scarborough St.
203-523-0334, FAX 203-233-6055

Hartford CT 06114
St. George Cathedral GOA
433 Fairfield Ave.
203-936-7586

Meriden CT 06450-0334
Ss. Peter & Paul OCA
54 Park Ave.
P.O. Box 334
203-634-9584

New Britain CT 06050-2876
Holy Trinity OCA
305 Washington St.
P.O. Box 2876
203-276-9793

New Britain CT 06050
St. George GOA
301 W. Main St.
P.O. Box 1753
203-229-0055

New Haven CT 06533
Greek Orthodox Community GOA
311 Temple St.
P.O. Box 9356
203-426-1298

New Haven CT 06515
Holy Transfiguration OCA
285 Alden Ave.
203-387-3882

New London CT 06320
St. Sophia GOA
200 Hempstead St.
203-442-2377

Norwalk CT 06851
St. George GOA
238 W. Rocks Rd.
203-849-0611

Norwich CT 06360-3517
Holy Trinity GOA
247 Washington St.
203-887-1458

Norwich CT 06360
St. Nicholas OCA
35 Convent Ave.
203-887-3623

Orange CT 06477
St. Barbara GOA
480 Race Brook Rd.
203-795-1347

Salisbury CT 06068
All Saints of America OCA
313 Twin Lakes Rd.
P.O. Box 45
203-387-3882

Southbury CT 06488
Christ the Savior OCA
1369 Southford Rd. (Rt. 68)
203-732-5057

Stamford CT 06905
Annunciation GOA
1230 Newfield Ave.
203-322-2093

Stamford CT 06905
Archangels GOA
13-27 Bedford St.
203-348-4216

Stamford CT 06903
Holy Assumption OCA
141 Den Rd.
203-329-9933

Stratford CT 06497
St. John the Baptist CRC
600 Silver Lane
203-386-8888

Stratford CT 06497
St. John the Baptist CRC
1240 Broadbridge Ave.
203-378-4007

Terryville CT 06786
Ss. Cyril & Methodius OCA
34 Fairview Ave.
203-582-3631

Trumbull CT 06611
St. George OCA
5490 Main St.
203-268-1968

Waterbury CT 06708
Holy Trinity GOA
937 Chase Pkwy.
203-754-5189

Waterbury CT 06704
Nativity of the Holy Virgin OCA
3125 N. Main St.
Box 4009
203-753-4866

Willimantic CT 06226
Holy Trinity OCA
414 Valley St.
203-423-3531

Delaware

Newark DE 19713
St. Athanasius ANT
22 Stature Dr.
302-737-9770

Wilmington DE 19806
Holy Trinity GOA
808 N. Broom St.
302-654-4446

Wilmington DE 19808
St. Michael the Archangel OCA
2300 W. Huntington Dr. & Kirkwood Hwy.
2231 E. Huntington Dr.
302-995-6775, FAX 302-995-8950

Dist. of Col.

Washington DC 20011
Ss. Constantine & Helen GOA
4115 16th Street N.W.
202-829-2910

Washington DC 20011
St. George ANT
4335 16th St. N.W.
202-723-5335, FAX 202-723-7924

Washington DC 20008
St. Luke NGM
P.O. Box 6468 Fr. Sta.
718-279-4010

Washington DC 20011
St. Luke SOC
5917 16th St. N.W.
202-829-4274

Washington DC 20007
St. Nicholas Cathedral OCA
3500 Massachusetts Ave. N.W.
202-333-5060

Washington DC 20007
St. Sophia Cathedral GOA
36th St. & Massachusetts Ave. N.W.
202-333-4730

Florida

Boca Raton FL 33431
St. Mark GOA
2100 N.W. 51st St.
407-994-4822

Bradenton FL 33508
St. Mark OCA
3415 9th St. E.
813-922-7551

Cape Coral FL 33904 MAIL
Holy Cross OCA
<Ft. Myers FL>
3704 S.E. 12th Ct.
813-549-0523

Clearwater FL 34625-4410
Holy Trinity GOA
409 Old Coachman Rd. S.
813-799-4605

Clearwater FL 34620
St. George NGM
15250 58th St. N.
813-531-0052

Coral Gables FL 33134
St. George Cathedral ANT
320 Palermo Ave.
305-444-6541, FAX 305-445-6530

Davie FL 33314
St. Phillip ANT
4870 Griffin Rd.
305-584-4030

Daytona Beach FL
Holy Cross ANT

Daytona Beach FL 32118
St. Demetrios GOA
129 N. Halifax Ave.
904-252-6012

De Land FL
Orthodox Mission OCA
@ St Peter's Roman Church
407-668-6020

DeBary FL 32713 MAIL
St. Stephen the Protomartyr OCA
<Longwood FL>
10 Monroe Ave.
407-260-6003

Destin FL 32541
St. John GOA
P.O. Box 277

Eustis FL 32726
St. Andrew ANT
2815 S. Bay St.
904-357-1549

Ft. Lauderdale FL 33065
St. Demetrios GOA
815 N.E. 15th Ave.
305-467-1515, FAX 305-467-0212

Ft. Lauderdale FL 33311-3918
St. Nicholas OCA
2001 N. Andrews Ave.
305-566-6358

Ft. Myers FL 33919-5116
Annunciation GOA
8210 Cypress Lake Dr.
813-481-2099

Ft. Myers FL 33905
Holy Cross OCA
2365 S. Olga Dr. S.E.
813-549-0523

Ft. Pierce FL 34981
St. Nicholas GOA
2525 S. 25th St.
407-464-7194

Florida

Ft. Walton Beach FL 32549
Ss. Markella & Demetrios GOA
Bryn Mawr @ Miracle Strip Pkwy.
P.O. Box 2135
904-244-0822

Gainesville FL
St. John the Theologian OCA

Gainsville FL 32606
St. Elizabeth GOA
5129 Millhopper Rd.
904-371-7258

Gulfport FL 33707
St. Mary's Protection UOA
6102 9th Ave. S
813-381-1619

Hollywood FL 33021
Presentation of Our Lord CRC
5801 Grant St.
305-987-8058

Hollywood FL 33021
St. George GOA
425 N. 58th Ave.
305-966-1898

Hollywood FL 33020
Three Saints OCA
5801 Grant St.

Inverness FL 34451-0241 MAIL
St. Michael the Archangel GOA
<Lecanto FL>
P.O. Box 241
904-527-0766

Jacksonville FL 32207
St. George ANT
1600 Ashland St.
904-398-1855

Jacksonville FL 32207
St. John the Divine GOA
3850 Atlantic Blvd.
904-396-5383, FAX 904-399-1547

Jacksonville FL
St. Justin Martyr OCA
407-668-6020, 904-269-3952, 904-273-3952

Lake Worth FL 33463-7507
St. Herman OCA
7099 S. Military Tr.
407-968-5343

Lantana FL 33460
Ss. Cyril & Methodius BEC
3829 Kewanee Rd.

Lecanto FL 34461
St. Michael the Archangel GOA
4705 W. Gulf-to-Lake Hwy.
904-527-0766

Longwood FL 32750
St. Petka SOC
1990 Lake Emma Rd.
407-831-SERB

Longwood FL 32750
St. Stephen Protomartyr OCA
1895 Lake Emma Rd.
407-260-6003

Maitland FL 32751
Holy Trinity GOA
1217 Trinity Woods Ln.
407-331-4687

Melbourne FL 32940
St. Katherine GOA
5965 Wickham Rd.
407-254-1045

Miami FL 33015
Christ the Savior Cathedral OCA
N.W. 166th St. & 77th Ct.
305-628-0413

Miami FL 33135-3208
Our Lady of Regla ANT
1920 S.W. 6th St.
305-642-7878

Miami FL 33135
Ss. Peter & Paul OCA
1411 S.W. 11th St.
305-858-2924

Miami FL 33156-7499
St. Andrew GOA
7901 N. Kendall Dr.
305-595-1343

Miami FL 33134
St. Jude GOA
4269 S.W. 6th St.
305-445-0915

Miami FL 33125-4562
St. Lazarus ANT
1778 N.W. 3rd St.
305-649-1519

Miami FL 33129
St. Sophia Cathedral GOA
2401 S.W. 3rd Ave.
244 S.W. 24th Rd.
305-854-2922

Miramar FL 33023
Holy Trinity OCA
6035 S.W. 60th St.
305-963-4790

Naples FL 33962
St. Demetrius OCA
140 Price St.
813-774-5757

Naples FL 33942-1710
St. Katharine GOA
7100 Airport Pulling Rd. N.
813-591-3430

New Port Richey FL 35642
St. Andrew OCA
4633 Glissade Dr.
813-862-8262

New Port Richey FL 34654
St. George GOA
9426 Little Rd.
813-868-5911

North Miami FL 33168
Annunciation GOA
12250 N.W. 2nd Ave.
305-681-1061

North Miami FL 33161
St. Peter ANT
1811 N.W. 4th Ct.
315 N.E. 131st St.
305-891-0425

North Miami FL 33169
St. Simeon SOC
175 N.W. 154th St.
305-944-6890

North Port FL 34287
St. Sava NGM
P.O. Box 7978
813-475-6811

Orlando FL
Holy Trinity OCA

Orlando FL 32801-1942
St. George ANT
24 N. Rosalind Ave.
407-422-3230

Palm Beach FL 32907
St. Barbara CRC
1533 Wake Forest Rd.
N.W.
407-952-2418

Panama City FL 32401
St. John the Theologian
GOA
136 Baldwin Rd.
P.O. Box 1933
904-769-3616

Pensacola FL 32501
Annunciation GOA
1720 W. Garden St.
904-433-2662

Pinellas Park FL 33764
St. Nicholas ANT
P.O. Box 1730
813-545-3797

Port Charlotte FL 33949
Holy Trinity GOA
P.O. Box 3534
813-624-4896

Port St. Lucie FL 34953
St. James OCA
2201 Airoso Blvd.
1712 S.W. Garnet St.
407-878-0338

Sarasota FL 34243
St. Barbara GOA
7671 N. Lockwood Ridge
Blvd.
813-355-2616

Silver Springs FL 32688
St. Basil ANT
5200 N.E. 29th St.
P.O. Box 898
904-236-2080

Spring Hill FL 34608
Holy Trinity CRC
11200 Elgin Blvd.
904-686-2869

St. Augustine FL 32085-0949
Holy Trinity GOA
7 Waldo St.
P.O. Box 949

St. Petersburg FL 33713
Holy Trinity OCA
301 38th St. N.
813-327-4373

St. Petersburg FL 33702
St. Sava SOC
530 77th Ave. N.
813-527-8738

St. Petersburg FL 33710
St. Stefanos GOA
3600 76th St. N.
813-345-8235, FAX 813-395-8286

Tallahassee FL 32308
Holy Mother of God GOA
1647 Phillips Rd.
904-878-0747

Tampa FL 33609
St. John the Baptist GOA
2418 Swann Ave.
813-876-8830

Tarpon Springs FL 33589
St. Michael GOA
113 Hope St.

Tarpon Springs FL 33589
St. Nicholas GOA
36 N. Pinellas Ave.
P.O. Box 248
813-937-3540

Titusville FL 32780
St. Simeon OCA
3175 Satterfield Rd.
407-268-8354

Venice FL 34293-1835
Holy Spirit OCA
700 Shamrock Blvd.
813-485-2752

West Palm Beach FL 33405
St. Catherine GOA
4000 Washington Rd.
110 Southern Blvd.
407-833-6387

West Palm Beach FL 33406
St. Mary ANT
1317 Florida Mango Rd.
407-965-5007

Winter Haven FL 33881-7424
St. Sophia GOA
1030 Bradbury Rd.
P.O. Box 7424
813-299-4532

Georgia

Alpharetta GA 30239-0264
Joy of All Who Sorrow OCA
477 Allyson Circle
P.O. Box 264
404-667-6407

Athens GA 30605
St. Philothea GOA
1196 S. Lumpkin St.
408 Sandstone Dr.
706-725-7331

Atlanta GA 30329
Annunciation Cathedral GOA
2500 Clairmont Rd. N.E.
404-633-5870

Atlanta GA 30307
St. Elias ANT
2045 Ponce de Leon Ave. N.E.
404-378-8191

Augusta GA 30901
Holy Trinity GOA
953 Telfair St.
706-724-1087

Avondale Estates GA 30002 MAIL
St. Mary of Egypt OCA
<Norcross GA>
1225 Berkeley Rd.
404-288-1556

Brunswick GA 31520
St. George GOA
401 Newcastle St.

Hiram GA 30141
St. Stephen ANT
4812 Mitchell Rd.
404-489-0010

Lilburn GA 30247-5822 MAIL
Ss. Constantine & Helen OCA
<Norcross GA>
5404 Oliver Ct. N.W.
215-365-3720

Macon GA 31208
Holy Cross GOA
3269 Bloomfield Dr.
P.O. Box 5692

Marietta GA 30066-4660
Holy Transfiguration GOA
3431 Trickum Rd.
404-977-1350

Norcross GA 30093
Ss. Constantine & Helen OCA
@St. Mary of Egypt Church; 925 Beaver Ruin Rd.
215-635-3720

Norcross GA 30093
St. Mary of Egypt OCA
925 Beaver Ruin Rd.
404-288-1556

Savannah GA 31416
St. Mary Magdalene OCA
2810 Skidaway Rd.
Box 15351
912-356-3545

Savannah GA 31401
St. Paul GOA
14 W. Anderson St.
912-236-8256

Hawaii

Honolulu HI 96822-3562
Ss. Constantine & Helen GOA
930 Lunalilo St.
808-521-7220, FAX 808-523-0429

Honolulu HI 96820
St. Lazarus SOC
P.O. Box 30224
808-422-8822

Idaho

Boise ID 83702
Ss. Constantine & Helen GOA
2618 Bannock St.
208-345-6147

Pocatello ID 83205-4567
Assumption GOA
528 N. 5th Ave.
P.O. Box 4567
208-232-5519

Twin Falls ID 83301
St. Ignatius of Antioch ANT
1751 Elizabeth Blvd.
P.O. Box 294
208-734-3664

Illinois

Aurora IL 60505
St. Athanasios GOA
1855 E. 5th Ave.
708-851-6106

Belleville IL 62221
Ss. Constantine & Helen GOA
405 Huntwood Rd.
618-277-0330

Bellwood IL 60104
St. John the Baptist NGM
405 Englewood St.
708-544-1524

Buckner IL 62819
Nativity of the Virgin Mary OCA
McDyby St.
618-984-2144

Burbank IL 60459
Archangel Michael OCA
5037 W. 83rd St.
708-423-2441

Champaign IL 61820
Three Hierarchs GOA
2010 Three Hierarchs Ct.
217-352-3452

Chicago IL 60610
Annunciation Cathedral GOA
1017 N. LaSalle Blvd.
312-664-5485

Chicago IL 60660-1124 MAIL
Archangels Michael and Gabriel OCA
<Ft. Wayne IN>
6352 N. Paulina St.
317-577-7838

Chicago IL 60644
Assumption GOA
601 S. Central Ave.
312-626-3114

Chicago IL 60617
Holy Archangel Michael SOC
9815 S. Commercial Ave.
312-375-3848, 312-375-3849

Chicago IL 60660
Holy Nativity OCA
6350 N. Paulina St.
312-743-9648

Chicago IL 60647
Holy Resurrection NGM
3062 Palmer Sq.
312-252-4452, 312-252-4545

Chicago IL 60631-2933
Holy Resurrection SOC
8035 W. Serbian Rd
5701 N. Redwood Dr.
312-693-3366, FAX 312-693-7615

Chicago IL 60639
Holy Trinity GOA
6041 W. Diversey
312-622-5979, FAX 312-622-8833

Chicago IL 60622-3502
Holy Trinity Cathedral OCA
1121 N. Leavitt St.
312-486-6064, 312-486-4545

Chicago IL 60622
Pokrov Cathedral UOA
2710 W. Iowa St.

Chicago IL 60609
Ss. Peter & Paul OCA
53rd St. & S. Western Ave.
708-963-1076

Chicago IL 60660
St. Andrew GOA
5649 N. Sheridan Rd.
312-334-4515

Chicago IL 60607
St. Basil GOA
733 S. Ashland Blvd.
312-243-3738

Chicago IL 60625
St. Demetrios GOA
2727 W. Winona St.
312-561-5992

Chicago IL 60614
St. George GOA
2701 N. Sheffield Ave.
312-525-1793

Chicago IL 60622
St. George Cathedral OCA
917 N. Wood St.
312-666-5179

Chicago IL 60634
St. Mary OCA
4225 N. Central Ave.
312-736-1153

Chicago IL 60639
St. Nicholas ADA
2701 N. Narragensett Ave.
312-889-4282

Chicago IL 60623
St. Nikola NGM
2754 S. Central Park Ave.
312-522-9643

Chicago IL 60617
St. Simeon Mirotocivi NGM
3737 E. 114th St.
312-731-2925

Chicago IL 60025
St. Stevan of Decani NGM
3543 W Leland Ave.
312-539-0818

Cicero IL 60148
St. George ANT
1220 S. 60th Ct.
708-656-2927, FAX 708-656-1166

Country Club Hills IL 60478 MAIL
St. Nicholas UOA
<Homewood IL>
17624 Maple Ave.
708-799-1023, 708-799-2221

DeKalb IL 60115
St. George GOA
320 S. 2nd St.
815-758-5731

Decatur IL 62522
Annunciation GOA
570 N. Union St.
217-429-7023

Des Plaines IL 60016
St. John the Baptist GOA
2350 Dempster St.
708-827-5519

East Moline IL 61244
Assumption GOA
4900 Kennedy Dr.
309-792-2912

Elgin IL 60120
St. Sophia GOA
525 Church Rd.
708-888-2822

Elmhurst IL 60126
St. Demetrios GOA
893 Church Rd.
708-834-7010

Glen Ellyn IL 60137
Holy Ancestors of Christ
Ss. Joachim & Anne UOA
1124 Londonberry Ln.
708-495-1807

Glenview IL 60025
Ss. Peter & Paul GOA
1401 Wagner Rd.
708-729-2235

Granite City IL 62040
Ss. Cyril & Methody OCA
4770 Maryville Rd. Box 1303
618-931-6465

Grayslake IL 60030-0496
Serbian Hierarchs NGM
P.O. Box 496
708-223-6513

Great Lakes IL 60088-5000
Three Hierarchs OCA
Recruit Memorial Chapel
Complex - Recruit Training Command, Bldg. 1301
708-688-2288, 708-688-2402

Hegewisch IL 60633
Assumption GOA
13631 Brainard Ave.
312-646-2999

Homewood IL 60430
St. Nicholas UOA
17935 Springfield Ave.
708-799-1023, 708-799-2221

Joliet IL 60435
All Saints GOA
102 N. Broadway
815-722-1727

Joliet IL 60436
St. George SOC
305 S. Midland Ave.
300 Stryker Ave.
815-725-5502

Joliet IL 60435-2918
St. Nicholas OCA
1000 Barber Ln.
1018 Barber Ln.
815-725-4742

Joliet IL 60433
St. Sava NGM
3457 Black Rd.

Justice IL 60458
Holy Cross GOA
7560 S. Archer Rd.
708-594-2040

Kankakee IL 60901
Annunciation GOA
296 N. Washington Ave.
815-933-5482

LaSalle IL
St. Christopher CRC
815-226-8089

Lansing IL 60438
New St. George RMA
17601 Wentworth Ave.
708-474-4810, 708-895-9672, 708-895-4810

Madison IL 62060
Holy Trinity BEC
1300 Grand Ave.

Madison IL 62060
Nativity of Virgin Mary OCA
5th St. & Ewing Ave.
416 Ewing Ave.
618-451-9995

Niles IL 60714-4503
Holy Taxiarchai-St. Haralambos GOA
7373 Caldwell Ave.
708-647-8880

Niles IL 60714
St. Michael CRC
7313 Waukegan Rd.
708-647-8398

Oak Lawn IL 60453-4892
St. Nicholas GOA
10301 S. Kolmar Ave.
708-636-5460, 708-636-5461

Olympia Fields IL 60461
Assumption GOA
20401 South Western Ave.
708-748-3040

Palatine IL 60078
Holy Resurrection OCA
1449 N. Quentin Rd.
P.O. Box 421
708-358-7321

Palatine IL 60067
St. Nectarios GOA
133 S. Roselle Rd.
708-358-5170

Palos Heights IL 60463
St. Spyridon GOA
12307 S. Ridgeland
708-385-0787

Palos Hills IL 60465
Ss. Constantine & Helen GOA
11025-45 S. Roberts Rd.
708-974-3400, 708-974-3401

Palos Hills IL 60465
St. Luke the Evangelist OCA
10700 S. Kean Ave.
708-594-0462

Palos Park IL 60464 MAIL
St. Joseph OCA
<Wheaton IL>
7900 W. 120th St.
708-361-1684

Peoria IL 61603
All Saints GOA
1812 N. Prospect Rd.
309-682-5824

Rock Island IL 61201-6398
St. George GOA
2930 31st Ave.
309-786-8163

Rockford IL 61109
Christ the Saviour CRC
1802 Pershing Ave.
815-398-2134

Rockford IL 61107
Ss. Constantine & Helen GOA
108 N. 5th St.
815-963-8625

Royalton IL 62983
Protection of the Holy Virgin Mary OCA
112 N. Fairdale Ave.
P.O. Box 307
618-984-2144

Spring Valley IL 61362-0165
St. George ANT
211 E. Minnesota St.
815-664-4540

Springfield IL 62704
St. Anthony GOA
1600 S. Glenwood Ave.
217-522-7010

Summit IL 60501
St. Panteleimon OCA
7545 W. 61st Pl.
708-458-2575

Sycamore IL
St. Michael ANT

Waukegan IL 60085
St. Demetrios GOA
1217 North Ave.
708-623-0190

Waukegan IL 60085
St. Nicholas SOC
228 N. County St.
708-336-9838

West Chicago IL 60185 MAIL
Holy Transfiguration ANT
<Wheaton IL>
247 N. Neltnor Blvd. Apt. F2H

Westchester IL 60154
Holy Apostles GOA
2501 S. Wolf Rd.
708-562-2744

Wheaton IL 60188
Holy Transfiguration ANT
1N075 Woods Ave.
708-510-9934, 708-876-9133

Wheaton IL 60187
St. Joseph OCA
412 Crescent St.
708-361-1684

Indiana

Bloomington IN
All Saints ANT

East Chicago IN 46312
Holy Ghost CRC
4413 Olcott Ave.
219-864-9820

East Chicago IN 46312
St. George NGM
4021 Elm St.
219-397-0240

Ft. Wayne IN
Archangels Michael and Gabriel OCA
2902 Evans St.
317-577-7838

Ft. Wayne IN 46806
Holy Trinity GOA
5420 S. Anthony Blvd.
219-456-9426

Ft. Wayne IN 46845
St. John Chrysostom ANT
639 Putnam St.
10821 Pine Mills Rd.
219-424-0615

Ft. Wayne IN
St. Mary RMA
708-895-4810

Ft. Wayne IN 46805
St. Nicholas OCA
3535 Crescent Ave.
219-484-2277

Gary IN 46408
Holy Resurrection ANT
4661 Harrison St.
219-884-2079

Gary IN 46409
Protection of Virgin Mary OCA
505 E. 45th Ave.
219-887-4663

Gary IN 46408
St. Nicholas CRC
47th Ave. & Pierce St.
219-962-2882

Goshen IN 46526
St. Mary ANT
66629 Pioneer St.
219-831-6347

Hammond IN 46324
St. Demetrios GOA
7021 Hohman Ave.
219-932-7347

Hobart IN 46342
Holy Resurrection ANT
305 E. 6th St.
219-942-2592

Indianapolis IN 46205
Holy Trinity GOA
4011 N. Pennsylvania St.
317-283-3816

Indianapolis IN 46222-2704
Ss. Constantine & Elena OCA
3237 W. 16th St.
317-638-4162

Indianapolis IN 46226
St. George ANT
4020 N. Sherman Dr.
317-547-9356

Indianapolis IN 46222
St. Nikola NGM
3626 W. 16th St.

Indianapolis IN 46222
St. Stephen BEC
1434 N. Medford

Kokomo IN
St. Thomas OCA
317-452-7535

Lake Station IN 46405-2278 MAIL
St. Nicholas CRC
<Gary IN>
2582 Newton St.
219-962-2882

Merrillville IN 46410
Descent of the Holy Ghost OCA
750 W. 61st Ave.
6075 Harrison St.
219-980-0374

Merrillville IN 46410
Ss. Constantine & Helen Cathedral GOA
8000 Madison St.
219-769-2481

Merrillville IN 46410
St. Clement of Ohrid OCA
5444 Harrison St.
219-884-3211

Merrillville IN 46410
St. Elijah Cathedral SOC
8700 Taft St.
219-769-2122

Merrillville IN 46410
St. Sava NGM
9191 Mississippi
P.O. Box 2106
219-736-9191, FAX 219-736-7836

Michigan City IN 46360
Holy Trinity UOA
7396 W. Johnson Rd.
219-879-7575

Michigan City IN 46360-5203
St. George ANT
303 Grace St.
127 S. Dickson St.

Schererville IN 46375
St. George SOC
905 E. Joliet St.
219-322-3355, FAX 219-322-9702

Schererville IN 46375
St. George GOA
528 77th Ave.
219-322-6168, 219-322-6165

South Bend IN 46614-3815
Ss. Peter & Paul SOC
59250 Keria Tr.
59262 Keria Tr.
219-291-0937

South Bend IN 46635
St. Andrew GOA
52455 N. Ironwood Rd.
219-277-4688, 219-277-4689

Terre Haute IN 47802
St. George ANT
1900 S. 4th St.
812-232-5244

Iowa

Cedar Rapids IA 52403
St. George ANT
3650 Cottage Grove Ave. S.E.
319-363-1559

Cedar Rapids IA 52401
St. John the Baptist GOA
501 A Ave. N.E.
319-364-5460

Des Moines IA 50311
St. George GOA
35th & Cottage Grove
515-277-0780

Dubuque IA 52001
St. Elias the Prophet GOA
1075 Rockdale Rd.
319-583-5902

Mason City IA 50401
Transfiguration of our Lord GOA
1311 2nd St. S.W.
515-423-6238

Sioux City IA 51101-0574
Holy Trinity GOA
900 6th St.
P.O. Box 574
712-255-5559

Sioux City IA 51102
St. Thomas ANT
1100 Jones St.
P.O. Box 1042
712-258-7166

Waterloo IA 50702
St. Demetrios GOA
613 W. 4th St.
319-232-4773

Kansas

Kansas City KS 66101
Holy Trinity OCA
558 Lowell Ave.
913-342-4552

Kansas City KS 66112
St. Archangel Michael NGM
310 N. 72nd St.
913-788-5845

Kansas City KS 66102
St. George SOC
50 S. Bethany
913-371-1648

Overland Park KS 66212
St. Dionysios GOA
8100 W. 95th St.
913-341-7373

Salina KS
All Saints ANT

Topeka KS 66614
Ss. Peter & Paul ANT
2516 S.W. Huntoon
3500 S.W. 29th #F158
913-271-6441

Wichita KS 67208
Holy Trinity GOA
805 N. Dellrose
316-681-1165

Wichita KS 67206-1223
St. George Cathedral ANT
7515 E. 13th at Broadmoor
316-636-4676

Wichita KS 67213
St. Mary ANT
344 S. Martinson
316-264-1576

Kentucky

Lexington KY 40502
Panagia Pantovasilissa GOA
920 Tates Creek Rd.
606-266-1921

Lexington KY 40503
St. Andrew ANT
1136 Higbee Mill Rd.
606-223-5091

Louisville KY 40203
Assumption GOA
932 S. 5th St.
502-587-6247

Louisville KY 40220
St. Michael ANT
3026 Hikes Ln.
502-452-1930, 502-454-3378

Louisiana

Baton Rouge LA 70821
Greek Orthodox Community GOA
P.O. Box 126

Baton Rouge LA
St. Mary Magdalene the Myrrbearer OCA

Lake Charles LA 70605
St. John the Divine ANT
5732 Bennie Ln.
318-474-2004

Metairie LA 70006-2808
St. Basil ANT
3916 Hudson St.
504-888-8114

Monroe LA 71201-3608
Ss. Constantine & Helen GOA
2011 Forsyth Ave.
318-325-1764

New Orleans LA 70003
Holy Trinity Cathedral GOA
1200 Robert E. Lee Blvd.
504-282-0259

New Orleans LA
St. Andrew of Crete OCA

Shreveport LA 71101
St. George GOA
1719 Creswell St.
318-222-5225

Maine

Bangor ME 04401
St. George GOA
90 Sanford St.
207-945-9588

Biddeford ME 04005
St. Demetrios GOA
35 Adams St.
P.O. Box 605
207-284-5651

Lewiston ME 04240
Holy Trinity GOA
155 Hogan Rd.
P. O. Box 1344
207-783-6795

Portland ME 04101
Holy Trinity GOA
133 Pleasant St.
207-774-0281

Maryland

Annapolis MD 21401
Ss. Constantine & Helen GOA
4 Constitution Ave.
410-263-2550

Baltimore MD 21201
Annunciation Cathedral GOA
24 W. Preston St.
410-727-1831

Baltimore MD 21229
Holy Cross ANT
602 Winans Way
410-956-3938

Baltimore MD 21231-1923
St. Andrew OCA
2028 E. Lombard St.
410-276-5541, FAX 410-276-3422

Baltimore MD 21234
St. Demetrios GOA
2504 Cub Hill Rd.
P.O. Box 28218
410-661-1090

Baltimore MD 21224
St. Nicholas GOA
520 S. Ponca St.
410-633-5020

Bethesda MD 20827
Ss. Peter & Paul ANT
7108 Bradley Blvd.
301-365-0932, FAX 301-365-3217

Bethesda MD 20817
St. George GOA
7701 Bradley Blvd.
301-469-7990

Bethesda MD 20817
St. Mark OCA
7124 River Rd.
301-229-6300, FAX 301-229-1559

Columbia MD 21045
St. Matthew OCA
P.O. Box 2003
410-992-0608

Cumberland MD 21502
St. John the Theologian OCA
@St. Paul Lutheran Church; Washington & Smallwood Sts.
301-424-7730

Frederick MD 21705
Greek Orthodox Church of Frederick GOA
108 W. Church St.
P.O. Box 4226

Hagerstown MD 21740
St. Catherine the Great Martyr OCA
433 Liberty St.
301-424-7730

Hunt Valley MD 21030
St. Mary ANT
P.O. Box 594
301-785-0909

Lanham MD 20706
St. Theodore GOA
7101 Cipriano Blvd.
301-552-3540

Ocean City MD 21842
St. George GOA
8805 Coastal Hwy.
301-524-0990

Potomac MD 20854
Holy Resurrection CRC
10201 Democracy Blvd.
301-299-5120

Rockville MD 20852 MAIL
St. John the Theologian OCA
<Cumberland MD>
825 Harrington Rd.

Massachusetts

Andover MA 01810
Ss. Constantine & Helen GOA
71 Chandler Rd.
P.O. Box 807
508-470-0919, 508-470-8715

Arlington MA 02174
St. Athanasius the Great GOA
735 Massachusetts Ave.
617-646-0705, FAX 617-648-6746

Boston MA
Annunciation Cathedral GOA
Parker & Ruggles Sts.
617-427-4500, 617-731-6633

Boston MA 02215
Holy Trinity Cathedral OCA
165 Park Dr.
617-262-9490

Boston MA 02132-0002
St. George ANT
55 Emmonsdale Rd.
P.O. Box 164
617-323-0323, FAX 617-323-6301

Massachusetts

Boston MA 02118
St. John the Baptist GOA
15 Union Park St.
617-536-5692

Boston MA 02131
St. Nektarios GOA
39 Belgrade Ave.
P.O. Box 12
617-327-1983

Boston MA
St. Sava SOC

Brockton MA 02401
Annunciation GOA
457 Oak St.
508-559-0910, 508-559-0911

Brookline MA 02146 MAIL
Annunciation Cathedral GOA
<Boston MA>
Cathedral Center, 162 Goddard Ave.
617-427-4500, 617-731-6633

Burlington MA 01803 MAIL
St. Sava SOC
<Boston MA>
4 Angela Cl.

Cambridge MA 02139
Ss. Constantine & Helen GOA
14 Magazine St.
617-876-3601

Cambridge MA 02139
St. Mary ANT
8 Inman St.
617-547-1234

Centerville MA 02632-3022
St. George GOA
1130 Falmouth Rd.
508-775-3045, 508-775-3091

Chelsea MA 02150
Nativity of the Virgin Mary OCA
8 Addison St.
508-697-3928

Chicopee Falls MA 01021
Ss. Constantine & Helen GOA
30 Grattan St.
P.O. Box 112
413-592-3401

Clinton MA 01510
St. Nicholas GOA
132 School St.
P.O. Box 81
508-365-9089

Cohasset MA 02025
Nativity-Assumption of the Virgin Mary GOA
811 Jerusalem Rd.
617-383-6380, 617-383-2975

Dedham MA 02026
St. John of Damascus ANT
300 West St.
617-326-3046

East Longmeadow MA 01028
St. Luke GOA
400 Prospect St.
P.O. Box 381
413-525-4551

Fall River MA 02720
St. Demetrios GOA
289 N. Main St.
508-672-2121

Fitchburg MA 01420-6922
Holy Trinity GOA
1319 Main St.
508-342-1216

Haverhill MA 01830
Holy Apostles Ss. Peter & Paul GOA
154-156 Winter St.
508-373-3311

Holyoke MA 01040
Holy Trinity GOA
410 Main St.
413-533-9880

Ipswich MA 01938
Assumption GOA
8 Lafayette Rd.
P.O. Box 6
508-356-9798

Kingston MA 02364
St. Mark of Ephesus OCA
261 Main St.
P.O. Box 261
617-585-8907

Lawrence MA
St. George ANT
8 Lowell St.
508-685-4052

Lexington MA 02173
St. Nicholas GOA
17 Meriam St.
617-862-6453

Massachusetts

Lowell MA 01853-1752
Assumption GOA
72 Butterfield St.
P.O. Box 1752
508-458-8684

Lowell MA 01854
Holy Trinity GOA
Lewis St.
508-458-8092

Lowell MA 01854
St. George ANT
41 Bowers St.
44 Bowers St.
508-452-8878

Lowell MA 01851
St. George GOA
44 Princeton Blvd.
508-459-9147

Lowell MA 01854-3599
Transfiguration of Our Savior GOA
Fr. John Serantos Way
508-458-4321

Lynn MA 01902
St. George GOA
11 Church St.
617-593-6162

Marlboro MA 01752
Ss. Anargyroi GOA
Cashman & Central Sts.
P.O. Box 381
508-485-2575

Maynard MA 01754-0604
Holy Annunciation OCA
15 Prospect St.
P.O. Box 604
617-395-7793

Methuen MA 01844 MAIL
St. George ANT
<Lawrence MA>
103 Pleasant St.
508-685-4052

New Bedford MA 02746
St. George GOA
87 Ashley Blvd.
508-996-5913

Newburyport MA 01950
Annunciation GOA
Harris & Park Sts.
P.O. Box 575
508-465-5757

North Natick MA 01760
Annunciation OCA
37 Washington St.
508-655-7927

Norwood MA 02062
St. George ANT
Atwood Ave.
617-762-4396

Peabody MA 01960-4452
St. Vasilios GOA
57 Paleologos St.
508-531-0777

Pittsfield MA 01201
St. George GOA
73 Bradford St.
413-442-8113

Pittsfield MA 01201
St. Nicholas OCA
76 Wahconah St.
413-442-2669

Quincy MA 02170
St. Catherine GOA
157 Beale St.
617-773-2545

Salem MA 01970
St. Nicholas OCA
64 Forrester St.
508-744-5869

Sharon MA 02067-1637
St. Gregory the Theologian GOA
1 Merchant St.
617-784-7822

Somerville MA 02143
Dormition of the Virgin Mary GOA
29 Central St.
617-625-2222

South Boston MA 02127
Holy Trinity ADA
245 D St.
P.O. Box 224
617-268-8708

South Boston MA 02127
St. George's Cathedral OCA
523 E Broadway
617-268-1275

South Boston MA 02127
St. John the Baptist OCA
410 W. Broadway
617-268-3564

Southbridge MA 01550
St. George GOA
55 North St.
P.O. Box 25
508-764-3398

Southbridge MA 01550
St. Michael RMA
16 Romanian Ave.
P.O. Box 823
508-765-5276

Southbridge MA 01550
St. Nicholas OCA
126 Morris St.
508-764-6226

Springfield MA 01101
Ss. Peter & Paul OCA
118 Carew St.
P.O. Box 2843
413-734-8472

Springfield MA 01104
St. George Cathedral GOA
8 Plainfield St.
413-737-1496

Watertown MA 02172
Taxiarchai GOA
25 Bigelow Ave.
617-924-8182

Webster MA 01570
Ss. Constantine & Helen GOA
Lake Parkway
P.O. Box 713
508-943-8361

West Hyannisport MA 02672
Our Lady of Kazan OCA
35 Patricia St.
Box 212
508-775-8978

Weston MA 02193
St. Demetrios GOA
57 Brown St.
P.O. Box 463
617-237-5561, FAX 617-237-8612

Woburn MA 01801
Annunciation GOA
70 Montvale Ave.
617-935-2424

Worcester MA 01609
Assumption of the Virgin Mary OCA
535 Salisbury St.
508-756-1690

Worcester MA 01604
St. George Cathedral ANT
30 Anna St.
617-752-9150

Worcester MA 01610-1513
St. Nicholas RMA
14 Hammond St.
508-799-0040

Worcester MA 01609
St. Spyridon GOA
102 Russell St.
508-791-7326

Michigan

Albion MI 49224-0367
Holy Ascension OCA
810 Austin Ave.
P.O. Box 367
517-629-3626, 517-321-0915

Ann Arbor MI 48104
St. Nicholas GOA
414 N. Main St.
313-769-2945

Battle Creek MI
Ss. Constantine & Helen GOA
1020 Goquac St.

Benton Harbor MI 49022
Annunciation GOA
725 Broadway
616-926-2972

Berkley MI 48072
St. Mary ANT
3212 W. Twelve Mile Rd.
313-545-9451

Bloomfield Hills MI 48013
St. George GOA
1515 Woodward Ave.
313-335-8869

Burton - Flint MI 48519
St. Nicholas OCA
2143 S. Center Rd.
313-744-0070

Dearborn MI 48126
Holy Trinity UOA
7103 Normile St.
313-581-8781

Dearborn MI 48128
St. Clement of Ohrid BEC
1900 Ford Rd.

Dearborn Heights MI 48127
Ss. Peter & Paul OCA
750 N. Beech Daly Rd.
313-274-9651

Dearborn Heights MI 48127
St. Paul Cathedral OCA
700 Beech Daly Rd.
313-565-9863

Detroit MI 48211
All Saints Cathedral OCA
2918 E. Hendrie Ave.

Detroit MI 48226
Annunciation Cathedral GOA
707 E. Lafayette Blvd.
313-965-2988

Detroit MI 48234-1458
Holy Trinity OCA
20500 Anglin
313-366-0677

Detroit MI 48206
Incarnation ANT
10331 Dexter
313-361-0110

Detroit MI 48210
Ss. Peter & Paul OCA
3800 Gilbert & Clayton Sts.
313-897-3308

Detroit MI 48234
St. Lazarus Cathedral
'Ravanica' SOC
4575 E. Outer Dr.
313-893-6025, FAX 313-892-6944

Detroit MI 48203
St. Nicholas GOA
17400 2nd Blvd.
313-868-1844

Detroit MI 48234
St. Petka SOC
18040 Van Dyke Ave.
313-893-4858

Detroit MI 48221
St. Spyridon GOA
19405 Renfrew Rd.
313-864-5433

Ecorse MI 48229
Holy Ascension NGM
4337 W. Jeffords St.
313-388-0386

Farmington Hills MI 48336
Holy Cross GOA
25225 Middlebelt
313-477-1677

Farmington Hills MI 48336-2814
St. Thomas OCA
29150 Ten Mile Rd.
313-471-1059

Flint MI 48532
Assumption GOA
G-3170 W. Beecher Rd.
313-732-2660

Flint MI 48507
St. George ANT
5191 Lennon Rd.
313-732-0720, FAX 313-732-0324

Grand Rapids MI 49503
Holy Trinity GOA
330 Lakeside Dr. N.E.
616-454-6563

Grand Rapids MI 49506
St. George ANT
334 La Grave S.E.
1413 Alexander S.E.
616-454-7558, 616-243-5705, FAX 616-454-8174

Grand Rapids MI 49506
St. Nicholas ANT
2148 Boston St. S.E.
616-452-2700

Grass Lake MI 49240-0309 MAIL
Nativity of the Blessed Virgin Mary OCA
<Jackson MI>
P.O. Box 309
517-522-4800

Gross Pointe Farms MI 48236 MAIL
St. Panteleimon GOA
<Lexington MI>
428 Calvin St.
313-884-0292

Haslett MI 48840 MAIL
St. James ANT
<Williamston MI>
5921 Bayonne Ave.
517-339-2130, 517-339-2184

Iron Mountain MI 49801
St. Mary ANT
309 W. 'D' St.
1313 Stockbridge
906-774-3772

Ironwood MI 49938
St. Simon ANT
P.O. Box 725
906-774-3772

Jackson MI 49201
Nativity of the Blessed Virgin Mary OCA
2522 Grey Tower Rd.
517-522-4800

Jackson MI 49204-0125
St. Demetrius OCA
3043 Seymour Rd.
P.O. Box 125
517-784-0116

Kalamazoo MI 49007
Annunciation GOA
507 S. Westnedge Ave.
616-345-5389

Lansing MI 48912
Holy Trinity GOA
1701 E. Saginaw St.
517-482-7315

Lexington MI
St. Panteleimon GOA
7143 Cedar Rd.
313-884-0292

Livonia MI 48152-3239
Holy Transfiguration OCA
36075 W. Seven Mile Rd.
313-477-4712

Livonia MI 48152
St. Mary ANT
18100 Merriman Rd.
313-422-0010

Marquette MI 49855
Assumption GOA
235 W. Ridge St.
906-226-6792

Monroe MI 48161
St. George SOC
2330 N. Monroe St.
312-241-1169

Mt. Clemens MI 48044
St. Andrew ANT
42250 Hayes Rd.
313-286-7212

Muskegon MI 49442
Annunciation GOA
1194 Terrace St.
616-725-8237

New Buffalo MI 49117-0099 MAIL
Annunciation GOA
<Benton Harbor MI>
P.O. Box 99

Plymouth Township MI 48170
Nativity of the Virgin Mary GOA
39851 Five Mile Rd.
313-420-0131

Pontiac MI
St. George RMA

Rochester MI 48307
St. Mark OCA
400 W. Hamlin
313-656-1630

Saginaw MI 48601
Holy Trinity UOA
3630 Wilkins St.
313-629-5400

Saginaw MI 48603
St. Demetrios GOA
4970 Mackinaw at McCarty
517-793-8822

Sault Ste. Marie MI 49783
St. George GOA
511 Court St.
906-632-6351

Southfield MI 48075
St. George Cathedral OCA
18405 W. Nine Mile Rd.
313-569-4833

Southgate MI 48195
St. George GOA
16300 Dix Toledo Hwy.
313-283-8820, 313-282-5700

St. Clair Shores MI 48080-2599
Assumption GOA
21800 Marter Rd.
313-779-6111

Sterling Heights MI 48077
St. John GOA
11455 Metro Pkwy.
313-977-6080

Troy MI 48098
Holy Trinity RMA
1850 E. Square Lake Rd.
313-879-2667

Troy MI 48083
St. George ANT
2240 E. Maple
810-589-0480

Troy MI 48098
St. Nicholas OCA
5353 Livernois Rd.
313-891-7857

Troy MI 48098-4500
St. Nicholas GOA
760 W. Waffles Rd.
313-362-9575

Warren MI 48092
Descent of Holy Ghost OCA
31500 Ryan Rd.
313-979-5193

Warren MI 48093
St. Stevan Decanski NGM
14235 E. 11 Mile Rd.
313-773-1940

Westland MI 48185
Ss. Constantine & Helen GOA
36375 Joy Rd.
P.O. Box 32
313-525-6789

Williamston MI 48895
St. James ANT
310 S. Putnam
517-339-2130, 517-339-2184

Minnesota

Chisholm MN 55719
St. Basil of Ostrog SOC
543 6th St. S.W.
P.O. Box 192
218-254-4874

Chisholm MN 55719
St. Nicholas OCA
402 2nd Ave. N.W.
218-254-4485

Duluth MN 55808-1616
Nativity of the Theotokos NGM
1129 101st Ave. W.
1519 99th Ave. W.
218-626-1580

Duluth MN 55808
St. George SOC
1216 104th Ave. W.
218-626-1856

Duluth MN 55805
Twelve Holy Apostles GOA
632 E. 2nd St.
218-722-5957

Hibbing MN 55746
Holy Archangel Michael SOC
701 E. 40th St.
P.O. Box 453
218-263-5027

Holdingford MN 56340
Nativity of Holy Virgin OCA
R.R. 1 Box 376

Minneapolis MN 55417
St. Herman OCA
5355 38th Ave. S.
612-722-2506

Minneapolis MN 55408-3399
St. Mary GOA
3450 Irving Ave. S.
612-825-9595, FAX 612-825-9283

Minneapolis MN 55413
St. Mary's Cathedral OCA
1701 5th St. N.E.
612-781-7667

Rochester MN 55902-6231
Holy Anargyroi GOA
703 W. Center St.
507-282-1529

South St. Paul MN 55075
St. Sava NGM
357 2nd Ave. S.
612-451-0775

St. Paul MN 55117
Falling Asleep of the Blessed Virgin Mary OCA
Atwater & Woodbridge Sts.
612-489-5618

St. Paul MN 55106
Holy Trinity OCA
956 Forest St.
612-771-5614

St. Paul MN 55104
Holy Trinity of the Twin Cities SOC
113 N. Saratoga St.
612-641-0828

St. Paul MN 55105
St. George GOA
1111 Summit Ave.
612-222-6220

St. Paul MN 55107
St. Mary ANT
678 S. Robert St.
612-224-5151

West St. Paul MN 55118-2601
St. George ANT
1250 Oakdale Ave.
612-457-0854, 612-457-3865

Mississippi

Biloxi MS 39531
Holy Trinity GOA
255 Beauvoir Rd.
601-388-6138

Clinton MS 39056
Holy Resurrection OCA
501 W. College St.
601-924-0292

Gulfport MS 39507
St. Mary ANT
3224 D Ave.
601-864-1568

Jackson MS 39203
Holy Trinity & St. John the Theologian GOA
1417 W. Capitol St.
601-355-6325

Jackson MS 39206-6652
St. Peter ANT
P.O. Box 16652
601-856-3894

Long Beach MS 39560 MAIL
St. Mary ANT
<Gulfport MS>
P.O. Box 742
601-864-1568

Vicksburg MS 39181-0342
St. George ANT
2709 S. Washington St.
P.O. Box 342
601-636-2483

Missouri

Desloge MO 63601
Nativity of Holy Virgin OCA
400 Tyler St.
314-431-4284

Kansas City MO 64145
Annunciation GOA
12001 Wornall Rd.
816-942-9100

Kansas City MO 64152
St. Theodore of Tarsus OCA
7409 N.W. Hwy. 9
816-587-9568

St. Louis MO 63104
Archangel Michael OCA
1901 Ann Ave.
314-776-4205

St. Louis MO 63104
Holy Trinity NGM
1900 -1910 McNair Ave.
314-776-3262, 314-776-9693

St. Louis MO 63122
St. John the Theologian SOC
1372 Beverly Ave.
314-962-2412

St. Louis MO 63108
St. Nicholas GOA
4967 Forest Park Blvd.
314-361-6924, 314-361-3539

St. Louis MO 63109
St. Thomas the Apostle OCA
6501 Nottingham Ave.
314-353-9785

Town & Country MO 63131
Assumption GOA
1755 Des Peres Rd.
314-966-2255

Montana

Billings MT
Orthodox Mission OCA

Billings MT 59104
St. Elijah SOC
2931 Colton Blvd.
P.O. Box 20842
406-259-3466

Billings MT 59105
St. Nicholas GOA
931 Silverbell Cl.

Butte MT 59701
Holy Trinity SOC
2300 Continental Dr.
406-723-7889

Great Falls MT 59401
Ss. Constantine & Helen GOA
1101 1st Ave. N.

Missoula MT 59807
Annunciation GOA
301 S. 6th St. W.
P.O. Box 9192
406-726-3445

Nebraska

Bayard NE 69334
Dormition of the Virgin Mary GOA
818 1st Ave.
P.O. Box 550
308-586-1926, FAX 308-586-1667

Grand Island NE 68802
Holy Trinity GOA
1015 W. 10th St.
P. O. Box 998
308-382-5290

Kearney NE 68847-6203
St. George ANT
1505 Avenue G
308-234-9456

Lincoln NE 68505-2286
Annunciation GOA
950 N. 63rd St.
402-464-2706

Omaha NE 68107
Holy Cross RMA
3221 'R' St.
715-455-1553

Omaha NE 68105
St. John the Baptist GOA
602 Park Ave.
402-345-7103

Omaha NE 68134
St. Mary ANT
10303 Boyd St.
402-496-0480

Omaha NE 68157
St. Nicholas SOC
5052 Harrison St.
402-734-4194

Omaha NE 68114
St. Vincent of Lerins ANT
1717 N. 106th St.
402-496-2406, 402-493-8102

Nevada

Ely NV
St. Alexios GOA

Las Vegas NV
Falling Asleep of the Virgin Mary OCA

Las Vegas NV 89118-1922
St. John the Baptist GOA
53005 El Camino Rd.
702-221-8245

Las Vegas NV 89115
St. Michael ANT
5719 E. Judson Ave.
702-452-1299

Las Vegas NV 89120
St. Paul OCA
5400 Annie Oakley Dr.
702-898-4800

Las Vegas NV 89103
St. Simeon SOC
3950 S. Jones Blvd.
702-367-7783

McGill NV 89318
St. Barbara GOA
4th St.
P.O. Box 1352
702-235-7341

Reno NV 89509
St. Anthony GOA
4795 Lakeside Dr.
702-825-5365

New Hampshire

Berlin NH 03570
Holy Resurrection OCA
20 Petrograd St.
603-752-2254

Claremont NH 03743
Holy Resurrection OCA
99 Sullivan St.
603-542-6273

Concord NH 03301
Holy Trinity GOA
68 N. State St.
603-225-2961

Dover NH 03820
Annunciation GOA
93 Locust St.
P.O. Box 851
603-742-7667

Franklin NH 03235
Transfiguration GOA
Sullowey St.

Keene NH 03431
St. George GOA
70 West St.
603-352-6424

Laconia NH 03246-2604
Greek Orthodox Church of Laconia NH GOA
811 N. Main St.
603-524-9415

Laconia NH 03246
Taxiarchai GOA
811 N. Main St.
617-872-8323

Manchester NH 03103
Assumption GOA
111 Island Pond Rd.
603-623-2045

Manchester NH 03104
St. George Cathedral GOA
650 Hanover St.
603-622-9113, 603-699-2167

Manchester NH 03104
St. Nicholas GOA
1168 Bridge St.
603-625-6115

Nashua NH 03062
St. Philip GOA
500 W. Hollis St.
603-889-4000

Newport NH 03773
St. Vasilios GOA
45 Winter St.
P.O. Box 428
603-292-1000

Portsmouth NH 03801-5448
St. Nicholas GOA
40 Andrew Jarris Dr.
603-436-2733

Somersworth NH 03878
Assumption GOA
4 Green St.
Bougrakos; Lily Pond Rd.

New Jersey

Alpha NJ 08865
St. John the Baptist OCA
1034 2nd Ave.
908-454-1553

Asbury Park NJ 07712
St. George GOA
700 Grand Ave.
908-775-2777

Atlantic City NJ 08401
St. Nicholas GOA
13 S. Mt. Vernon Ave.
P.O. Box 641
609-348-3495

Bargaintown NJ
Holy Trinity GOA
Mill Rd. & Ridge Ave.
609-653-8092

Bayonne NJ 07002
Ss. Peter & Paul OCA
98 W. 28th St.
201-436-3244

Bayonne NJ 07602
St. Mary CRC
90 W. 30th St.
201-436-5549

Bergenfield NJ 07621
St. Anthony ANT
385 Ivy Ln.
203-768-0324

Brick Town NJ 08724
Annunciation OCA
360 Van Zile Rd.
908-458-9032

Cherry Hill NJ 08002 MAIL
Holy Cross OCA
<Medford NJ>
24 Colmar Rd.
609-665-2491, FAX 609-265-0864

Cherry Hill NJ 08002
St. Thomas GOA
615 Mercer St.
609-665-1731

Clifton NJ 07013
Assumption of the Holy Virgin OCA
35 Orange Ave.
201-365-9671

Clifton NJ 07013
St. George GOA
818 Valley Rd.
201-779-2626

Demarest NJ 07627 MAIL
St. Anthony ANT
<Bergenfield NJ>
59 Columbus Rd.
203-768-0324

Dover NJ 07801
St. Andrew GOA
Sussex Turnpike; Randolph Township
P.O. Box 336
201-584-0388

Elizabeth NJ 07207
Holy Ascension NGM
117 Liberty St.
201-354-4134

Elizabeth NJ 07202
St. George SOC
654 S. Broad St.
908-352-8990

Elizabeth NJ 07202-2602
St. Nicholas CRC
668 S. Broad St.
908-354-1384

Englewood NJ 07631
St. John Chrysostom ANT
358 Mountain Rd
201-871-1355, 201-871-1356, FAX 201-871-7954

Fairview NJ 07022
Ascension GOA
Anderson Ave. & Henry St.
201-945-6448

Flemington NJ 08822 MAIL
St. Gregory Palamas OCA
<Stanton NJ>
P.O. Box 634
908-788-3887

Freehold NJ 07728-3288
St. Paul the Apostle CRC
24 Burke Rd.
3587 Hwy. 9 #214
908-780-3158, 908-364-2942

Holmdel-Hazlet NJ 07733-0367
Kimisis Tis Theotokou GOA
20 Hillcrest Rd.
P.O.Box 367
908-739-1515, 908-566-4449

Jackson NJ 08527
Nativity of the Holy Virgin OCA
P.O. Box 146
908-928-3223

Jersey City NJ 07306
Evangelismos GOA
661 Montgomery St.
201-432-2488

Jersey City NJ 07302-4428
Ss. Peter & Paul OCA
109 Grand St.
201-434-1986

Jersey City NJ 07306
St. Demetrios GOA
524 Summit Ave.
201-792-0697

Little Falls NJ 07424
St. George ANT
237 Long Hill Rd.
201-256-8961

Manville NJ 08835
Holy Ghost CRC
249 S. 7th Ave.
201-725-3385

Manville NJ 08835
Ss. Peter & Paul OCA
605 Washington Ave.
908-685-1452

Mays Landing NJ 08330-0398
Mother of God 'Joy of All Who Sorrow' OCA
Hudson St. & Cedar Ave.
P.O. Box 398

Medford NJ 08055
Holy Cross OCA
127 Medford Mt. Holly Rd. (Rt. 541 N.)
609-654-4865, 609-665-2491

Newark NJ 07105
St. Michael OCA
227 Oliver St.
201-589-8712

Newark NJ 07102
St. Nicholas GOA
555 High St.
201-623-6211

North Wildwood NJ 08262-0277
St. Demetrios GOA
301 Anglesea Ave.
P.O. Box 277
609-522-0152

Northfield NJ 08225 MAIL
Holy Trinity GOA
<Bargaintown NJ>
P.O. Box 769
609-653-8092

Ocean City NJ 08226
St. John Chrysostom OCA
1914 Central Ave.
609-398-3207

Orange NJ 07050
Ss. Constantine & Helen GOA
510 Linden Pl.
201-674-6600

Paramus NJ 07652
Christ the Savior OCA
365 Paramus Rd.
201-652-6633

Paramus NJ 07652
St. Athanasios GOA
51 Paramus Rd.
201-368-8881

Passaic NJ 07055
St. John the Baptist OCA
170 Lexington Ave.
201-473-1928

Paterson NJ 07501
St. John the Baptist SOC
119 Carlisle Ave.
718-389-7296

Perth Amboy NJ 08862-1068
St. Demetrios GOA
Sadowski Pkwy. & Wisteria St.
P.O. Box 1068
908-826-4466

Perth Amboy NJ 08861
St. John the Baptist CRC
145 Broad St.
908-826-4442

Piscataway NJ 08854
St. George GOA
1101 River Rd.
908-463-1642

Princeton NJ 08544
Orthodox Christian Fellowship / Holy Transfiguration OCA
Murray Dodge Hall; Princeton Univ.
109 Rollingmead
609-924-7368

Rahway NJ 07065
St. John the Baptist CRC
211 W. Grand Ave.
908-382-8844

Rahway - Clark NJ 07065
Holy Trinity OCA
830 Jefferson Ave.
908-574-1234

Randolph NJ 07801
Holy Trinity OCA
120 Dover-Chester Rd.
201-366-8360

Rockaway NJ 07866-3514
Ss. Peter & Paul CRC
64 Beach St.
201-627-1462

Saddlebrook NJ 07662
Holy Apostles OCA
17 Platt Ave.
201-444-8580

South Plainfield NJ 07080
Nativity of the Blessed Virgin UOA
416 Delmore Ave.
201-756-7223

South Plainfield NJ 07080-3516
St. Stephen ANT
609 Lane Ave.
908-756-0410

South River NJ 08882-2314
Ss. Peter & Paul OCA
76 Whitehead Ave.
153 Kamm Ave.
908-257-0102

Stanton NJ 08885
St. Gregory Palamas OCA
Hwy. 31; Stanton Pl.
908-788-3887

Stanton NJ 08885
St. Luke's Priory ANT
P.O. Box 84
908-236-7890

Tenafly NJ 07670
St. John the Theologian Cathedral GOA
353 E. Clinton Ave.
201-567-5072

Toms River NJ 08753
St. Barbara GOA
2200 Church Rd.
908-255-5525

Trenton NJ 08619
St. George GOA
1200 Klockner Rd.
609-586-4448

Trenton NJ 08610
St. Vladimir OCA
812 Grand St.
609-393-1234

Union NJ 07083
St. Demetrios GOA
721 Rahway Ave.
908-964-7957

Vernon NJ 07462
Holy Spirit OCA
@VFW Lower Hall; Rts. 94 & 515
P.O. Box 399

Vineland NJ 08360
St. Anthony GOA
430 W. Wheat Rd.
609-696-0917

Wayne NJ 07470
Holy Resurrection OCA
285 French Hill Rd.
201-696-6572

Westfield NJ 07090
Holy Trinity GOA
250 Gallows Hill Rd.
908-233-8533

Wyckoff NJ 07481
St. Nicholas GOA
467 Grandview Ave.
201-652-4774, FAX 201-652-0789

New Mexico

Albuquerque NM
Ss. Cosmas & Damian OCA

Albuquerque NM
St. Catherine GOA
@Cannon A.F.B.

Albuquerque NM 87102
St. George GOA
308 High St. S.E.
505-247-9411

Clovis NM 88101 MAIL
St. Catherine GOA
<Albuquerque NM>
3609 Palmer Ct.

Santa Fe NM 87502
Dormition of the All-Holy Theotokos OCA
885 El Caminito
Box 4596
505-271-1515

Santa Fe NM 87505
St. Elias the Prophet GOA
85 Moya Rd.
505-982-8586

Santa Fe NM 87504
St. Joseph ANT
P.O. Box 602
505-988-9835

New York

Albany NY 12209
St. George ANT
St. George Pl. & S. Dove St.
P.O. Box 9060
518-462-0579

Albany NY 12208
St. Sophia GOA
440 Whitehall Rd.
518-489-4442

Astoria NY 11106-1407
Ss. Constantine & Helen GOA
14-54 31st Rd.
35-18 31st Ave #3A
718-721-3810

Astoria NY 11105
St. Catherine - St. George GOA
22-28 33rd St.
718-728-1100

Astoria NY 11102
St. Demetrios Cathedral GOA
30-11 30th Dr.
718-728-1718

Auburn NY 13021
St. Nicholas OCA
28 Cross St.
315-252-3423

Binghamton NY 13905
Dormition of the Virgin Mary OCA
53 Baxter St.
607-797-1058

Binghamton NY 13901
Holy Trinity GOA
214 Court St.
607-723-9662, 607-798-0963

Binghamton NY 13905
St. Michael CRC
280 Clinton St.
607-797-4471

Blue Point NY 11715
St. John GOA
77 Montauk Hwy.
516-363-6450

Bronx NY 10463
Greek Orthodox Community of Kingsbridge and Riverdale GOA
Kingsbridge Ave.
P.O. Box 356

Bronx NY 10461
Zoodochos Peghe GOA
3573 Bruckner Blvd.
718-823-2030

Brooklyn NY 11209
Holy Cross GOA
8401 Ridge Blvd.
718-836-3510

Brooklyn NY 11211
Holy Trinity UOA
185 S. 5th St.
718-388-4723

Brooklyn NY 11215
Kimisis tis Theotokou GOA
224 18th St.
718-788-0152

Brooklyn NY 11201
Ss. Constantine & Helen Cathedral GOA
64 Schermerhorn St.
718-624-0595

Brooklyn NY 11229
Three Hierarchs GOA
1724 Ave. P
718-339-0280

Brooklyn (Bay Ridge) NY 11209-3587
St. Mary ANT
8100 Ridge Blvd.
718-238-8008

Brooklyn (Downtown) NY 11209-0003
St. Nicholas Cathedral ANT
355 State St.
P.O. Box 090-147
718-855-6225, FAX 718-855-3608

Brooklyn - E. New York NY 11207
Holy Trinity OCA
400 Glenmore Ave.
718-498-0518

Brooklyn - Greenpoint NY 11211
Transfiguration Cathedral OCA
228 N. 12th St.
718-387-1064

Brooklyn-Glendale NY 11385
Three Hierarchs OCA
7105 Cooper Ave. @ Myrtle and 71st Sts.
718-366-1358

Brooklyn-Ridgewood NY 11385
Descent of Holy Spirit OCA
@St. Bridget Church; 409 Linden St.
60-23 Catalpa Ave.
718-628-6145

Brooklyn-Ridgewood NY 11385 MAIL
Three Hierarchs OCA
<Brooklyn-Glendale NY>
6332 Forest Ave.
718-366-1358

Buffalo NY 14222
Annunciation GOA
146 W. Utica St.
716-882-9485, 716-882-9495

Buffalo NY 14206-1402
Ss. Peter & Paul OCA
45 Ideal St.
44 Benzinger St.
716-893-0044, FAX 716-896-4159

Buffalo NY 14216
St. George OCA
2 Nottingham Terrace
716-873-9106

Buffalo NY 14217 MAIL
St. Nicola BEC
<Lackawanna NY>
1496 Kenmore

Cheektowaga NY 14227
St. Mary CRC
940 Losson Rd.
81 Fairoaks Ln.
716-668-4465, 716-892-3150

Cohoes NY 12047
St. Nicholas OCA
67 Saratoga St.
518-237-5335

Corning NY 14830
St. Mary CRC
254 Sunset Dr.
607-936-9284

Corona NY 11368
Transfiguration GOA
38-05 98th St.
718-458-5251

Dix Hills NY 11746
St. Andrew OCA
1095 Carll's Straight Path
516-586-1611

East Herkimer NY 13350
Ss. Peter & Paul OCA
R.D. 1; Main St.
315-866-3272

East Meadow NY 11554
Holy Trinity OCA
369 Green Ave.
516-483-3649

Ellenville NY 12428
St. Mary's Dormition Chapel UOA
c/o Ukrainian Youth Association
914-647-9680

Elmhurst NY 11373
St. Mary OCA
42-14 74th St.
718-726-6113

Elmira Heights NY 14903
Holy Trinity OCA
140 Horseheads Blvd.
607-732-3980

Elmira-Corning NY 14904
St. Athanasios GOA
210 Franklin St.
607-734-0771

Endicott NY 13760
Ss. Peter & Paul OCA
210 Hill Ave.
607-745-0249

Endicott NY 13760
St. Mary CRC
1907 Jenkins St.
607-754-8952

Flushing NY 11358
St. Nicholas GOA
196-10 Northern Blvd.
718-357-4200

Garrison NY 10524-9742
St. Basil GOA
Rt. 2; Box 8A
914-424-3500

Geneva NY 14456
St. Michael ANT
98 Genesee St.
P.O. Box 185
315-789-3060

Glen Cove NY 11542
Resurrection GOA
34 Cedar Swamp Rd.
516-671-5200

Gloversville NY 12078
Ss. Theodoroi GOA
70 Washington St.

Greenlawn NY 11740
St. Paraskevi GOA
Shrine Pl.
516-261-7272

Hempstead NY 11550
St. Paul Cathedral GOA
110 Cathedral Ave.
516-483-5700

Hicksville NY 11801
Holy Trinity GOA
20 Field Ave.
516-433-4522

New York

Hicksville NY 11801
St. Mary UOA
40 W. Carl St.
516-541-8977

Island Park NY 11558
Kimisis Tis Theotokou GOA
83 Newport Rd.
P.O. Box 308
516-432-4086

Ithaca NY 14850
St. Catherine GOA
120 W. Seneca St.
607-273-2767

Jackson Heights NY 11372
Ss. Constantine & Helen GOA
37-57 72nd St.
718-639-0611

Jamaica NY 11435
St. Andrew Cathedral UOA
90-34 139th St.
718-297-2407

Jamaica NY 11432
St. Demetrios GOA
84-35 152nd St.
718-291-2420

Jamaica Estates NY 11432-1433
St. Nicholas OCA
181-14 Midland Pkwy.
718-380-5684

Jamestown NY 14701
St. Elia OCA
101 Palmer St. Box 1274
716-487-0728

Jamestown NY 14701
St. Nicholas GOA
Mt. Vernon Pl. & Francis St.
P.O. Box 264
716-483-0022, 716-484-7737

Kingston NY 12401
St. George GOA
294 Greenkill Ave.
U.P.O Box 3062
914-331-3522

Lackawanna NY
St. Nicola BEC

Lackawanna NY 14218-2837
St. Stephen SOC
177 Weber Rd.
716-823-2846

Latham NY 12110 MAIL
Christ the Savior OCA
<Milton NY>
22 Fairlawn Dr.
518-885-4681, 518-786-3100

Long Island City NY 11102 MAIL
St. Catherine-St. George GOA
<Astoria NY>
30-11 30th Dr.
718-728-1100

Mattituck NY 11952
Transfiguration of Christ GOA
1950 Breakwater Rd.
P.O. Box 1162
516-298-9652

Merrick NY 11566
St. Demetrios GOA
2421 Hewlett Ave.
24 Kenney Ave.
516-379-1368

Middletown NY 10940
Greek Orthodox Church of Orange County GOA
R.D. 6 Box 109
Goshen Turnpike
914-695-1976

Milton NY 12020
Christ the Savior OCA
3425 Galway Rd.
518-885-4681, 518-786-3100

New Rochelle NY 10804
Holy Trinity GOA
10 Mill Rd.
914-235-6100

New York City NY 10003
All Saints UOA
206 E. 11th St.
212-475-9534

New York City NY 10024
Annunciation GOA
302 W. 91st St.
212-724-2070

New York City NY 10021
Christ the Savior OCA
340 E. 71st St.
212-744-8502

New York City NY 10021
Holy Trinity Cathedral GOA
319-337 E. 74th St.
212-288-3215

New York City NY 10003-9270
Protection of the Holy Virgin Cathedral OCA
59 E. 2nd St.
212-420-0667

New York City NY 10040
Ss. Anargyroi GOA
1547 St. Nicholas Ave.
212-568-0367

New York City NY 10108
Ss. Kirill & Methody Cathedral BEC
552 W. 50th St.
P.O. Box 83 Times Square Station
212-586-7636

New York City NY 10002
St. Barbara GOA
27 Forsyth St.
212-226-0499

New York City NY 10024
St. Dumitru OCA
50 W. 89th St.
212-874-4490

New York City NY 10011
St. Eleftherios GOA
359 W. 24th St.
212-924-3919

New York City NY 10019
St. George Tropeoforos GOA
307 W. 54th St.
212-265-7808

New York City NY 10029
St. George-St. Demetrios GOA
140 E. 103rd St.
212-722-6750

New York City NY 10025
St. Gerasimos GOA
153 W. 105th St.
212-749-0017

New York City NY 10003
St. John the Baptist GOA
143 E. 17th St.
212-473-0648

New York City NY 10009
St. Mary CRC
121 E. 7th St.
212-674-1066

New York City NY 10033
St. Mary Magdalen OCA
@ Union Theological Seminary; 121st St. W.
100 Bennett Ave. 5J
212-927-0596

New York City NY 10006
St. Nicholas GOA
155 Cedar St.
212-227-0773

New York City NY 10009
St. Nicholas CRC
288 E. 10th St.
212-254-6685

New York City NY 10025
St. Sava Cathedral NGM
P.O. Box 687 Cathedral Station
212-242-9240

New York City NY 10010
St. Sava Cathedral SOC
15 W. 25th St.
20 W. 26th St.
212-242-9240

New York City NY 10033
St. Spyridon GOA
124 Wadsworth Ave.
212-795-5870

Newburgh NY 12550
St. Nicholas GOA
19 Fullerton Ave.
P.O. Box 2004
914-561-2556

Niagara Falls NY 14301
Holy Trinity OCA
3920 Pine Ave.
716-284-9596

Niagara Falls NY 14302
St. George ANT
1073 Saunders Settlement Rd. (Rte. 31)
P.O. Box 713
716-773-3896

Pearl River NY 10965
Transfiguration OCA
Sickletown & Orangeburg Rds.
P.O. Box 960
914-735-7024

Port Jefferson NY 11776
Assumption GOA
430 Sheep Pasture Rd.
516-473-0894

Poughkeepsie NY 12603
Kimisis Tis Theotokou GOA
140 S. Grand Ave.
914-452-0772, FAX 914-452-0114

Ridgewood NY
St. George OCA

Rochester NY 14607
Annunciation GOA
962 East Ave.
716-244-3377

Rochester NY 14613
Ss. Peter & Paul OCA
30 Riverside St.
508-754-3451

Rochester NY 14620
St. John the Baptist OCA
855 S. Goodman St.
716-442-6860

Rochester NY 14605
St. Nicholas UOA
64 Niagara St.

Roslyn Heights NY 11577
Archangel Michael GOA
108 Warner Ave.
516-625-0900

Rye NY 10580
Our Savior GOA
2195 E. Westchester Ave.
914-967-2838

Schenectady NY 12305
St. George GOA
107 Clinton St.
518-393-0742

Schenectady NY 12303 MAIL
St. Nicholas OCA
<Cohoes NY>
1906 Evva Dr.
518-237-5335

Sea Cliff NY 11579-1932
Our Lady of Kazan OCA
Willow Shore Ave.
516-671-6616, FAX 516-671-3720

Seaford NY 11783
St. Gregory of Nyssa CRC
1100 Hicksville Rd.
516-541-8977

South Glens Falls NY 12803-5236
Archangel Gabriel ANT
5 McHugh St.
518-792-4985

South Glens Falls NY 12803
St. George ANT
55 Main St.
P.O. Box 1344
518-792-2359

Southampton NY 11969
Kimisis Tis Theotokou GOA
St. Andrew's Rd.
P.O. Box 2550
516-283-6169

Spring Valley NY 10977-0498
St. John the Baptist OCA
West & Church Sts.
P.O. Box 498
914-425-0259

Staten Island NY 10314
Holy Trinity-St. Nicholas GOA
1641 Richmond Ave.
718-494-0658

Staten Island NY 10303-2239
St. Ireney OCA
2099 Forest Ave.
718-720-8800

Syosset NY
St. Sergius of Radonezh Chapel, Metropolitan's Residence OCA
6850 Route 25A
516-922-0550, FAX 516-922-0954, TELEX 400245564

Syracuse NY 13204
Ss. Peter & Paul OCA
401 Hamilton St.
315-468-0442, 315-468-1715, FAX 315-468-5668

Syracuse NY 13215
St. Elias ANT
4988 Onondaga Rd.
315-488-0388

Syracuse NY 13215-0125
St. Michael OCA
411 Oswego & Fabius Sts.
P.O. Box 125
315-468-0442, 315-468-1715

Syracuse NY 13224
St. Sophia GOA
325 Waring Rd.
315-446-5222

Troy NY 12180
St. Basil GOA
909 River St.
518-273-8923

Uniondale NY 11553
St. John the Baptist ANT
560 Uniondale Ave.
516-485-8934

Utica NY 13501
St. George ANT
1104 Brinkerhoff Ave.
315-735-7465

Vestal NY 13903
Annunciation GOA
1 Hellenic Center
607-797-0824

Wantagh NY 11793-0199
St. Markella GOA
1960 Jones Ave. N.
P.O. Box 11
516-783-5760

Wappingers Falls NY 12590
St. Gregory the Theologian OCA
1824 Rt. 376
914-462-3887

Watertown NY 13601
St. Vasilios GOA
516 Franklin St.
315-788-4920

Watervliet NY 12189
St. Basil OCA
36 Archibald St.
518-273-6262

West Babylon NY 11704
St. Nicholas GOA
200 Great East Neck Rd.
516-587-1150, 516-587-1253

West Nyack NY 10994
Ss. Constantine & Helen GOA
1 Mary Crest Rd.
914-623-4023

West Point NY 10996
St. Herman Community OCA
U.S. Military Academy;
Office of Cadet Chaplains

Whitestone NY 11357
Holy Cross GOA
150-05 12th Ave.
718-767-2943

Whitestone NY 11357-2643
St. Nicholas OCA
14-65 Clintonville St.
718-767-7292

Windham NY 12496
Assumption GOA
P.O. Box 454
518-734-4631

Woodside NY 11377
St. John Chrysostom OCA
70-29 45th Ave.
718-429-8245

Woodside NY 11377
St. Nicholas RMA
45-03 48th Ave.
718-784-4453

Yaphank NY 11980
St. John the Theologian OCA
@ Yaphank Presbyterian Church; Main St.
P.O. Box 274
516-475-7146

Yonkers NY 10701
Holy Trinity OCA
46 Seymour St.
914-965-6815

Yonkers NY 10705
Prophet Elias GOA
15 LeRoy Ave.
914-963-3638

Yonkers NY 10701-1923
St. Mary CRC
485 N. Broadway
914-963-5549

Yonkers NY 10703
Virgin Mary ANT
77 High St.
914-476-1072

North Carolina

Asheville NC 28814
Holy Trinity GOA
227 Cumberland Ave.
P.O. Box 8369
704-253-3754

Asheville NC
Orthodox Mission ANT

Burlington NC 27215
St. Katherine GOA
2150 W. 4th St.
P.O. Box 1004
919-226-8243

Cary NC
All Saints ANT
919-851-5335

Charlotte NC 28203
Holy Trinity Cathedral GOA
600 East Blvd.
704-334-4771

Charlotte NC 28213
Nativity of the Holy Theotokos OCA
1700 Mineral Springs Rd.
704-596-8252

Durham NC 27702
St. Barbara GOA
1316 Watts St.
P.O. Box 1149
919-682-1414

Fayetteville NC 28305
Ss. Constantine & Helen GOA
614 Oakridge Ave.
919-484-2010

Fayetteville NC 28302
St. Nicholas OCA
P.O. Box 31
914-484-7771

Greensboro NC 27410
Dormition of the Theotokos GOA
800 Westridge Rd.
919-292-8013

High Point NC 27262
St. George GOA
808 N. Hamilton St.
919-888-9028

Raleigh NC 27607 MAIL
All Saints ANT
<Cary NC>
7404-M Chapel Hill Rd.
919-851-5335

Raleigh NC 27612-3434
Holy Trinity GOA
5000 Lead Mine Rd.
919-781-4548

Raleigh NC 27609
St. Gregory the Great OCA
@Episcopal Diocesan House; 201 St. Alban's Dr.
125 Salem Circle B-4
919-781-5477

Wilmington NC 28403
St. Nicholas GOA
608 S. College Rd.
919-392-4484

Winston-Salem NC 27104
Annunciation GOA
435 Keating Dr. S.W.
919-765-7145

North Dakota

Fargo ND 58102-2619 MAIL
All Saints ANT
1362 N. 9th St.
701-293-0694

Minot ND 58701
St. Mary GOA
109 6th St. S.E.
P.O. Box 845
701-838-3094

Minot ND 58702
St. Peter the Aleut OCA
109 6th St. S.E.
P.O. Box 845
701-838-3094

Ohio

Akron OH 44304
Annunciation GOA
129 S. Union St.
216-434-0000

Akron OH 44333-3197
Presentation of Our Lord OCA
3365 Ridgewood Rd.
216-666-8054

Akron OH 44312
St. Archangel Michael SOC
2552 Pickle Rd.
216-644-1571

Akron OH 44309
St. Demetrius NGM
3106 Ridgewood Rd.
P.O. Box 151
216-666-7852

Akron OH 44313
St. George ANT
3204 Ridgewood Rd.
216-666-7116, FAX 216-456-6207

Akron OH 44306-2651
St. Mary CRC
1357 Coventry St.
216-724-5828

Akron OH 44301
St. Prophet Elia OCA
64 W. Wilbeth Rd.
216-724-7129, 216-724-7009

Akron OH 44320
St. Thomas BEC
870 Copley Rd.

Alliance OH 44601
St. Nicholas OCA
1035 E. Grant St.
216-499-3432

Amsterdam OH 43903-9801
All Saints OCA
R.D. 1; Wolf Run
614-543-3671

Barton OH 43905
St. Nicholas CRC
P.O. Box 777
614-695-9533

Bellaire OH 43906
Ss. Cyril & Methodius OCA
527 44th St.
412-343-4394

Berea OH 44017-2522 MAIL
St. Matthew ANT
<North Royalton OH>
192 Prospect
216-826-0662

Broadview Heights OH 44147
Archangel Michael OCA
5025 E. Mill Rd.
216-526-5192

Broadview Hgts. OH 44147
St. Sava NGM
2151 Wallings Rd.
216-237-2260

Brooklyn OH 44144 MAIL
St. Theodosius Cathedral OCA
<Cleveland OH>
8200 Biddulph Rd.
216-741-1310

Byesville OH 43723
Christ the Savior OCA
282 S. 5th St.
513-422-1213

Campbell OH 44405
Archangel Michael GOA
401 12th St.
216-755-3596

Campbell OH 44405
St. John the Baptist OCA
301 Struthers-Liberty Rd.
216-755-4931

Canton OH 44705-2175
Holy Assumption OCA
2027 18th St. N.E.
216-455-9146

Canton OH 44711
Holy Cross ANT
5015 Ridge Ave. S.E.
P.O. Box 8034
216-484-1284

Canton OH 44709
Holy Trinity GOA
4705 Fairhaven Ave. N.W.
216-494-8770

Canton OH 44709
St. George OCA
144 30th St. N.W.
216-492-4592

Canton OH 44704-1036
St. George ANT
1118 Cherry Ave. N.E.
216-455-8482, 216-492-4592

Canton OH 44709
St. Haralambos GOA
251 25th St. N.W.
216-454-7278

Cincinnati OH 45212
Christ the Savior / Holy Spirit OCA
4285 Ashland Ave.
513-351-0907

Cincinnati OH 45231
Holy Ghost BEC
10014 Lake Park Dr.

Cincinnati OH 45224
Holy Trinity-St. Nicholas GOA
7000 Winton Rd.
513-591-0030, FAX 513-591-0034

Cincinnati OH 45223
St. Andrew RMA
837 Dayton St.
513-681-6230

Cincinnati OH 45224
St. George NGM
5830 Glenview Ave.
513-542-4452

Cleveland OH 44113
Annunciation GOA
2187 W. 14th St.
216-861-0116

Cleveland OH 44111
Falling Asleep of the Blessed Virgin Mary OCA
3256 Warren Rd.
216-941-5550

Cleveland OH 44121
St. Dimitri BEC
115 S Green Rd.

Cleveland OH 44111
St. E. Premte OCA
10716 Jasper Rd.
216-941-1508

Cleveland OH 44113-4487
St. George ANT
2587 W. 14th St.
216-781-9020

Cleveland OH 44144-3203
St. Theodosius Cathedral OCA
733 Starkweather Ave.
8200 Biddulph Rd.
216-741-1310

Cleveland Heights OH 44118
Ss. Constantine & Helen Cathedral GOA
3352 Mayfield Rd.
216-932-3300

Columbus OH 43215
Annunciation Cathedral GOA
555 N. High St.
614-224-9020, 614-224-3984

Columbus OH 43214-3825
St. Gregory of Nyssa OCA
Ohio State Univ.
271 Brevoort Rd.
614-268-4186

Columbus OH 43219
St. Stephen of Decani SOC
1840 N. Cassady Ave.
614-475-0922

Dayton OH 45405-4797
Annunciation GOA
500 Belmonte Park N.
513-224-0601

Dayton OH 45420
St. Paul the Apostle OCA
2382 Kennedy Ave.
513-254-7900

Lakewood OH 44107
Ss. Peter & Paul OCA
12711 Madison Ave.
216-521-0923

Lakewood OH 44107
St. Nicholas Pro-Cathedral UOA
2101 Quail St.
216-226-5506

Lorain OH 44055
Ss. Cyril & Methodius OCA
1795 E. 31st St.
216-277-5195

Lorain OH 44005
Ss. Cyril & Methodius BEC
31 East

Lorain OH 44055
Ss. Peter & Paul OCA
Gary Ave. & 32nd St.
216-277-5281

Lorain OH 44055
St. George SOC
3335 Grove Ave.
216-781-9020

Lorain OH 44053
St. Nicholas GOA
2000 Tower Blvd.
216-960-2992

Mansfield OH 44902
Ss. Constantine & Helen GOA
265 W. 3rd St.
419-526-0129

Maple Heights OH 44137
St. Andrew OCA
16069 Maple Park Dr.
216-475-9365

Marblehead OH 43440
Holy Assumption OCA
114 E. Main St.
419-798-4591

Martins Ferry OH 43935
Zoodochos Peghe GOA
314-316 N. 5th St.
614-633-3707

Massillon OH 44648-0438
St. George GOA
364 1st St. S.E.
P.O. Box 438
216-832-3659

Massilon OH 44648
Holy Spirit Chapel OCA
@Massilon State Hospital;
3000 S. Erie
P.O. Box 540
216-833-3135 ext. 241 or 238

Mentor OH 44060
St. Nicholas OCA
9650 Johnnycake Ridge Rd.
216-946-9571

Middletown OH 45042
Ss. Constantine & Helen GOA
2500 Grand Ave.
513-422-2312

Mingo Junction OH 43938
St. Andrew OCA
Cemetery Rd.
614-535-0128

Mogadore OH 44260-3547
St. Nicholas OCA
755 S. Cleveland Ave.
216-628-1333

Niles OH 44446
St. John Chrysostom OCA
135 S. Chestnut St.
216-369-3908

North Canton OH 44720
St. George SOC
4663 Wayview Ave. N.W.
216-494-7888, 216-494-2712

North Olmsted OH 44070
MAIL
St. Innocent OCA
<Westlake OH>
25151 Mitchell
216-979-9622

North Royalton OH 44133
Christ the Saviour CRC
10000 State Rd.
216-886-4609

North Royalton OH 44133
St. Matthew ANT
10383 Albion Rd.
P.O. Box 33183
216-826-0662

North Royalton OH 44133
St. Paul GOA
4548 Wallings Rd.
216-237-8998, FAX 216-237-8999

Norton OH 44203
Ss. Peter & Paul NGM
3532 Clark Mill Rd.
P.O. Box 1318
206-763-3968, FAX 216-745-0189

Parma OH 44134
Holy Trinity OCA
6822 Broadview Rd.
216-524-4859

Parma OH 44134
St. Sava Cathedral SOC
6306 Broadview Rd.
216-749-0064

Rocky River OH 44116
Bunavestire Cathedral RMA
3300 Wooster Rd.
216-356-1126

Rocky River OH 44116
St. Demetrios GOA
22909 Center Ridge Rd.
216-331-2246

Sheffield OH 44054
St. Mark NGM
1434 Lake Breeze Rd.
216-949-7719

Springfield OH 45501
Assumption of the Blessed Virgin GOA
1127 E. High St.
P.O. Box 1694
513-322-8169

Steubenville OH 43952
Holy Resurrection SOC
530 N. 4th St.
614-282-4463

Steubenville OH 43952
Holy Transfiguration OCA
206 N. 10th St.
614-282-2493

Steubenville OH 43952
Holy Trinity GOA
300 S. 4th St.
P.O. Box 788
614-282-9835

Sylvania OH 43560
St. Elias ANT
4940 Harroun Rd.
419-882-4037

Toledo OH 43604
Holy Trinity Cathedral GOA
802 Superior St.
740 Superior St.
419-243-9189

Toledo OH 43605
St. George Cathedral OCA
137 Oswald St.
419-691-8913

Toledo OH 43606-1159
St. George Cathedral ANT
3754 Woodley Rd.
419-475-7054, FAX 419-475-3502

Warren OH 44483-3699
Holy Resurrection OCA
1836 North Rd. N.E.
216-372-1159, 216-372-3721

Warren OH 44481
St. Demetrios GOA
429 High St. N.E.
216-394-9021

Warren OH 44484
St. Elija NGM
P.O. Box 2304
216-369-8092

Warren OH 44483-0946
St. John the Baptist OCA
2220 Reeves Rd. N.E.
P.O. Box 946
216-372-3895

Warren OH 44485
St. Nicholas CRC
2280 N. Leavitt Rd.
216-898-7507

Westlake OH 44145
St. Innocent OCA
25800 Hilliard Rd.
216-979-9622

Youngstown OH 44509
Holy Ghost OCA
18 S. Richview Ave.
216-792-9119

Youngstown OH 44509
Holy Trinity SOC
39 Laird St.
216-792-2022

Youngstown OH 44502
Holy Trinity OCA
626 Wick Ave.
216-746-4424

Youngstown OH 44515
Old Holy Trinity NGM
420 N. Racoon Rd.
216-799-0075

Youngstown OH 44512
St. John GOA
4955 Glenwood
216-788-5257, 216-788-4802

Youngstown OH 44501
St. Mark ANT
3560 Logan Way
P.O. Box 1414
216-759-8383

Youngstown OH 44509
St. Michael CRC
125 Steel St.
216-799-8133

Youngstown OH 44503
St. Nicholas GOA
220 N. Walnut St.
216-743-5493

Oklahoma

Hartshorne OK 74547
Ss. Cyril & Methodius OCA
3rd & Modoc

Jones OK 73049
St. Mary UOA
P.O. Box 793
405-524-2924

Oklahoma City OK 73107
St. Elias ANT
2101 N.W. 16th St.
405-524-2625, FAX 405-528-1832

Oklahoma City OK 73134
St. George GOA
2101 N.W. 145th St.
405-751-1885, 405-751-1889

Tulsa OK 74101-1491
Holy Trinity GOA
1222 S. Guthrie Ave.
P.O. Box 1491
918-583-0417

Tulsa OK 74104
St. Antony ANT
2645 E. 6th St.
918-584-7300

Oregon

Albany OR
Holy & Righteous Anne Mother of the All-Pure Theotokos OCA
@St. Mary Roman Church Rectory Chapel;728 Elsworth S.W.
503-928-9240

Ashland OR
Orthodox Mission OCA

Eugene OR 97401
St. George GOA
202 Hillview #1
P.O. Box 70132
503-683-3519

Portland OR 97232
Holy Trinity GOA
3131 N.E. Glisan St.
503-234-0468

Portland OR 97236
Nativity of the Most Holy Theotokos SOC
16838 S.E. Kelly St.
503-760-2330

Portland OR 97215
St. George ANT
11510 S.E. Holgate Blvd.
5834 S.E. Lincoln St.
503-761-7292

Portland OR
St. Mary OCA
@St. Nicholas Church;
2210 S.W. Dolphin St.
503-254-8376

Portland OR 97219
St. Nicholas OCA
2210 S.W. Dolph Ct.
503-245-2403

Pennsylvania

Alden Station PA 18634
Holy Resurrection OCA
17 E. Kirmar Ave.
717-735-0546

Aliquippa PA 15001
Kimisis Tis Theotokou GOA
2111 Davidson St.
412-375-5341

Aliquippa PA 15001
St. Elijah SOC
12200 Irwin St.
412-375-4074, FAX 412-375-1018

Pennsylvania

Allentown PA 18102
Protection of the Blessed Virgin Mary CRC
703 N. 6th St.
215-439-9589, 215-432-0272

Allentown PA 18102
St. George ANT
1011 Catasauqua Ave.
215-439-9972

Allentown PA 18102
St. Mary's Cathedral UOA
1031 Fullerton Ave.
215-439-4810

Allison Park PA 15101
St. Alexander Nevsky Cathedral OCA
1600 Guyton Rd.
412-366-4647

Altoona PA 16601
Holy Trinity GOA
1433 13th Ave.
814-943-0091

Altoona PA 16601
Ss. Peter & Paul OCA
2027 13th Ave.
814-944-4387

Altoona PA 16602
St. George ANT
519 58th St.
814-944-7187, 814-944-2080

Ambridge PA 15003-2516
Holy Ghost OCA
210 Maplewood Ave.
412-266-5009

Ambridge PA 15003
Holy Trinity GOA
2930 Beaver Rd.
412-266-5336

Ambridge PA 15003
St. John the Baptist CRC
450 Glenwood Dr.
412-266-2879

Beaver Falls PA 15010
St. John the Evangelist ANT
221 Oakville Rd.
412-847-1111

Belle Vernon PA 15012
Holy Resurrection OCA
Mary St.
412-929-9194

Berwick PA 18603
Holy Annunciation OCA
1228 2nd Ave.
717-752-3184

Bethlehem PA 18017
St. Nicholas OCA
980 Bridle Path Rd.
215-867-0402, 215-866-6057

Bethlehem PA 18018
St. Nicholas GOA
1607 W. Union Blvd.
215-867-1327

Blairsville PA 15717
St. John the Baptist OCA
801 Blaire Rd.; Black Lick
Box 464
412-248-3822

Bolivar PA 15923-9664
St. Ignatius ANT
R.D. 1 Box 307
412-238-9565, 412-238-3677

Boswell PA 15531
Ss. Peter & Paul OCA
814-754-4054

Bridgeville PA 15017
St. George ANT
610 Dewey Ave.
412-221-2277

Broomall PA 19008
St. Luke GOA
35 N. Malin Rd.
P.O. Box 198
215-353-1592

Brownsville PA 15417
St. Ellien ANT
506 Spring St.
412-785-9431

Butler PA 16001
St. Anthony ANT
400 S. 6th Ave.
412-287-6893

Camp Hill PA 17011
Holy Trinity Cathedral GOA
1000 Yverdon Dr.
717-763-7441, FAX 717-763-7458

Canonsburg PA 15317
All Saints GOA
411 Blaine Ave.
412-745-5205, FAX 412-745-3599

Canonsburg PA 15317
St. John the Baptist OCA
601 Boone Ave.
412-745-9776

Carmichaels PA 15320
St. George SOC
R.D. 1 Box 91
412-966-7428

Carnegie PA 15106
Intercession of the Holy Virgin OCA
214 Mansfield Blvd.
412-276-6234

Catasauqua PA 18032-2202
Holy Trinity OCA
1023 5th St.
215-264-0822

Central City PA 15926
Holy Assumption OCA
635 Sunshine Ave.
814-754-4054

Central City PA 15926
Ss. Peter & Paul CRC
149 Wheeler St.
814-754-4442

Charleroi PA 15022
Holy Trinity OCA
1000 Lookout Ave.
412-483-4441

Clairton PA 15025
St. Anthony GOA
424 Miller Ave.
P.O. Box 31
412-621-0581

Clairton PA 15025
St. Mary SOC
524-526 3rd St.
412-929-8052

Clarkes Summit PA 18411 MAIL
St. Basil OCA
<Simpson PA>
1107 Sunset Dr.
717-937-4411

Clymer PA 15728
St. Michael CRC
65 Morris St.
412-254-4343

Coaldale PA 18218-1602
St. Mary (Nativity) OCA
1st & Phillips Sts.
717-645-2772

Coatesville PA 19320
St. Nicholas OCA
Oak St. & 1st Ave.
215-384-0783

Colver PA 15927
Holy Ascension OCA
5th St.
814-944-4387

Curtisville PA 15032
St. Michael OCA
P.O. Box 92
412-265-1005

Dallas PA 18612
St. Andrew OCA
Huntsville-Idetown Rd.
P.O. Box 147
717-675-1541, 717-344-6189

Dickson City PA 18519
St. Mary CRC
522 Main St.
717-489-7023

Donora PA 15033
St. Nicholas OCA
St. Nicholas Dr.
412-379-4827

Du Bois PA 15801
St. Nicholas OCA
108 N. 3rd St.

DuBois PA 15801
Ss. Peter & Paul OCA
102 N. 3rd St.
814-375-0459

Dundaff PA
St. John the Baptist OCA
717-937-4860

Duquesne PA 15110
St. Nicholas OCA
507 Catherine St.
412-466-1180

East Pittsburg PA 15112
Presentation of Christ GOA
1672 Electric Ave.
P.O. Box 87
412-824-5540, 412-824-9740

East Pittsburgh PA 15112
St. John the Baptist CRC
211 Cable Ave.
412-824-0246

Easton PA 18042
Evangelismos GOA
20th St. & Hay Terrace
215-253-8147

Edinboro PA 16412-9802
Ss. Peter & Paul OCA
R.D. 2; Crossingville
814-734-3801

Pennsylvania

Edwardsville PA 18704
St. John the Baptist OCA
93 Zerby Ave.
717-287-7186

Elkins Park PA 19117
Annunciation GOA
7921 Old York Rd.
215-635-0316

Elkins Park PA 19117
Descent of Holy Ghost OCA
323 Ashbourne Rd.
326 Gerard Ave.
215-635-3720

Ellwood City PA 16117
Holy Trinity OCA
Short Ave.; Elport
412-758-9745

Ellwood City PA 16117
MAIL
Holy Trinity OCA
<New Castle PA>
Short Ave.; Elport
412-758-9745

Ellwood City PA 16117
St. Elias OCA
425 Cherry Way
412-758-9530

Ellwood City PA 16117
St. John the Baptist CRC
528 1st Ave.
412-652-7602

Emmaus PA 18049-2655
St. Paul ANT
45 S. 4th St.
610-965-2298

Erie PA 16503-1111
Holy Trinity OCA
631 Parade St.
814-459-2599

Erie PA 16505
Koimisis Tis Theotokou
GOA
4376 West Lake Rd.
814-459-4390

Erie PA 16503
St. Nicholas CRC
1115 East Ave.
814-452-4176

Farrell PA 16121
Evangelismos GOA
1007 Washington St.
412-342-2070

Forest Hills PA 15221
Holy Resurrection OCA
716 Atlantic Ave.
412-271-4738

Frackville PA 17931
Holy Ascension OCA
209 S. Lehigh Ave.
717-874-3162

Freeland PA 18224
Ss. Peter & Paul UOA
921 Walnut St.
717-636-0291

Freeland PA 18224
St. Michael CRC
451 Fern St.
717-636-2085

Ganister PA 16642
Holy Assumption OCA
814-944-4387

Greensburg PA 15601-5398
St. Michael ANT
Ashland Ave. Ext.
601 Wirsing Ave.
412-834-1311, 412-837-5113

Harrisburg PA 17109-5623
Christ the Savior OCA
5501 Locust Ln.
717-652-1825

Hawk Run PA 16840-0203
St. John the Baptist CRC
Fulton St.
P.O. Box 203
814-342-0163

Hazelton PA
Entrance into Jerusalem
OCA

Hermitage PA 16148
Holy Cross OCA
950 Maple Dr.
412-346-3151

Hermitage PA 16148
St. George SOC
65 S. Keel Ridge Rd.
P.O. Box 1052
412-342-2600

Homer City PA 15748
Ss. Peter & Paul CRC
419 S. Main St.
412-479-3656

Homestead PA 15120
St. Gregory OCA
214 E. 15th Ave.
412-461-2426

Homestead PA 15120
St. Nicholas CRC
903 Ann St.
412-461-3264

Irvona PA 16656
St. Michael OCA
814-672-3846

Jeannette PA 15644
Ss. Cyril & Methodius OCA
520 Scott Ave.
412-523-3628

Jenners PA 15546
St. Mary CRC
190 Front St.
814-629-5292

Jermyn PA 18433
St. Michael OCA
Walnut & Hudson Sts.
717-876-1241

Johnstown PA 15906
Christ the Saviour Cathedral CRC
249 Butler Ave.
814-536-4207

Johnstown PA 15907
St. George NGM
P.O. Box 1096

Johnstown PA 15909
St. John the Baptist OCA
427 1st St.
814-539-8613

Johnstown PA 15905-2005
St. Mary ANT
111 Alberta Ave.
1346 Menoher Blvd.
814-255-4077

Johnstown PA 15901
St. Mary GOA
435 Somerset St.
814-535-5056

Johnstown PA 15905
St. Nicholas SOC
971-1001 St. Clair Rd.
814-255-1853

Lancaster PA 17603
Annunciation GOA
64 Hershey Ave.
717-394-1735

Lansford PA 18232
St. Nicholas CRC
125 W. Bertsch St.
717-645-4311

Latrobe PA 15650
St. Stephen CRC
1520 Susan Dr.
412-238-9783

Lebanon PA 17042
Holy Resurrection NGM
122 E. Weidman St.
P.O. Box 1419
717-272-8132

Levittown PA 19057
Ss. Peter & Paul CRC
1313 Randall Ave.
215-943-8222

Ligonier PA 15658-0638
Ss. Peter & Paul ANT
Rt. 711 N.
P.O. Box 638
412-238-3677, 412-238-9565

Ligonier PA 15658
St. John the Baptist CRC
R.D. 1; Box 241-I
412-238-9783

Ligonier PA 15658 MAIL
St. Stephen CRC
<Latrobe PA>
R.D. 1; Box 241-I
412-238-9783

Lopez PA 18628
St. Vladimir OCA
211 Main St.
717-928-8909

Lykens PA 17048
Holy Ascension OCA
752 N. 2nd St.
717-544-2690

Lyndora PA 16045
St. Andrew OCA
201 Penn Ave.
412-285-6010

Madera PA 16661
Nativity of the Theotokos OCA
814-672-3846

Masontown PA 15461
Nativity of the Blessed Virgin Mary OCA
309 S. Washington St.
412-583-9740

McAdoo PA 18237
Holy Trinity OCA
223 S. Kennedy Dr.
717-929-2733

McKees Rock PA 15136
St. Nicholas OCA
320 Munson Ave.
412-331-1053

McKeesport PA 15131
Annunciation GOA
1128 Summit Ave.
412-673-1224

McKeesport PA 15132-4001
St. Michael CRC
424 9th Ave.
412-678-0517

McKeesport PA 15132
St. Sava SOC
901 Hartman St.
412-672-1872

Mechanicsburg PA 17055
St. John Chrysostom ANT
26 Winding Hill Dr.
717-795-7170

Media PA 19063
St. George GOA
30 E. Forge Rd.
215-459-0366

Midland PA 15059
St. George 'Lazarica' SOC
30 10th St.
412-643-1396

Minersville PA 17954-1016
Ss. Peter & Paul OCA
558 Sunbury St.
717-544-2690

Monessan PA 15062
St. Michael ANT
1201 Patton Ave.
141 Pennsylvania Blvd.
412-684-7460

Monessen PA 15062
St. John the Divine OCA
42 McKee Ave.
P.O. Box 91
412-684-3932

Monessen PA 15062
St. Spyridon GOA
Reeves Ave.
P.O. Box 327
412-684-4841

Monongahela PA 15063
Nativity of the Blessed Virgin Mary OCA
508 High St.
412-258-5621

Monongahela PA 15063
St. Nicholas CRC
314 6th St.
412-258-5072

Monroeville PA 15146
St. Archangel Michael NGM
4472 Northern Pike
P.O. Box 392
412-373-2726

Monroeville PA 15146-4322
St. Nicholas SOC
2110 Haymaker Rd.
412-372-4454

Mount Carmel PA 17851
St. Michael OCA
131 N. Willow St.
717-339-1200

Mount Union PA 17066
Ss. Peter & Paul CRC
20 W. Sherman St.

Nanticoke PA 18634
St. John the Baptist OCA
106 Welles Sts.
717-735-2263

Nesquehoning PA 18240
St. John the Baptist CRC
9 W. Railroad St.
717-669-6623

New Castle PA 16101
Holy Trinity OCA
1709 Moravia St.
412-758-9745

New Castle PA 16101-4329
St. Elias ANT
915 Lynn St.
412-658-1712, 412-658-1146, 412-652-3529

New Castle PA 16105
St. George GOA
315 W. Englewood Ave.
412-654-8521

New Castle PA 16101
St. Nicholas CRC
205 E. Reynolds Ave.
412-652-7602

New Kensington PA 15068
Annunciation of the Virgin Mary GOA
805 Walnut St.
412-339-2003

New Kensington PA 15068-5605
St. George ANT
1150 Leishman Ave.
412-335-5223, 412-335-9988

New Kensington PA 15068-4636
St. John the Baptist OCA
150 Elmtree Rd.
412-337-8162

New Salem PA 15468
Holy Trinity OCA
R.D. 1 Box 14
412-245-9251

Norristown PA 19403-3217
St. Sophia - Ss. Faith, Hope, & Agape GOA
75 Centre Ave.
215-539-4586

Oakmont PA 15139
Dormition of the Theotokos GOA
12 Washington Ave.
412-828-4144, 412-828-2888

Oberlin-Steelton PA 17113
St. Nicholas SOC
601 S. Harrisburg St.
717-939-0251

Old Forge PA 18518
St. Michael OCA
512 Summer St.
717-457-3703

Olyphant PA 18447
All Saints OCA
210 Susquehanna Ave.
717-489-0942

Olyphant PA 18447
St. Nicholas OCA
Lackawanna & Gravity Sts.
717-489-3891

Osceola Mills PA 16666
St. Mary Nativity OCA
414 French St.
814-339-6554

Patton PA 16668
Ss. Peter & Paul OCA
1005 N. 5th Ave.
R.D. 1 P.O. Box 451

Philadelphia PA 19145
Assumption of the Holy Virgin OCA
28th St. & Snyder Ave.
P.O. Box 20083
215-468-3535, 215-237-6985, FAX 215-461-1031

Philadelphia PA 19149
Evangelismos GOA
6501-05 Bustleton Ave.
215-743-7982

Philadelphia PA 19115-1910
Holy Trinity RMA
9865 Jeanes St.
215-671-1075

Philadelphia PA 19115
Ss. Peter & Paul OCA
9230 Bustleton Ave.
215-676-3311

Philadelphia PA 19107
St. George Cathedral GOA
256 S. 8th St.
215-627-4389

Philadelphia PA 19103
St. John Chrysostom OCA
5 Franklin Plaza
215-563-0979

Philadelphia PA 19122
St. Nicholas SOC
1231-39 N. Hancock St.
215-425-2128

Philadelphia PA 19123
St. Nicholas OCA
817 N. 7th St.
P.O. Box 16459; Spring Garden Sta.
215-922-3037

Philadelphia PA 19111
St. Stephen Cathedral OCA
8598 Verree Rd.
215-745-3232

Philipsburg PA 16866-2520
St. John the Baptist OCA
420 Laura St.
814-342-2011

Phoenixville PA 19460
Holy Ghost CRC
Starr St.; Phoenix Pk.
P.O. Box 66
215-933-3336

Pine Hill PA
Ss. Peter & Paul OCA

Pittsburgh PA 15203
Holy Assumption OCA
105 S. 19th St.
412-431-6428

Pittsburgh PA 15228
Holy Cross GOA
123 Gilkeson Rd.
412-833-3355

Pittsburgh PA 15212
Holy Trinity GOA
302 W. North Ave.
412-321-9282

Pittsburgh PA 15236-2259
Holy Trinity Cathedral SOC
4920 Clairton Blvd.
412-882-3900, FAX 412-882-6391

Pittsburgh PA 15243 MAIL
Intercession of the Holy Virgin OCA
<Carnegie PA>
334 Rockfield Rd.
412-276-6234

Pittsburgh PA 15213
St. George ANT
3400 Dawson St.
412-681-2988

Pittsburgh PA 15212
St. John the Baptist CRC
2695 Woodland Ave.
412-766-3460

Pittsburgh PA 15219
St. Michael OCA
43 Reed St.
412-261-2314

Pittsburgh PA 15213
St. Nicholas Cathedral GOA
419 S. Dithridge St.
412-682-3866

Pittsburgh PA 15210
St. Sava NGM
185 Knox Ave.

Portage PA 15946
St. Michael OCA
915 Blair St.
814-736-3051

Pottstown PA 19464
Holy Trinity OCA
Mervin & Juniper Sts.
215-323-4183

Rankin PA 15104
St. Michael CRC
146 3rd St.
412-271-2725

Reading PA
Orthodox Mission OCA

Reading PA 19611
Ss. Constantine & Helen GOA
1001 E. Wyomissing Blvd.
215-374-7511

Reading PA 19601
St. Matthew GOA
N. 5th & Elm Sts.
215-372-1031

Scranton PA 18509
Annunciation GOA
505 N. Washington Ave.
717-342-0566

Scranton PA 18510
St. Nicholas CRC
621 Vine St.
717-344-5917

Sharon PA 16146
St. John the Baptist CRC
725 Cedar St.
412-346-4457

Shillington PA 19607
St. Herman of Alaska OCA
133 W. Broad St.
215-777-3553

Simpson PA
St. Basil OCA
717-937-4411

Souderton PA 18964
St. Philip ANT
1970 Clearview Rd.
P.O. Box 565
215-721-4947

St. Clair PA 17970
Assumption of the Blessed Virgin Mary OCA
Nicholas & Lawton Sts.
717-929-2733

St. Clair PA 17970
St. Michael CRC
106 N. Morris St.
717-429-0670

State College PA
Holy Trinity OCA
@Eisenhower Chapel;
Penn. State Univ.

State College PA
Holy Trinity GOA

Steelton PA 17113
Holy Annunication BEC
721 N. Front St.
717-939-7525

Stroudsburg PA 18360
Holy Cross GOA
135 Stokes Ave.
717-421-5734

Stroudsburg PA 18360
Holy Trinity OCA
Chipperfield Dr.
Box 832
717-842-7333

Taylor PA 18517
St. George CRC
745 S. Keyser Ave.
717-562-1170

Uniondale PA 18470
Ss. Peter & Paul OCA
R.D. 2
717-488-6567

Upper Darby PA 19082
St. Demetrios GOA
229 Powell Ln.
215-352-7212

Upper Darby PA 19082
St. George ANT
8210 W. Chester Pike
215-853-1171

Urey PA 15742
Ss. Peter & Paul OCA
R.D. 1; Glen Campbell
814-375-0459

Vandergrift PA 15690
Ss. Constantine & Helen GOA
167 Lincoln Ave.
P.O. Box 282
412-568-2998

Vintondale PA 15961
Ss. Peter & Paul OCA
3rd St.
P.O. Box 204
814-736-3051

Wallingford PA 19086
St. Herman of Alaska OCA
403 Moore Rd.
Box 373
215-876-6077

West Brownsville PA 15417
Holy Resurrection OCA
118 Main St.
412-785-4245

Whitehall PA 18052-6007 MAIL
Protection of the Virgin Mary CRC
<Allentown PA>
1231 N. 14th St.
215-432-0272

Wilkes-Barre PA 18702
Annunciation GOA
32 E. Ross St.
717-823-4805

Wilkes-Barre PA 18705
Holy Resurrection Cathedral OCA
591 N. Main St.
717-822-7725

Wilkes-Barre PA 18705
Holy Trinity OCA
401 E. Main St.
717-825-6139

Wilkes-Barre PA 18702-3470
St. Mary Dormition ANT
905 S. Main St.
717-824-5016

Williamsburg PA 16693 MAIL
Holy Assumption OCA
<Ganister PA>
R.D. 1 Box 230C
814-944-4387

Williamsport PA 17701
Elevation of the Holy Cross OCA
1725 Blair St.
717-322-3020

Windber PA 15963
Ss. Peter & Paul CRC
RD 2; Box 6
814-467-7444

Wood PA 16694
St. Michael CRC
Box 47
814-635-3752, 412-479-2376

Wrightstown PA 18940-9633
St. Mark OCA
452 Durham Rd.
215-860-9640

York PA 17403
Annunciation GOA
2500 Pine Grove Rd.
717-741-4200

York PA 17405
St. John Chrysostom ANT
P.O. Box 86
717-795-7170

Youngwood PA 15697
Holy Ascension SOC
24 N. 3rd St.
412-925-6353

Rhode Island

Cranston RI 02920
Annunciation GOA
175 Oaklawn Ave.
401-942-4188

Cumberland RI 02864
Dormition of the Holy Theotokos OCA
71 Manville Hill Rd.
401-658-0874

Newport RI 02840
St. Spyridon GOA
Thames & Brewer Sts.
P.O. Box 427
401-846-0555

Pawtucket RI 02860
Assumption GOA
97 Walcott St.
401-725-3127

Pawtucket RI 02860
St. Mary ANT
249 High St.
401-726-1202

Woonsocket RI 02895
St. John the Baptist OCA
501 E. School St.
401-766-3343

South Carolina

Charleston SC 29403
Holy Trinity GOA
30 Race St.
803-577-2063

Columbia SC 29201
Holy Trinity GOA
1931 Sumter St.
803-252-6758

Florence SC 29501
Transfiguration GOA
2990 S. Cashua Dr.
803-662-5471

Greenville SC 29601
St. George GOA
15 De Camp St.
803-233-8531

Greenville SC
St. John of the Ladder OCA
314 Lloyd St.
803-878-5815

Hilton Head SC 29925
Holy Resurrection GOA
P.O. Box 22888
912-352-4019

Myrtle Beach SC 29578-2247
St. John the Baptist GOA
3301 33rd Ave. N.
P. O. Box 2247
803-448-3773

Spartanburg SC 29304
St. Nicholas GOA
697 Asheville Hwy.
P.O. Box 1107
803-585-5961

West Columbia SC 29169
Holy Apostles OCA
931 N. Lucas St.
803-926-8744, 803-781-6296

South Dakota

Sioux Falls SD 57105
Transfiguration GOA
1936 S. Summit Ave.
605-334-5301

Tennessee

Bristol TN 37620
Holy Trinity GOA
108 Maxwell Dr.
615-652-1628

Chattanooga TN 37422
Annunciation GOA
722 Glenwood Dr.
P.O. Box 23502
615-629-4881

Franklin TN 37064-7614
St. Ignatius ANT
4671 Peytonsville Rd.
615-791-0658

Knoxville TN 37919-5245
St. George GOA
4070 Kingston Pike
615-522-5043

Memphis TN 38122
Annunciation GOA
573 N. Highland
901-327-8177

Memphis TN 38107-5047
St. John ANT
1663 Tutwiler Ave.
901-274-4119

Memphis TN
St. Peter the Aleut OCA

Nashville TN 37220
Holy Trinity GOA
4905 Franklin Pike
615-333-1047

Texas

Amarillo TX 79106
St. John the Prodromos GOA
1101 Bell Ave.
806-355-0683

Austin TX 73701-2617
St. Elias ANT
408 E. 11th St.
512-476-2314, FAX 512-858-1630

Austin TX 78716
Transfiguration GOA
2008 Justin Ln.
P.O. Box 160632
512-454-2143

Beaumont TX 77706
St. Michael ANT
690 15th St.
4490 Folsom Dr.
409-838-4951

Colleyville TX 76034
Falling Asleep of Virgin OCA
3801 Glade Rd.
817-545-0753

Corpus Christi TX
Orthodox Mission ANT

Corpus Christi TX 78403
St. Nicholas GOA
502 S. Chaparral St.
P.O. Box 343
512-883-9843

Cypress TX 77429
St. Sava SOC
16900 Cypress Rosehill Rd.
713-373-1769

Dallas TX 75240-5412
Holy Trinity GOA
13555 Hillcrest Rd.
214-991-1166

Dallas TX 75229-6100
Ss. Constantine & Helen ANT
3755 Walnut Hill Ln.
214-350-2104

Dallas TX 75214
St. Gregory ANT
P.O. Box 140772
214-823-7830

Dallas TX 75219
St. Seraphim of Sarov Cathedral OCA
4112 Throckmorton
214-528-3741

El Paso TX 79902
St. George ANT
915 N. Florence
915-532-7845

El Paso TX 79912
St. Nicholas GOA
124 S. Festival
915-833-0882

Euless TX 76040
St. John the Baptist GOA
303 Cullum Dr.
817-283-2291

Ft. Worth TX 76133-5037
St. Barbara OCA
6525 Dan Danciger Rd.
6929 Winifred Dr.
817-294-0325

Ft. Worth TX 76106
St. Demetrios GOA
2022 Ross Ave.
817-626-5578

Galveston TX 77550
Assumption GOA
1824 Ball St.
P.O. Box 655
409-762-7591

Galveston TX 77550
Ss. Constantine & Helen SOC
4109 Ave. L
P.O. Box 3280
409-762-4363

Galveston TX 77551
Ss. Constantine & Helen NGM
6914 Youpon
409-744-3966

Gladewater-Longview-Tyler TX
St. John of Damascus OCA

Houston TX 77006-4388
Annunciation Cathedral GOA
3511 Yoakum Blvd.
713-526-5377, FAX 713-526-1010

Houston TX 77005-2125
St. George ANT
5311 Mercer at Bissonnet
713-665-5252

Houston TX
St. Mary Magdala OCA

Houston TX
St. Michael the Archangel OCA

Katy TX 77449 MAIL
St. Sava SOC
<Cypress TX>
19149 Glenway Falls
713-373-1769

Lubbock TX 79493
St. Andrew GOA
6001 81st St.
P.O. Box 93705
806-798-1828

Midland TX 79710-1722
Holy Annunciation OCA
@Holy Trinity Episcopal School; 3500 W. Wadley Ave.
P.O. Box 51722

Paris TX
St. Thomas OCA

Pharr TX 78577
St. George the Great Martyr OCA
784 W. Sam Houston
P.O. Box 667
512-781-6114

Plano TX 75086-5081
St. Sava OCA
@Prince of Peace Roman Community
P.O. Box 865081
214-494-2623

Port Arthur TX 77643
St. George GOA
3146 Thomas Blvd.
P.O. Box 3035
409-983-7360

San Angelo TX 76904
Assumption GOA
801 Montecito Dr.
2702 Oak Forest
915-653-6074

San Antonio TX 78210
St. Anthony the Great OCA
103-105 Carolina St.
210-533-2492

San Antonio TX 78212
St. Sophia GOA
2504 N. St Mary's St.
210-735-5051

Spring TX 77388
St. Anthony the Great ANT
18823 Mirror Lake Dr.
713-350-6784

Waco TX 76707
St. Nicholas GOA
617 N. 17th St.
817-754-6519

Wichita Falls TX 76309
Holy Cross GOA
3804 Old Seymour Rd.
817-692-0860

Utah

Draper UT 84020
OCA Mission of Greater Salt Lake City OCA
516 E. 13800 S.
801-572-5323

Midvale UT
Orthodox Mission OCA

Ogden UT 84403
Transfiguration GOA
674 42nd St.
801-399-2231

Price UT 84501
Assumption GOA
61 S. 2nd East St.
P.O. Box 688
801-637-0704

Salt Lake City UT 84101
Holy Trinity Cathedral GOA
279 South 300 West
801-328-9681

Salt Lake City UT 84101
Prophet Elias GOA
5335 S. Highland Dr.
279 South 300 West
801-277-2693, 801-328-9681

Salt Lake City UT 84111
Ss. Peter & Paul ANT
355 S. 300 E.
P.O. Box 17896
801-272-7920

Vermont

Burlington VT 05401
Dormition of the Mother of God GOA
600 S. Willard Ave.
30 Ledge Rd.
802-863-2455

Rutland VT 05701
St. Nicholas GOA
8 Cottage St.
P.O. Box 939

Springfield VT 05156
Holy Trinity OCA
90 Park St.
802-885-2615

Virginia

Alexandria VA 22302
Holy Cross OCA
5150 Leesburg Pike
(Bailey's Crossroads)
703-671-1919

Alexandria VA 22312
Nativity of Our Lord CRC
4317 Dahill Pl.
703-256-1658

Arlington VA 22204
St. George OCA
800 S. Buchanan St.
703-761-4316

Charlottesville VA 22902
Transfiguration GOA
100 Perry Dr.
P.O. Box 94
804-295-5337

Danville VA 24541
St. Peter GOA
116 Jefferson Ave.
P.O. Box 3392
804-793-5382

Falls Church VA
Protection of the Mother of God OCA
@ St. Philip's School; 7506 St. Philip Ct. (Beltway Exit 8E & Rte. 50E)
703-670-0867

Falls Church VA 22041
St. Katherine GOA
3149 Glen Carlyn Rd.
703-671-1515

Fredricksburg VA 22404
Nativity of the Theotokos GOA
102 Caison Rd. Rte 603
P.O. Box 8418

Hopewell VA 23860
St. Elpis GOA
107 Memorial Ave.
P.O. Box 1204
804-458-4142

Lynchburg VA 24501
St. George GOA
1724 Langhorne Rd.
P.O. Box 2061
804-384-7585

McLean VA 22101
St. Luke OCA
6801 Georgetown Pike
P.O. Box 178
703-893-1759

Newport News VA 23606
Ss. Constantine & Helen GOA
60 Traverse Rd.
804-872-8119, 804-874-6958

Norfolk VA 23505-4002
Annunciation GOA
7220 Granby St.
804-440-0500, FAX 804-423-6429

Norfolk VA 23518 MAIL
Dormition of the Theotokos OCA
<Tidewater VA>
Box 14073
804-587-6369

Reston VA 22090
Holy Trinity OCA
@The Glade Room;
Soapstone & Glade
P.O. Box 3708
703-758-7914

Richmond VA 23221
Ss. Constantine & Helen Cathedral GOA
30 Malvern Ave.
804-355-3687

Richmond VA 23229-4157
St. Cyprian of Carthage OCA
3820 Chamberlayne Ave.
8419 Zell Ln.
804-288-9363

Roanoke VA 24012
Holy Trinity GOA
30 Huntington Blvd. N.E.
P.O. Box 5055
703-362-3601

Roanoke VA 24019
St. Ambrose of Milan OCA
8115 Williamson Rd.
703-982-7710

Tidewater VA 23503
Dormition of the Theotokos OCA
1051 E. Bayview Blvd.
804-587-6369

Virginia Beach VA 23464
St. Ignatius of Antioch ANT
824 Gammon Sq.
804-523-9424

Virginia Beach VA 23451
St. Nicholas GOA
621 First Colonial Rd.
804-422-5600

Winchester VA 22601
Dormition of the Virgin Mary GOA
Rt. 50 W. - Amherst St.
703-667-1416

Woodbridge VA 22193 MAIL
Protection of the Mother of God OCA
<Falls Church VA>
15111 Catalpa Ct.
703-670-0867

Washington

Bellingham WA 98225
St. Sophia GOA
510 E. Sunset Dr.
206-734-8745

Brier WA 98036
St. Paul ANT
21226 Poplar Way
206-771-1916

Everson WA 98247
St. Innocent ANT
7592 Oat Coles
206-966-3937

Issaquah WA 98027
St. Sava SOC
14619 239th Pl. S.E.
206-391-2240

Pasco WA 99301-1161
St. Nektarios GOA
627 W. Bonneville
P.O. Box 1161
509-547-3968

Puyallup WA 98371 MAIL
Holy Trinity / Holy Resurrection OCA
<Wilkeson WA>
P.O. Box 1332
206-848-7505

Seattle WA 98122-2515
Assumption GOA
1804 13th Ave.
206-323-8557

Seattle WA 98112
St. Demetrios GOA
2100 Boyer Ave. E.
206-325-4347

Seattle WA 98109
St. Spiridon Cathedral OCA
400 Yale Ave. N.
206-624-5341

Seattle WA
Three Holy Hierarchs OCA

Spokane WA 99205-4769
Holy Trinity GOA
1703 N. Washington
509-328-9310

Tacoma WA 98405
St. Nicholas GOA
S. 16th & Yakima Ave.
206-272-0466

Wilkeson WA
Holy Trinity/Holy Resurrection OCA
Long St.
206-848-7505

Yakima WA 98902
Holy Cross ANT
706 Stewart St.
618 S. 3rd St.
509-575-0145

West Virginia

Beckley WV 25801-4321
St. Nicholas ANT
211 S. Heber St.
105 Lilly St.
304-252-5821, 305-265-5547

Charleston WV 25327-2044
St. George ANT
Lee & Court Sts.
P.O. Box 2044
304-346-0106, 304-346-0146

Charleston WV 25304
St. John GOA
3512 MacCorkle Ave. S.E.
304-925-3906

Clarksburg WV 26301
St. Spyridon GOA
340 S. 2nd St.
P.O. Box 1703
304-624-5331

Elkhorn WV 24831
Dormition of the Mother of God CRC
Box 221
304-862-3313

Fairmont WV 26554
St. Andrew the Apostle CRC
501 Cleveland Ave.
304-366-8523

Huntington WV 25703-2095
Holy Spirit ANT
2109 10th Ave.
304-529-6693

Huntington WV 25701
St. George GOA
701 11th Ave.
304-522-7890

Morgantown WV 26505
Assumption GOA
447 Spruce St.
304-292-9048

Morgantown WV 26505
Nativity of the Blessed Virgin Mary CRC
19 W. Park Ave.
304-296-4319

Moundsville WV 26041
Ss. Peter & Paul OCA
1109 Morton Ave.
614-535-1379

Weirton WV 26062
All Saints GOA
3528 West St.
304-797-9884

Weirton WV 26062-5006
St. Nicholas OCA
604 Colliers Way
304-723-9746

Wheeling WV 26003
St. John the Divine GOA
2215 Chapline St.
304-233-0757

Wisconsin

Appleton WI 54911
St. Nicholas GOA
3333 N. French Rd.
414-734-2305

Clayton WI 54004
Holy Trinity OCA
R.R. 1
715-948-2493

Clayton WI 54004 MAIL
St. Mary OCA
<Cornucopia WI>
Rt. #1 Box 17

Cornucopia WI 54827
St. Mary OCA

Cudahy WI 53110
St. Nikola NGM
3802 E. Squire Ave.
P.O. Box 564
414-747-9246

DePere WI
St. Matthew OCA
@ Crypt Chapel, St Norbert's Abbey, 1016 N. Broadway
414-432-0840, 414-433-6777

Fond Du Lac WI 54935-0011
Holy Trinity GOA
198 N. Macy St.
P.O Box 11
414-921-4364

Green Bay WI 54305-0652 MAIL
St. Matthew OCA
<DePere WI>
P.O. Box 652
414-432-0840, 414-433-6778

Kenosha WI 53140-2707
St. Nicholas OCA
4313 18th Ave.
414-657-3415

La Crosse WI 54601-3176
St. Elias ANT
716 Copeland Ave.
P.O. Box 3176
608-782-8641

Lublin WI 54447-9634
Holy Assumption OCA
N1249 County Rd. F
715-669-3855

Madison WI 53704
Assumption GOA
11 N. 7th St.
608-244-1001

Mequon WI 52092
St. Nicholas ANT
3906 W. Mequon Rd.
P.O. Box 114
414-241-9041

Mequon WI 53092-2799 MAIL
St. Nicholas ANT
<Mequon WI>
1235 W. Baldwin Ct.
414-241-9041

Milwaukee WI 53225-4812
Annunciation GOA
9400 W. Congress
414-461-9400

Milwaukee WI 53215
Ss. Cyril & Methodius OCA
2505 S. 30th St.
414-671-5819

Milwaukee WI 53219
St. Sava Cathedral SOC
3201 S. 51st St.
414-545-4080

Minocqua WI 54548-0074
St. Andrew OCA
@St. Matthias Episcopal Church, 403 Chicago Ave.
P.O. Box 74
715-669-3855, 715-356-9214

Prairie Farm WI 54762
St. James Hermitage RMA
505 One Half Ave.
715-455-1553

Racine WI 53406
Kimisis Tis Theotokou GOA
1335 S. Green Bay Rd.
414-632-5682

Racine WI 53404
St. George NGM
826 State St.
414-634-9512

Racine WI 53403
St. George SOC
6108 Braun Rd.
414-554-7998

Sheboygan WI 53081
St. Spyridon GOA
1427 S. 10th St.
414-452-2585

Stanley WI 54768
St. John the Baptist OCA
R.R. 2

Wauwatosa WI 53213-1798
Ss. Constantine & Helen
GOA
2160 Wauwatosa Ave.
414-778-1555

Wyoming

Casper WY 82602
Holy Trinity GOA
1350 E. 'C' St.
P.O. Box 1465
307-237-9969

Cheyenne WY 82001
Ss. Constantine & Helen
GOA
501 W. 27th St.
307-635-5929

Harriman WY 82059
Ss. Anargyroi Cosmas &
Damian / St. John GOA
54 Harriman Rd.
307-638-6642, 307-638-
0611

Rock Springs WY 82901
Holy Trinity GOA
405 'N' St.
302 'M' St.
307-362-2930

Worland WY 82041
St. George GOA
12th St. & Robertson

Parishes and Missions in Canada

Alberta

Andrew AB T0B 0C0 MAIL
Archangel Michael OCA
<Sochava AB>
Ewanowich; Box 425
403-365-3521

Andrew AB T0B 0C0 MAIL
Nativity of the Holy Virgin OCA
<Kysylew AB>
Ewanchuk; Box 148

Andrew AB T0B 0L0
Ss. Peter & Paul UOC

Andrew AB T0B 0C0 MAIL
St. Tikhon of Moscow OCA
<Lakeland AB>
P.O. Box 255
403-365-2340

Athabasca AB T0G 0B0
Ss. Peter & Paul UOC

Barrhead AB T0G 0E0
All Saints UOC

Bellis AB T0A 0J0
All Saints UOC

Berwyn AB T0H 0E0
St. John the Baptist UOC

Big Meadow AB
St. John the Baptist UOC

Boian (Willingdon) AB
St. Mary RMA
403-456-7737

Bonnyville AB T0A 0L0
Ss. Peter & Paul OCA

Bonnyville AB T0A 0L0
St. Elias UOC

Borwicl AB
St. Mary UOC

Boyle AB T0A 0M0
Holy Ghost UOC

Boyne Lake AB T0A 3E0
Holy Cross UOC

Brinsley AB
Holy Trinity UOC

Brosseau AB T0B 0P0
Holy Trinity UOC

Brunderheim AB T0B 0S0
St. Demetrius UOC

Calgary AB
Annunciation ANT

Calgary AB T3B 4P4
Nativity of the Holy Virgin Mary OCA
4727 17th Ave. N.W.
403-288-4699

Calgary AB T3C 3B7
St. Demetrios GOA
1 Tamarac Crescent S.W.
403-249-8876

Calgary AB T2T 1T3
St. Simeon Mirotocivi SOC
2001 31st Ave. S.W.
403-244-3586

Calgary AB T2E 5A6
St. Vladimir UOC
400 Meredith Rd.

Calmar AB T0C 0U0
Holy Trinity UOC

Camrose AB
All Saints UOC

Craigend AB T0A 2G0
St. Demetrius UOC

Dawning AB
St. Paraskeva UOC

Deadwood AB T0H 1A0
St. Vladimir UOC

Desjarlais AB T0B 4R0
St. Nicholas OCA
403-365-2340

Dickie Bush AB
Ss. Peter & Paul OCA

Edmonton AB T5W 1E4
All Saints GOA
5824 118th Ave.
403-471-2781

Edmonton AB T5E 0Y1
Ss. Constantine & Helen RMA
9005 - 132nd Ave.
403-475-1422

Edmonton AB T6E 0J4
St. Andrew UOC
9755 64th Ave. N.W.

Edmonton AB T5K 1R2
St. George GOA
10831 124th St.
403-452-7329

Edmonton AB T5N 3C3
St. Herman of Alaska OCA
10320 147th St.
403-454-8335

Edmonton AB T5K 1G4
St. John UOC
10945 107th St.

Alberta

Edmonton AB T6C 3K4
St. Michael UOC
8541 89th St. N.W.

Edmonton AB T5P 0G8
St. Phillip ANT
15804 98th Ave.
403-489-7943

Edmonton AB T5E 6J8
St. Sava SOC
12904 112th St.
P.O. Box 71040 Nortwood Mall
403-455-2147

Egremont AB T0A 0Z0
St. John UOC

Elk Point AB T0A 1A0
St. Vladimir UOC

Enshaw AB
St. Vladimir UOC

Farusy AB
St. John the Baptist OCA

Fedorah AB T0A 1N0
St. John UOC

Gefford AB
Ss. Peter & Paul UOC

Glendon AB T0A 1P0
Holy Ghost UOC

Hairy Hill AB T0B 1S0
St. Mary RMA

Hamlin AB T0B 1T0
Descent of the Holy Ghost RMA

Hamlin AB T0B 1T0
St. Mary UOC

Innisfree AB T0B 2G0
St. John the Baptist UOC

Ispas AB T0B 4K0
Holy Ascension UOC

Jasper AB T0E 1E0
Greek Orthodox Community GOA
P.O. Box 85
403-852-3137

Kahwin AB T0B 0C0
Holy Trinity UOC

Kaleland AB T0B 4K0
Ss. Peter & Paul UOC

Kysylew AB T0B 0C0
Nativity of the Holy Virgin OCA

Lac La Biche AB T0A 2C0
St. Andrew UOC

Lakeland AB
St. Tikhon of Moscow OCA
403-365-2340

Lamont AB T0B 2R0 MAIL
St. Michael OCA
<Peno AB>
Staciuk; R.R. 1

Lethbridge AB T1J 0P6
Holy Trinity UOC
1417 9th Ave.

Lethbridge AB T1J 3Y6
St. Sava SOC
P.O. Box 794
403-244-3586

Luzany-Toporiwsti AB
St. Elias UOC

Malin AB
Holy Cross RMA

Manning-Peace River AB
Descent of the Holy Ghost RMA

Musidora AB T0B 3J0
Assumption UOC

Myrnas AB T0B 3K0
Holy Trinity UOC

Newbrook AB T0A 2P0
Assumption UOC

Noral AB T0A 0R0
St. John the Baptist UOC

North Bank AB
Holy Transfiguration OCA
403-365-2340

Oyen AB T0J 2J0
Ss. Peter & Paul UOC

Pakan AB T0A 3C0
St. Elijah OCA

Peace River AB
St. Elias UOC

Peno AB T0B 4B0
St. John the Baptist UOC

Peno AB T0B 4B0
St. Michael OCA

Poplar Ridge AB T0H 3G0
Ss. Peter & Paul UOC

Prut-Luzany AB
St. Demetrius UOC

Radway AB T0A 2V0
Holy Ascension UOC

Red Water AB T0A 2W0
Holy Ghost UOC

Richmond Park AB T0G 0B0
Holy Trinity UOC

Sangudo AB T0E 2A0
Assumption UOC

Sarrail AB T0A 0M0
Ss. Peter & Paul UOC

Seba Beach AB T0E 2B0
Ss. Peter & Paul UOC

Serediaky AB
St. Demetrius of Thessalonika OCA

Shandro AB T0B 4R0
Holy Assumption OCA

Shepentzi AB
St. Mary UOC

Sich-Kolmiya AB
St. Mary UOC

Slawa AB T0B 3K0
All Saints UOC

Slawa AB T0B 3K0
Assumption UOC

Smoky Lake AB T0A 3C0
Holy Ghost UOC

Smoky Lake AB T0A 3C0
Holy Trinity OCA

Sochava AB
Archangel Michael OCA
403-365-3521

Spedden AB T0A 3E0
St. John the Baptist UOC

Spirit River AB
St. Elias UOC

St. Paul AB T0A 3A0
All Saints UOC

Star AB T0B 4E0
Holy Transfiguration OCA
403-365-2340

Stary Vostok AB
Holy Trinity OCA
403-365-2340

Stry AB
Holy Ghost UOC

Suchawa AB
Ukrainian Orthodox Church UOC

Sunland AB T0B 0C0
Holy Trinity OCA
403-365-2340

Therien AB T0A 3H0
St. Michael UOC

Two Hills AB T0B 4K0
Holy Trinity UOC

Vegreville AB T0B 4L0
St. Vladimir UOC

Vilna AB T0A 3L0
St. Demetrius UOC

Wandering River AB T0A 3M0
St. Elias UOC

Warspite AB T0A 3N0
Assumption UOC

Wasel AB T0B 4R0
Holy Ascension OCA

Waskatanau AB T0A 3P0
St. Vladimir UOC

Westlock AB T0G 2L0
St. Vladimir UOC

Wildwood AB T0E 2M0
Holy Fathers UOC

Willingdon AB T0B 4R0 MAIL
Holy Ascension OCA
<Wasel AB>
Katarenchuk; R.R. 1

Willingdon AB T0B 4R0 MAIL
Ss. Peter & Paul OCA
<Dickie Bush AB>
Shapka; R.R. 1

Wostok-Bukovina AB
St. Nicholas OCA
403-365-2340

Zawale AB T0B 0C0
St. Michael UOC

British Columbia

Agassiz BC V0M 1A0
Holy Transfiguartion UOC

Burnaby BC V5G 1M2
Ss. Peter & Paul UOC
7137 Grand Hwy.

Calgary BC T2W 5G3
St. Peter the Aleut OCA
3107 40th St. S.W.
527 Woodridge Terr.
403-242-6754

Chilliwack BC V2P 4P1
St. Demetrius UOC

Kamloops BC V2B 4G9
Greek Orthodox Community GOA
756 Ridgeview Terr.

Kelowna BC V1P 7J4
Ss. Peter & Paul UOC

Kitimat BC V8C 1T1
Metamorfosis GOA
71 Finch St.
604-632-7475

Langley BC
St. Herman of Alaska OCA
216th St. & Glover Rd.
604-588-6166

Mission City BC V2V 2B5
St. Mary UOC

New Westminster BC V3M 5E7
Mar Elias OCA
1398 Ewen Ave.
604-941-8498

New Westminster BC V3M 2T4
St. George RMA
1932 - 8th Ave.
604-522-4360

North Vancouver BC V1L 4J8
North Shore Hellenic Community GOA
604-632-7475, 604-632-3221

Penticton BC V2A 6S6
Greek Orthodox Community GOA
1489 Leir St.
486 Alder St.

Port Alberni BC V9Y 5N4
St. Mary UOC

Prince George BC V2M 6W7
Koimisis GOA
511 Tabor Blvd.
604-564-2766

Revelstoke BC V0E 2S0
Holy Trinity UOC

Surrey BC V3R 0J7
Greek Orthodox Church of Surrey and Fraser Valley GOA
89985 154th St.
P.O. Box 55514
604-583-0554

Surrey BC V3T 1G4 MAIL
St. Herman of Alaska OCA
<Langley BC>
13268-99A Ave.
604-588-8911

Vancouver BC V6K 3N9
Holy Annunciation RMA
1805 Larch St.

Vancouver BC V5W 1S7
Holy Resurrection OCA
75 E. 43rd Ave.
604-325-1922

Vancouver BC V5W 1S7
Holy Trinity OCA
@Holy Resurrection Church; 75 E. 43rd Ave.

Vancouver BC V5Y 2G4
Holy Trinity UOC
126 E. 10th St.

Vancouver BC V5L 1T2
St. Archangel Michael NGM
1806 E. Hastings St.
604-253-8121

Vancouver BC V6J 4A2
St. George GOA
4500 Arbutus St.
604-266-7148

Vancouver BC V5R 2N5
St. Nicholas GOA
4641 Boundary Rd.
604-438-6432

Vancouver BC V5X 2K3
St. Sava SOC
505 E. 63rd Ave.
604-321-6572

Vernon BC V1T 5E6
Assumption UOC

Victoria BC V8W 2K5
All Saints of Alaska OCA
604-588-6166

Victoria BC V8V 4G3
Hellenic Orthodox Community of Victoria & Vancouver Islands GOA
420 Linden Ave. #201
604-382-5650

Victoria BC V8W 1P6
St. George UOC

Walley BC
St. Mary UOC
13512 108th Ave.
604-581-2768

Manitoba

Arbakka MB R0E 0E0
Ss. Peter & Paul UOC

Arbakka MB R0E 0E0
St. Nicholas UOC

Augusville MB
Holy Ascension UOC

Beausejour MB R0E 0C0
St. Vladimir UOC

Blue Wing MB
St. George OCA

Bohdan-Boian MB
Holy Assumption UOC

Brandon MB R7A 6A2
Holy Ghost UOC
2204 MacDonald Ave.

Dauphin MB R7N 0E7
St. George UOC
810 Main St. E.

Drifting River MB R0L 0X0
St. John the Baptist UOC

Dufrost MB R0E 0K0
St. Mary UOC

Durban MB R0L 0P0
Holy Trinity UOC

Ethelbert MB
Ss. Peter & Paul UOC

Ethelbert MB R0L 0T0
Ss. Peter & Paul UOA
Box 78
204-742-3349

Flin Flon MB R8A 1G5
St. George UOC
52 Hill St.

Gardenton MB R0E 0M0
St. Demetrios UOA
213 Claremont Ave.

Gardenton MB R0L 0M0
St. John the Baptist UOC

Garland MB R0L 0W0
St. John the Baptist UOC

Gilbert Plains MB R0L 0X0
Ss. Vladimir & Olga UOC

Gonoi MB
St. Nicholas UOC

Grandview MB R0l 0Y0
All Saints UOC

Kosiw MB
Ss. Peter & Paul UOC

Ledwyn MB
Holy Assumption UOC

Lennard MB R0S 0X0
Holy Trinity UOC

Lennard-Inglis MB R0S 0X0
St. Elias OCA
306-642-3201

Menzie MB R0J 1C0
Transfiguration UOC

Minitonas MB
St. Lavrentius the Martyr OCA
Hwy. 286

Oakburn MB R0J 1L0
St. Vladimir UOC

Petlura MB R0L 1W0
Holy Ghost UOC

Pine River MB R0L 1M0
Transfiguration UOC

Poplar Field MB R0C 2N0
Holy Trinity UOC

Poplar Park MB R0E 1C0
Holy Trinity UOC

Portage La Prairie MB
St. Nicholas UOC

Renwer MB R0L 1N0
St. Mary UOC

Roblin MB R0L 1P0
St. John the Baptist UOC

Roblin MB R0L 1P0
St. Stephen the First Martyr OCA
219 1st St. N.W.
Box 1397
204-937-4673

Rorketon MB R0L 1R0
St. Mary UOC

Rosa MB R0A 1N0
Ss. Peter & Paul UOC

Rossburn MB
Holy Assumption UOC

Rossburn MB
St. Elias UOC

Russell MB
St. Vladimir UOC

Sandhill MB R0E 0C0
St. Michael UOC

Sandy Lake MB R0J 1X0
St. Nicholas OCA
County Hwy. 250 N.

Sarto MB R0A 1X0
Ss. Peter & Paul UOC

Seech MB R0J 1L0
Ss. Peter & Paul UOC

Selkirk MB R1A 1R8
St. Michael UOC

Senkiw MB R0A 1P0
St. Mary UOC

Shell Valley MB R0J 0X0
St. John the Baptist UOC

Shortdale MB R0L 1W0
Holy Ghost UOC

Sifton MB R0L 1X0
Holy Resurrection OCA

Sifton MB R0M 1P0
Holy Trinity UOC

Sirko MB R0A 2C0
St. Elias UOC

Stead MB R0E 1Z0
St. John UOC

Sundown MB R0A 2C0
Ss. Peter & Paul UOC

Swan River MB R0I 1Z0
Holy Ascension UOC

The Pas MB R9A 1L5
Holy Assumption UOC

Thompson MB R8N 1M9
St. John the Baptist UOC

Tolstoi MB R0A 2E0
Holy Ghost UOC

Transconia MB
All Saints UOC

Tyndall MB R0E 2B0
Ss. Peter & Paul UOC

Valley River MB R0L 2B0
Holy Trinity UOC

Vanlaw MB R0L 0X0
St. Michael UOC

Vista MB R0J 2E0
Holy Trinity UOC

Vita MB R0A 2K0
Holy Trinity UOC

Vita MB R0A 2K0 MAIL
St. Demetrios UOA
<Gardenton MB>
Pohychuk, Box 245

Ward MB R0L 0T0
St. Mary UOC

Winnepegosis MB R0L 2G0
Holy Cross UOC

Winnipeg MB R2W 3S4
Holy Trinity Cathedral UOC
1175 Main St.

Winnipeg MB R2W 2H1
Holy Trinity Sobor OCA
643 Manitoba Ave.
204-589-6223

Winnipeg MB R3P 0S2
St. Demetrios GOA
2255 Grant Ave.
204-889-8723

Winnipeg MB R3C 2A4
St. Demetrius RMA
103 Furby St.
204-775-6472

Winnipeg MB R3T 4Y9
St. George OCA
121 Harvard Ave. E.
3 Prestwood Pl.
204-269-3743, 204-222-1116

Winnipeg MB R2W 3P2
St. Ivan Suchavsky Cathedral UOA
939 Main St.
204-942-3655

Winnipeg MB R3E 0S1
St. Mary ANT
903 Winnipeg Ave.
204-775-9084

Winnipeg MB R2X 0R4
St. Mary Cathedral UOC
840 Burrows Ave.

Winnipeg MB R2W 3J5
St. Michael UOC
110 Disraeli St.

Winnipeg MB R2W 0R2
St. Sava SOC
226 Atlantic Ave.
204-582-1389

Winnipeg (North Winnipeg) MB R3C 2E7
St. Nicholas OCA
5635 Henderson Hwy.
Box 2 Grp. 352 R.R. 2
204-786-3262

New Brunswick

St. John NB E2L 3H7
St. Nicholas GOA
33 Dorchester St.
506-642-1258

Newfoundland

St. John's NF A1C 5X3
Greek Orthodox Community of Newfoundland and Labrador GOA
P.O. Box 6302; Station C
709-579-0612

Nova Scotia

Glace Bay NS B1A 2P2
Ss. Anargyroi GOA
15 Marconi St.
902-849-9554

Halifax NS B3K 5B9
St. Anthony ANT
2455 Windsor St.
902-422-5056

Halifax NS B3N 1R4
St. George GOA
38 Purcell's Cove Rd.
902-479-1271

Ontario

Atikokan ON
St. Michael UOC

Belleville ON K8N 5B2
Holy Trinity GOA
P.O. Box 483
613-968-3327

Brantford ON N3R 7K8
Hellenic Community of Brantford GOA
475 Park Rd. N.
P.O. Box 651
519-759-7353

Brantford ON N3T 3G9
St. Michael UOC

Brockville ON K6V 6E6
Analipsis GOA
P.O. Box 1521
613-345-5525

Chatham ON N7M 5K1
St. Nectarios GOA
P.O. Box 34A
519-352-6266

Cornwall ON K6G 1H1
Greek Orthodox Community GOA
436 2nd St. W.
613-933-1000

Ft. Frances ON P9A 2C4
St. George UOC
804 McKenzie Ave.

Goulais River ON P0S 1E0 MAIL
Holy Resurrection GOA
<Wawa ON>
Mantle; R.R. 1

Goulais River ON P0S 1E0 MAIL
Panagia GOA
<Sault Ste. Marie ON>
Mantle; R.R. 1

Grimsby ON L3M 4G3
St. George UOC
16 Adelaide St.

Guelph ON N1H 6R7
Hellenic Canadian Community GOA
P.O. Box 1591
519-836-8101

Hamilton ON L8L 1B1
Holy Resurrection RMA
278 McNab St. N.
416-529-1663

Hamilton ON
Holy Trinity UOA
73 Mohawk Rd. E.

Hamilton ON L9A 4G1
Koimisis GOA
233 E. 15th St.
416-385-9815

Hamilton ON L8R 1P9
St. Demetrios GOA
22 Head St.
416-529-9651

Hamilton ON L8K 4J9
St. Nicholas Cathedral SOC
153 Nash Rd. S.
416-560-0563

Hamilton ON L8H 2W6
St. Nikola NGM
1415 Barton St. E.
416-549-0876

Hamilton ON
St. Vladimir UOC
851 Barton St. E

Kenora ON P9N 2C2
St. Vladimir UOC

Kingston ON K7L 1X9
Koimisis GOA
121 Johnson St.
613-546-9841

Kingston ON
St. Gregory of Nyssa OCA
@Queens University
613-542-5832

Kirkland Lake ON P2N 3K3
St. Michael UOC

Kitchener ON N2E 1K3
Holy Trinity SOC
700 Fischer Hallman Rd.
519-578-2715

Kitchener ON
Ss. Peter & Paul RMA
313-893-0385

Kitchener ON N2K 1N6
Ss. Peter & Paul GOA
527 Bridgeport Rd. E.
519-579-4703

Kitchener ON N2G 4A2
St. George Martyr NGM
P.O. Box 473 Sta. C
519-884-0311

Kitchener ON N2G 3M4
St. John the Baptist OCA
335 Lancaster St. W.
126 Madison St. S.
519-576-8953

Kitchener ON N2G 4G7
St. Sophia UOC

Lambeth ON N0L 1S3
Holy Transfiguration ANT
4647 Colonel Talbot Rd.
P.O. Box 1163
519-432-1461

Leamington ON N8H 3L2
St. Mary UOC
2529 Buckingham Dr.

London ON N6G 1H6
Holy Cross OCA
@ St. Mark's Anglican
Church; 1320 Wilton Ave.
420 Fox Ave.
519-434-8572

London ON N6A 3K5
Holy Trinity GOA
1114 Richmond St.
519-438-7951

London ON N6A 4L9
Holy Trinity UOC
151 King Edward Ave.

London ON N6C 3C7
St. Sava SOC
Bostwick Rd. @ 401
P.O. Box 62 Sta. 'B'
519-652-2771

Markham ON
St. Panteleimon GOA
416-472-2452

Mississauga ON L4W 1M4
Prophet Elias GOA
4030 Dixie Rd.
416-238-9491, 416-238-5943

Mississauga ON L5A 2Z7
St. Barbara GOA
352 Michelle Row
416-848-6069

Nepean ON K2E 6M4 MAIL
Christ the Saviour CRC
<Ottawa ON>
26 Bowmoor Ave.
613-727-7790

Niagara Falls ON L2E 2J5
St. Archangel Michael NGM
4992 Huron St.
416-358-7363

Niagara Falls ON L2H 1L4
St. George SOC
6085 Montrose Rd. S.
416-356-0090

North Bay ON
St. George GOA
705-566-1059

Oakville ON L6J 6L6
Ss. Peter & Paul SOC
P.O. Box 7408
416-829-0659

Orillia ON L3Y 6H2
Holy Cross-St. Nektarios GOA
Heliotis; R.R. 2

Oshawa ON L1H 3M3
Evangelismos-St. Gerasimos-St. Nektarios GOA
261 Bloor St. E.
416-728-5965

Oshawa ON L1G 1G9
St. Mary UOC
261 Bloor St. E

Ottawa ON K1S 2R6
Annunciation / St. Nicholas Cathedral OCA
55 Clarey Ave.
613-236-5596

Ottawa ON
Christ the Saviour CRC
@All Saints Anglican Church, 347 Richmond Rd.
613-727-7790

Ottawa ON K2A 0J3
Holy Assumption UOC
1000 Byron Ave.

Ottawa ON K1R 7B9
Holy Trinity Sobor OCA
721 Somerset St. W.
58 Arthur St.
613-230-4113

Ottawa ON K2C 1N2
Koimisis GOA
1315 Prince of Wales Dr.
613-225-8545, 613-225-8016

Ottawa ON K1V 6N1
St. Elias ANT
700 Ridgewood Ave.
613-738-2222

Ottawa ON K1Y 2R1
St. Matthew RMA
289 Spencer St.
313-893-0385

Ottawa ON K1N 1C4
St. Nicholas OCA
@Ascension Anglican Church; 253 Echo Dr.
724 Chapel Cres.
613-565-0275

Ottawa ON K2A 2H1
St. Stephen SOC
361 Dominion Ave.
613-729-0244 Tel/FAX

Pembroke ON K8A 3L7
Greek Orthodox Community GOA
526 Alfred St.

Peterborough ON K9J 7X7
Greek Orthodox Community GOA
P.O. Box 1985
705-742-5664

Rainy River ON P0W 1L0
Ss. Peter & Paul UOC

Richmond Hill ON L4C 7B5
St. George ANT
9116 Bayview Ave.
416-731-7210

Richmond Hill ON L4B 2N5 MAIL
St. Panteleimon GOA
<Markham ON>
1-81 Granton Dr.
416-472-2452

Sarnia ON N7T 7C2
Holy Trinity UOC
14 Lisgar St.

Sarnia ON N7T 6X7
St. Demetrios GOA
204 N. East St.
519-336-1420

Sault Ste. Marie ON P6B 2LI
Panagia GOA

Sault Ste. Marie ON
St. Mary UOC

Scarboro ON M1F 4N7
St. Anne UOC

Scarborough ON M1R 2S3
St. John GOA
1385 Warden Ave.
416-759-9259

Scarborough ON M1W 4R6
St. Nicholas GOA
3840 Finch Ave. E.
416-291-4367

Sioux Lookout ON P0V 2T0
St. Vladimir UOC

Smithville ON
St. Charalambos GOA
416-386-6224

Spencerville ON K0E 1X0
Bishop's Chapel of St. Silouan the Athonite OCA
Box 179
613-658-2901, FAX 613-925-1521

St. Ann's ON L0R 1Y0 MAIL
St. Charalambos GOA
<Smithville ON>
Antoniou; R.R. 2
416-386-6224

St. Catherine's ON L2R 7C2
St. George UOC

St. Catherines ON L2R 2Z6
St. Katherine GOA
124 Queenston St.
416-685-3028

Sudbury ON P7B 4M9
Ss. Peter & Paul SOC
515 Antwerp St.

Sudbury ON P3C 4M9
Ss. Peter & Paul NGM
515 Antwerp St.
705-674-2578

Sudbury ON P3B 3J2 MAIL
St. George GOA
<North Bay ON>
99 Shappert St.
705-566-1059

Sudbury ON P3E 5C4
St. Nicholas GOA
486 Ester Rd.
705-522-5181

Sudbury ON P3A 5P3
St. Vladimr UOC
190 Baker St.

Thunder Bay ON P7B 5X1
Holy Trinity GOA
651 Beverly St.
807-623-1033

Thunder Bay ON P7B 2A4
St. George SOC
1237 John St.
807-767-8359

Thunder Bay ON P7A 7E4
St. Mary UOA
716 Pacific Ave.
807-767-3515

Timmins ON
St. Mary RMA
705-264-8276

Toronto ON M6G 2W9
Christ the Savior Sobor OCA
823 Manning Ave.
416-534-1763

Toronto ON M6R 2E4
Evangelismos GOA
136 Sorauren Ave.
416-537-2665

Toronto ON M4H 1H8
Greek Community of Metropolitan Toronto Inc. GOA
30 Thorncliffe Park Dr.
416-425-2485

Toronto ON M6G 2Y3
Holy Trinity-Panagia Grigoroussa GOA
54 Clinton St.
416-537-1351

Toronto ON M4J 3N6
Metamorphosis GOA
40 Donlands Ave.
416-465-2345

Toronto ON M6M 4N6
Ss. Constantine & Helen GOA
1 Brookhaven Dr.
416-241-2470

Toronto ON M5A 3G1
Ss. Cyril & Methodius BEC
237 Sackville

Toronto ON M6K 2P8
St. Andrew UOC
30 O'Hara St.

Toronto ON M6H 2T1
St. Archangel Michael NGM
212 Delaware Ave.
416-531-0275

Toronto ON M4H 1H8
St. Demetrios GOA
30 Thorncliffe Park Dr.
416-425-2485

Toronto ON M8W 2S8
St. Demetrius UOC
3338 Lakeshore Blvd. W.

Toronto ON M6H 2X8
St. Euphrosynia GOA
1008 Dovercourt Rd.
416-536-4449

Toronto ON M5B 1Y2
St. George GOA
115 Bond St.
416-977-3342

Toronto ON M5A 3N4
St. George OCA
17 Regent St.
416-366-1810

Toronto ON M6M 3K9
St. George OCA
247 Rosethorn Ave.
416-651-1321

Toronto ON M4K 3N8
St. Irene Chrysovalantou GOA
66 Cough Ave.
416-465-8213

Toronto ON M5A 3P9
St. Sava SOC
203 River St.
416-967-9885

Toronto ON M8Y 4M6
Three Hierarchs SOC
5A Stockbridge Ave.
416-231-4409

Wawa ON
Holy Resurrection GOA

West Lorne ON N0L 2P0
St. Ilija NGM
P.O. Box 130

Willowdale ON M2K 1G2
All Saints GOA
3125 Bayview Ave.
416-221-4611

Windsor ON N9B 2G7
All Saints RMA
1242 McEwan Ave.
519-252-2269

Windsor ON N8Y 1Y1
Descent of the Holy Ghost RMA
2895 Seminole St.
519-948-0818

Windsor ON N8W 4E2
Dormition of the Theotokos - 'Gracanica' SOC
1960 Meldrum Rd.
519-945-8555

Windsor ON N8X 2G8
Holy Cross GOA
65 Ellis St. E.
519-252-3435

Windsor ON N8Y 1X7
St. Dimitrije NGM
2690 Seminole St.

Windsor ON N8W 1E1
St. George Cathedral RMA
1960 Tecumseh Rd. E.
519-258-1824

Windsor ON N8S 1X1
St. Ignatius of Antioch ANT
283 St. Rose St.
519-945-2280

Windsor ON N8Y 2P8
St. John the Divine OCA
1094 Drouillard Rd.
313-263-0986

Windsor ON N9E 2X8
St. Paul UOA
519-966-3905

Windsor ON N8W 1M5
St. Vladimir UOC
1905 Alsace Ave.

Quebec

Chomedey-Laval PQ H7W 1E1
Holy Cross GOA
4865 Du Souvenir
514-973-3773

Chomedey-Laval PQ H7V 1X3
St. Nicholas GOA
3780 Du Souvenir
514-688-2080

Dollard Des Ormeaux PQ H9B 2N8
Ss. Constantine & Helen GOA
20 Brunswick Rd.
514-684-6462

Labelle PQ J0T 1H0
St. Sergius of Radonezh OCA
Troubetskoy; R.R. 2

Montreal PQ H4J 1R7
Archangels GOA
11801 Elie Blanchard Blvd.
514-334-6868

Montreal PQ H3N 2K3
Evangelismos GOA
777 St. Roch St.
514-340-3552

Montreal PQ H3M 3B5
Fraternite Missionaire de St. Serafin de Sarov OCA
1605 Blvd. Henri Bourassa Oest #308
514-493-8915

Montreal PQ H3S 2V7
Hellenic Community of Montreal GOA
5777 Wilderton Ave.
514-738-2421

Montreal PQ H3N 1Z5
Holy Trinity GOA
7570 Tenasse St. Rock

Montreal PQ H3Z 2J7
Holy Trinity SOC
351 Melville Ave.
514-932-8529

Montreal PQ H3N 2E6
Koimisis GOA
7700 De L'Epee St.; Park Ext.
514-340-3555

Montreal PQ H2L 2R7
Ss. Peter & Paul Sobor OCA
1175A rue Champlain
514-522-2801

Montreal PQ H3M 3B5 MAIL
St. Benoit de Nursie OCA
<Montreal North PQ>
1605 Blvd. Henri Bourassa Oest #308
514-321-3591

Montreal PQ H3T 1A8
St. George GOA
2455 Cote St. Catherine Rd.
514-340-3550

Montreal PQ H2R 1T8
St. George ANT
575 Jean-Talon St. E.
514-276-8533, FAX 514-276-6740

Montreal PQ H2H 1A1
St. John the Baptist RMA
1841 Masson St.
514-527-3314

Montreal PQ H2T 2X1
St. Markella GOA
5390 St. Urbain St.
514-270-4513

Montreal PQ H2G 1T6
St. Mary UOC
2246 Rosemount Blvd.

Montreal PQ H2R 1P2
St. Nicholas ANT
80 de Castelnau St. E.
514-270-9788, 514-276-3102

Montreal PQ H1X 3A5
St. Sophia UOC
6250 12th Ave.
6270 12th Ave.
514-727-2236, FAX 514-728-9834

Montreal PQ H5A 1H3 MAIL
The Sign of the Theotokos OCA
<Westmount PQ>
C.P. 1390; Place Bonaventure
514-934-5093, FAX 514-481-2256

Montreal PQ H3L 3P1
Virgin Mary ANT
C.P. 532; Succ. Ahuntsic
514-858-7004

Montreal North PQ H1H 4X1
St. Benoit de Nursie OCA
2014 St. Urbain St.
514-337-0559

Quebec PQ
Holy Trinity Mission OCA

Quebec City PQ G1R 2A3
Evangelismos GOA
17 St. Cyrille St. E.
418-523-8564

Rawdon PQ J0K 1S0
St. Seraphim Skete & Chapel OCA
15th & Petrograd Aves.
C.P. 1521
514-834-8331, 514-834-3302

St. Hubert PQ J3Y 1V1
St. John the Baptist GOA
4350 Montee St. Hubert
514-676-4027

St. Hubert PQ J3Y 1A1
St. Marina GOA
5220 Grande Allee
514-656-4832

St.-Eusebe; Comte de Temiscouata PQ G0Y 2Y0
Ermitage de la Protection de la Mere de Dieu OCA

Ville LaSalle PQ H8P 1Y5
St. Dionysios GOA
7707 LaSalle Blvd.
514-364-5442

Westmount PQ
The Sign of the Theotokos OCA
330 Clarke Ave.
514-934-5093, FAX 514-481-2256

Saskatchewan

Alvena SK S0K 0E0
All Saints UOC

Arran SK S0A 0B0
Holy Trinity UOC

Arran-Kozbar SK S0A 0B0
Holy Ascension UOC

Assiniboia SK S0H 0B0
Descent of the Holy Ghost OCA
504 6th Ave E.
P.O. Box 285
306-642-3201

Biggar SK S0K 2M0
All Saints UOC

Borden SK S0K 0N0
Holy Assumption UOC

Brooksby SK S0E 0K0
Ss. Peter & Paul UOC

Burgis SK S0A 0L0
Holy Ascension UOC

Calder SK S0A 0K0
Ss. Peter & Paul UOC

Candiac SK S0G 0N0
St. Michael UOC

Cando SK S0K 0V0
St. Michael UOC

Canora SK S0A 0L0
Holy Trinity UOC

Canora SK S0A 0L0
Ss. Peter & Paul OCA
306-642-3201

Canora SK S0A 0L0
St. Michael UOC

Clair SK S0A 0N0
Transfiguration UOC

Codette SK S0A 0N0
Ss. Peter & Paul UOC

Cudworth SK
Holy Trinity UOC

Danbury SK S0A 0P0
St. Vladimir UOC

Donwell SK S0A 0L0
Transfiguration UOC

Doroboy SK
St. Nicholas UOC

Dysart SK
St. George OCA
306-761-2379

Edmore SK S0A 1A0
St. Mary UOC

Elm Spring SK
Ascension of Our Lord RMA
306-642-5844

Endeavor SK S0A 0W0
All Saints UOC

Endeavor SK
St. John the Baptist OCA
306-783-2153

Erwood SK S0E 0Y0
St. John the Baptist UOC

Fenwood SK
Ss. Peter & Paul UOC

Flintoft SK S0H 1R0
Ss. Peter & Paul OCA
306-642-3201

Foam Lake SK S0A 1A0
Ss. Peter & Paul UOC

Fosston SK S0E 0V0
Holy Trinity UOC

Glaslyn SK S0M 0Y0
Ss. Peter & Paul UOC

Goodeve SK S0A 1C0
Holy Ghost UOC

Gorlitz SK S0A 0L0
Ss. Peter & Paul UOC

Gorlitz SK S0A 0L0
St. Basil OCA
306-783-2153

Gronlid (South) SK
Holy Ascension UOC

Halford SK S0J 1A0
Holy Trinity UOC

Hatherleigh SK
Holy Trinity UOC

Honeymoon SK
Ss. Peter & Paul UOC

Hubbard SK S0A 1J0
St. Nicholas UOC

Hudson Bay SK S0E 0Y0
St. Nicholas UOC

Hyas SK S0A 1K0
St. John UOC

Insinger SK S0A 1L0
Holy Ghost UOC

Ituna SK S0A 1N0
Holy Ghost UOC

Kamsack SK S0A 1S0
All Saints UOC

Kayville SK S0H 2C0
Holy Trinity OCA
P.O. Box 12

Kayville SK S0H 2C0
St. Mary / Ss. Peter & Paul RMA
P.O. Box 74
306-475-2345

Kindersley SK S0L 1S0
Holy Ghost UOC

Krydor SK S0J 1K0
Ss. Peter & Paul UOC

Lady Lake SK S0A 3B0
St. Dimitrius OCA
306-783-2153

MacDowell SK S0K 2S0
Holy Ascension UOC

MacNutt SK S0A 2K0
Holy Trinity OCA
306-642-3201

MacNutt SK S0A 2K0
St. Nicholas UOC

Mamornitz SK
Holy Ascension UOC

Marcelin SK S0J 1R0
St. John the Baptist RMA
306-475-2345

Mazeppa SK
Holy Ghost UOC

Meacham SK S0K 2V0
Holy Assumption UOC

Meadow Lake SK S0M 1V0
All Saints UOC

Melfort SK S0E 1A0
All Saints UOC
P.O. Box 3520

Melville SK S0A 2P0
St. Mary UOC

Montmarte SK S0G 3M0
St. Michael UOC

Montmartre SK S0G 3M0
St. Michael UOA

Montmartre SK S0G 3M0
St. Michael OCA
Box 28
306-424-2067

Moose Jaw SK S6H 5X2
Holy Trinity OCA
725 9th Ave. S.W.
306-692-7582

Moose Jaw SK S6H 2E9
St. Vladimir UOC

Naybridge SK
Holy Trinity UOC

Niapwin SK S0E 1E0
St. Mary UOC

Norquay SK S0A 2V0
Ss. Peter & Paul UOC

North Battleford SK S9A 2B9
St. John UOC
972 108th St.

Parkerview SK S0A 2Y0
St. Elias UOC

Pierceland SK S0M 2K0
Descent of the Holy Ghost RMA

Prairie River SK S0E 1J0
St. Michael UOC

Prelate SK S0N 2B0
St. John the Baptist UOC

Prince Albert SK S6V 7P3
Holy Trinity UOC
305 6th St.

Prince Albert SK
St. Peter the Aleut OCA

Punichy SK
St. Mary UOC

Rama SK S0A 3H0
St. Michael UOC

Redfield SK S0M 1S0
St. Vladimir UOC

Regina SK S4P 1M8
Holy Ghost UOC
1920 Toronto St.

Regina SK S4N 0K7
Holy Trinity SOC
928 11th Ave.
FAX 306-352-6276

Regina SK S4P 3J8 MAIL
Orthodox Christian Centre Inc. OCA
<Ft. Qu'Appelle SK>
Box 3512

Regina SK S4N 3K5
St. George OCA
3005 Edgar St.
421 Victoria St.
306-352-0112

Regina SK S4N 2Y4
St. Michael UOA
2075 McDonald St.
306-522-9004

Regina SK S4N 3K5
St. Nicholas OCA
1770 St. John St.
306-789-4143

Regina SK S4S 2B2
St. Paul GOA
3000 Argyle St.
306-586-6402

Rhein SK S0A 3K0
All Saints UOC

Rhein SK S0A 3K0
Holy Assumption OCA
306-783-2153

Samburg SK
Holy Trinity UOC

Saskatoon SK
Holy Ghost UOC

Saskatoon SK S7J 0R9
Holy Resurrection OCA
2202 Lorne Ave.
306-354-5967, FAX 306-477-3718

Saskatoon SK S7H 2C1
Koimisis GOA
1020 Dufferin Ave.
306-244-2802

Saskatoon SK S7M 0C4
St. Vincent of Lerins ANT
224 25th St. W.
306-934-1695

Sheho (Fedaky) SK S0A 3T0
St. Mary UOC

Sheho (Melynchuk) SK S0A 3T0
Ss. Peter & Paul UOC

Sheho (South) SK S0A 3T0
Holy Assumption UOC

Sheho (Town) SK S0A 3T0
Holy Trinity UOC

Shipman SK S0J 2M0
All Saints UOC

Smuts SK S0K 4N0
Holy Ghost UOC

St. Julien SK
St. Mary UOC

St. Walbourg SK S0M 2T0
Ss. Peter & Paul OCA
P.O. Box 356

St. Walburg SK S0N 2T0
Ss. Peter & Paul UOC

Stenen SK S0A 3X0
Holy Assumption OCA
Kindratsky
306-548-4280

Stenen SK S0A 3X0
St. Demetrius UOC

Stornoway SK S0A 3Z0
Ss. Peter & Paul UOC

Sturgis SK
Holy Trinity UOC

Swan Plain SK S0A 2V0
Ss. Peter & Paul UOC

Swift Current SK S9H 1C6
Lifegiving Font GOA
301 N. Railway St. E.
306-773-3735

Swydowa SK
St. Michael UOC

Tarnopol SK
Holy Trinity UOC

Theodore SK S0A 4C0
St. Mary UOC

Theodore River SK
St. John the Baptist UOC

Tiaziw SK
Ss. Vladimir & Olha UOC

Verigin SK S0A 4H0
Assumption UOA
P.O. Box 113
306-542-3385

Verigin SK S0A 4H0
St. Michael OCA
306-783-2153

Vonda SK
St. Mary UOC

Wadena SK S0A 4J0
All Saints UOC

Wakaw SK S0K 4P0
Holy Assumption UOC

Watson SK
St. Michael UOC

Weirdale SK
St. John the Baptist UOC

Westbrook SK
St. Mary UOC

Whitebeach SK
Holy Ghost UOC

Whitkow SK S0M 1S0
Holy Ghost UOC

Wimmer SK S0N 1A0
Holy Ascension UOC

Wishart SK
St. Michael UOC

Wood Mountain SK S0H 4L0
Holy Transfiguration RMA
306-266-4325

Wroxton SK S0A 4S0
St. Elias UOC

Wynyard SK S0A 4T0
St. Mary UOC

Yellow Creek SK
Ss. Peter & Paul UOC

Yorkton SK S3N 1M5
Ss. Anargyroi GOA
160 Betts Ave.
306-773-3735

Yorkton SK S3N 3R2
St. Mark OCA
160 Betts Ave.
306-786-6216, 306-783-2153

Yorkton SK S3N 0S8
Transfiguration UOC

Parishes and Missions in Mexico and the Carribean

Bahamas

Nassau
Annunciation GOA
P.O. Box N-823; West St.
809-322-4382

Cuba

La Havana
Santos Constantino y Elena GOA
20 Paseo Marti

Mexico

Mexico City
Santa Sofia GOA

El Aguacate; Mazatlan Chiapas
San German OCA

Centro Mexico D.F. 06000
Heraldo de la Orthodoxia OCA
Cancelleria de la Iglesia Orthodoxa Catolica en Mexico
Apartado Postal M-8576

Mexico City D.F. 15520
Catedral de la Ascension del Senor OCA
Av. Rio Consulado e Irapuato #53; Penon de los Banos; Delg. V. Carranza

Mexico City DF
Santisimo Salvador y San Nicolas OCA

Guadalajara Jalisco
San German OCA

Chalco Mexico
Transfiguracion OCA

Colonia la Glorieta Mexico
Santa Cruz OCA

San Pablo Xalpa Mexico
San Pedro y San Pablo OCA

Mexico City Mexico C.P. 11000
Santa Sofia - Catedral de GOA
Agua Caliente Esq. Saratoga Col. Lomas-Hipodromo
525-589-6700

Ciudad Lago Mexico City
Santisima Trinidad OCA

Apipilhuasco Veracruz
Santa Maria OCA

Pisaflores Veracruz
Santa Cruz OCA

Poblado de San Martin Veracruz
San Martin OCA

Poblado de San Pedro Veracruz
San Pedro OCA

Parishes and Missions in Jurisdictions not affiliated with SCOBA

Parishes and Missions in the United States of America

Alabama

Birmingham AL 35207
All Saints ROR
3537 N. 27th St.

Brookside AL 35036
St. Nicholas PER
P.O. Box 271
205-674-1325

Arizona

Glendale AZ 85304-3818
Holy Trinity ROR
5814 W. Shangri-La Rd.
602-979-5537

Phoenix AZ 85002
St. Gregory PER
P.O. Box 25233
602-420-9415

Phoenix AZ 85006
St. Mary Protectress UCU
1102 N. 10th St.
602-254-3752

Phoenix AZ 85016-7926
St. Nectarios CHR
3044 N. 27th St.
602-957-3054

Tucson AZ 85714-2525
St. Germain of Alaska - Miracleworker ROR
501 W. Columbia St.
602-889-0154

California

Burlingame CA 94010-5005
All Saints of Russia ROR
744 El Camino Real
415-343-7935, 415-348-9688

Calistoga CA 94515-1609
St. Simeon Verkhotursky ROR
1421 Cedar St.
707-942-6697

Chico CA 95927-3858
St. Sergius & Herman of Valaam VAS
252 E. 4th St.
916-343-2859

Claremont CA 91711
St. George BAM
830 W. Bonita Ave.
909-981-2882, FAX 909-798-5545

Colma CA 94014
St. John Chrysostomos CYP
1801 Hillside Blvd.

Etna CA 96027
Orthodox Community of Etna CYP
P.O. Box 677

Garden Grove CA 92642
St. Athanasios CYP
P.O. Box 2833

Guerneville CA 95446-9120
Holy Virgin of Kazan ROR
17370 Neeley Rd.
707-869-2637

Los Angeles CA 90027-5603
Holy Transfiguration Cathedral ROR
5432 Fernwood Ave.
213-464-2623

Los Angeles CA 90068-3305
Protection of the Holy Virgin ROR
2049 Argyle Ave.
213-466-4845

Los Angeles CA 90026
St. Andrew UCU
1456 Sutherland St.
213-250-4285

Los Angeles CA 90029-3607
St. Vladimir UCU
4025 Melrose Ave.
619-952-2968

Monterey CA 93944-0813 MAIL
St. Seraphim of Sarov ROR
<Seaside CA>
P.O. Box 5813
408-394-1611, 408-373-6364

Oxnard CA 93030-1735
Holy Trinity ROR
2784 Alvarado St.
805-983-4472

Palo Alto CA 94303-4412
Protection of the Holy Virgin ROR
3475 Ross Rd.
415-494-6397

Pomona CA 91766
St. Demetrios AUX
1495 Reservoir St. S.
909-623-9563

Ramona CA 92065
St. Mark VAS
1425 Main St. Suite 144

Redding CA 96001-4825
Theotokos Icon - Surety of Sinners ROR
1972 Jewell Ln.
916-241-1732

Sacramento CA 95814-1903
Ascension of Christ ROR
714 13th St.
916-443-2271

Sacramento CA 95842
Our Lady of Prayer UIU
4748 Greenholme

Sacramento CA 95815
Sacramento Mission VAS
3181 High St.
916-929-4898

San Diego CA 92105
Our Lady of Kazan PER
3703 Central Ave.
619-281-6446, 619-589-8182

San Diego CA 92165
St. John of Kronstadt ROR
5131 Rex Ave.
P.O. Box 5611
619-282-3304, 619-284-9346

San Diego CA 92077
St. Mary Protectress UCU
9558 Campo Rd.
619-464-1830

San Francisco CA 94117
Christ the Savior VAS
720 DuBose Ave.

San Francisco CA 94109
Holy Archangels Michael, Gabriel, & Raphael VAS
1065 Sutter St.
415-474-4621

San Francisco CA 94117
Holy Theotokos VAS
20 Steiner St.

San Francisco CA 94121
Holy Virgin Cathedral ROR
6210 Geary Blvd.
415-221-3255

San Francisco CA 94121-2210
Mother of God of Kazan ROR
5717 California St.
415-752-2502

San Francisco CA 94117-1752
Old Holy Virgin Cathedral ROR
864 Fulton St.
415-346-4952

San Francisco CA 94118-1325
Resurrection of Christ ROR
109 6th Ave.
415-386-0452

San Francisco CA 94118
St. Francis UIU
130 11th Ave.

San Francisco CA
St. George VAS

San Francisco CA 94103
St. Michael UCU
345 7th St.
415-861-4066

San Francisco CA 94114
St. Nicholas Cathedral PER
2005 15th St.
415-621-1849

San Francisco CA 94122-2214
St. Sergius of Radonezh ROR
1346 12th Ave.
415-664-8442

San Francisco CA 94118-3531
St. Tikhon of Zadonsk ROR
598 15th Ave.
415-221-0234

Santa Barbara CA 93101-3619
Holy Resurrection ROR
411 W. Victoria St.
805-966-1453, 805-966-0151

Santa Rosa CA 95407
Dormition of the Mother of God VAS
1468 Gloria Dr.

Santa Rosa CA 95407-8046
Ss. Peter & Paul ROR
850 St. Olga St.
707-584-4092

Santa Rosa CA
St. George VAS

Seaside CA 93944
St. Seraphim of Sarov ROR
1159 Canyon Del Ray & Francis Ave.
408-394-1611, 408-373-6364

Sonoma CA 95476
St. Demetrios the Physician VAS
22666 Broadway Ave.

Sunnyvale CA 94086-5061
St. Herman of Alaska ROR
161 N. Murphy St.
408-733-9475

Whittier CA
St. Mary MOC
10550 E. Whittier Blvd.

Willits CA 95490
St. John the Almsgiver ROR
24200 Redwood Hwy. N.
P.O. Box 302
707-459-5424

Colorado

Colorado Springs CO 80908
Rocky Mt. Mission VAS
16755 Southwood Dr.
303-495-0005

Denver CO 80210-5510
All Russian Saints ROR
3274 E. Iliff Ave.
303-757-3533

Denver CO 80218
St. Mary Protectress UCU
1136 Ogden St.
303-831-0497

Connecticut

Bridgeport CT 06610
Holy Trinity UCU
99 York St.
203-729-1887

Clinton CT 06514
St. Barbara GMA
27 Brickyard Rd.

Danbury CT 06811-4737
St. Peter & St. Paul VAS
12 Alan Ave.

Hartford CT 06114-2402
St. Panteleimon ROR
19 Becket St.
203-956-0561

Hartford CT 06106
St. Volodymyr UCU
110 Russ St.
203-246-0248

New Britain CT 06051
St. Mary UCU
54 Winter St.
203-229-3833

New Haven CT 06515
St. Mary Protectress UCU
50 Fowler St.
203-387-4305

Pawcatuck CT 06379
Holy Epiphany VAS
43 Liberty St.

Southbury CT 06488-0029
St. Sergius ROR
Russian Village Rd.
P.O. Box 29
203-264-8808

Stratford CT 06497-4931
Presentation of Christ ROR
5 Wheeler Terrace
203-375-8342

Stratford CT 06497-6402
St. Nicholas ROR
1 Honeyspot Rd.
203-375-2786

Waterbury CT 06710
St. Mary Protection UOD
74 Fairview Ave.

Delaware

Wilmington DE 19809
Ss. Peter & Paul UCU
1406 Philadelphia Pike
302-798-4588

Dist. of Col.

Washington DC 20011-5302
St. John the Baptist Cathedral ROR
4001 17th St. N.W.
202-726-3000, 202-726-4989, FAX 301-565-0848

Washington DC 20017
St. Moses the Black SGP
1223 Girard St. N.E.
202-832-6750

Florida

Clearwater FL 34615
Holy Dormition of the Theotokos CHR
1910 Douglas Ave.
813-443-3999, FAX 813-446-0290

Clearwater FL 34625-1406
St. Nectarios ROR
1845 Asbury Dr.
813-724-9140

Cooper City FL 33328
St. Nicholas UCU
5031 S.W. 100th Ave.
305-434-2461

Dover FL 33527
Protection of the Most Holy Mother of God UCU
3820 Moores Lake Rd.
P.O. Box 738
813-659-0123

Dunnellon FL 32630
St. Demetrios VAS
10606 N. Citrus Springs Blvd.
901-489-2147

Melbourne FL 32935
St. Gerasimos VAS
2223 Dordon St.

Miami FL 33126-5361
St. Vladimir ROR
101 N.W. 46th Ave.
305-448-7087

Palm Harbor FL 34683
Holy Sepulchre VAS
P.O. Box 2177

Pinellas Park FL 34666
St. Michael UCU
9201 60th St. N.
813-531-8804

St. Petersburg FL 33701
Holy Theotokos of Vladimir ROR
310 13th Ave.

St. Petersburg FL 33711-2326
St. Andrew ROR
4668 15th Ave. S.
813-321-1639

Tampa FL 33610-5927
St. Gregory the Theologian PER
9615 E. Hillsborough Ave.
813-628-0026

Georgia

Atlanta GA
St. Andrew UCU
404-476-0351, 912-897-4378

Atlanta GA 30312
St. John the Wonderworker VAS
543 Cherokee Ave.
404-624-1442

Atlanta GA 30306-3311
St. Michael the Archangel ROR
1160 Reeder Circle N.E.
404-875-1447

Augusta GA 30909
Ss. Cyril & Methodius ROR
3110 Edinburgh Dr.
706-738-0698

Duluth GA 30136 MAIL
St. Andrew UCU
<Atlanta - Savannah GA>
2755 Kenwood Court
404-476-0351, 912-897-4378

Norcross GA 30092-6105
Holy Resurrection AUX
508 Glenleaf Dr.
404-447-0785

Savannah GA
St. Andrew UCU
7207 Golden Isles Way
912-897-4378

Hawaii

Honolulu HI 96815-1616
Iveron Mother of God ROR
1778 Ala Moana Blvd. Apt. 1908
808-947-6605

Waianae HI 96792
St. Sophia GMA
88-660 Homestead Rd.

Idaho

Boise ID 83702-3122
St. Seraphim of Sarov ROR
872 N. 29th St.
208-345-1553, 208-384-2153

Osburn ID 83849
Holy Apostles UIU
Box 309

Post Falls ID 83854
Holy Cross UIU
1295 N. Syringa Rd.

Illinois

Benld IL 62009-1306
Holy Dormition PER
304 N. 4th St.
217-835-2202

Bloomingdale IL 60108
St. Andrew UCU
300 E. Army Trail Rd.
708-894-9717

Centralia IL 62801
St. Basil DHE
217 S. Maple St.
618-532-4456

Chicago IL 60613
Ss. Athanasius & John the Baptist GMA
1415 W. Waveland Ave.

Chicago IL
Ss. Raphael & Markella VAS

Chicago IL 60622
St. George BYC
1500 Maplewood Ave.
312-486-7209

Chicago IL 60656
St. Sophia UCU
6655 W. Higgins St.
312-631-3112

Chicago IL 60622
St. Volodymyr Cathedral UCU
2230-50 W. Cortez St.
708-596-7316

Des Plaines IL 60018-2024
Holy Protection Cathedral ROR
1800 Lee St.
708-824-6531, 708-298-4144

Palos Park IL 60464-2122
Ss. Peter & Paul UCU
8410 W. 131st St.
708-448-1350, 708-361-5165

Rock City IL 61070
St. Vladimir ROR
Vladimorovo-Lost Lake
815-968-6351

Rockford IL 61101-9003
St. Vladimir ROR
<Rock City IL>
4859 Huxley Dr.
815-968-6351

Worth IL 60452
Ss. Anargyroi-St. Nectarios CHR
11360 S. Lawler
708-371-1800, 708-460-5051

Indiana

Ft. Wayne IN 46806
Holy Ascension UCU
2902 Evans St.
219-440-0269

Ft. Wayne IN 46803-3450
Holy Trinity ROR
2402 Smith St.
219-432-9742

Ft. Wayne IN 48606
St. Volodymyr UOD
Drezel & St. Anthony

Gary IN 46409
Ss. Peter & Paul MOC
51st & Virginia

Goshen IN 46526
Holy Trinity UCU
61302 C.R. 21

Goshen IN 46526
Protection of the Holy Virgin ROR
County Rd. 21; Box 61355
219-534-2375

Hammond IN 46324
St. Michael UCU
7074 Columbia Ave.
219-844-6483

Iowa

Cedar Rapids IA 52403-1612
St. John the Baptist ROR
3635 Cottage Grove Ave. S.E.
319-362-8601, FAX 319-363-4252

Radcliffe IA 50230
Radcliffe Orthodox Mission VAS
R.R. 1, Box 87

Louisiana

Harahan LA 70123
Holy Innocents HOC
311 Hickory Ave.
504-738-3502

Maine

Gardiner ME 04345-1817
St. Alexander Nevsky ROR
<Richmond ME>
33 Mt. Vernon St.
207-737-2365

Richmond ME 04357
Holy Cross UOD

Richmond ME 04357
St. Alexander Nevsky ROR
17 Church St.
207-737-2365

South Portland ME 04106
Holy Nativity VAS
16 Channel Rd.

Maryland

Baltimore MD 21231-2002
Holy Transfiguration ROR
2201 E. Baltimore St.
301-732-1022

Baltimore MD 21231
Holy Trinity PER
1723 E. Fairmount Ave.
301-732-1824

Baltimore MD 21231
St. Michael UCU
2019 Gough St.
301-327-2840

Laurel MD 20708-2830
MAIL
St. Cosmas Aitolos AUX
<Riverdale MD>
11812 Randy Ln.
301-776-3189

Riverdale MD 20737-1210
St. Cosmas Aitolos AUX
6300 Kenilworth Ave.
301-776-3189

Silver Spring MD 20904
St. Andrew Cathedral UCU
15100 New Hampshire Ave.
301-384-2407

Whaleysville MD 21872
Holy Trinity UCU
Box 44 Circle Rd.
301-835-8661

Massachusetts

Allston MA 02134
Holy Resurrection VAS
64 Harvard Ave.
617-787-7625

Boston MA
Greek Orthodox Mission
MAT

Dorchester MA 02124
Bethany VAS
25 Ocean St.

Haverhill MA 01832-5536
St. Xenia ROR
55 Wingate St.
508-521-0253

Ipswich MA 01938-1251
St. John the Confessor
AUX
244 High St.
508-356-5303

Ipswich MA 01938-2116
St. John the Russian ROR
16 Mt. Pleasant Ave.
508-356-1207

Jamaica Plain MA 02130
St. Andrew UCU
24 Orchardhill Rd.
617-522-3323

New Bedford MA 02744
MAIL
Greek Orthodox Mission
MAT
<Boston MA>
60 Mott St.

New Bedford MA 02744
House Chapel MAT
60 Mott St.

Roslindale MA 02131-2309
Holy Epiphany ROR
963 South Street
617-327-3663

Roslindale MA 02131
Holy Protection GMA
22 Cedrus Ave.
617-524-4724, FAX 617-524-7142

Roslindale MA 02131-2448
St. Anna AUX
852 South St.
617-327-5300

Roslindale MA 02131-0129
St. Mark of Epesus
Cathedral AUX
850 South St. Box 129
617-469-2380

West Springfield MA 01089-2722
St. Nicholas ROR
23 Southworth St.

Worcester MA 01605-3069
Holy Resurrection AUX
63 Laurel St.
508-752-7813

Michigan

Ann Arbor - Dexter MI 48130
St. Vladimir ROR
9900 Jackson Rd.
313-761-7311

Battle Creek MI 49017
St. Elias PER
5066 B. Drive S.
616-979-2146

Benton Harbor MI 49022-3339
Christ the Saviour ROR
817 Thresher Ave.
616-429-0133

Detroit MI 48212
St. Andrew UOD
5130 Prescott St.

East Detroit MI 48021
Holy Spirit BAM
14873 Collinson

East Lansing MI 48823
St. Andrew PER
1222 Greencrest
517-351-4627

Ecorse MI 48229
Great Martyr George & St.
Nectarios CHR
4592 W. Jefferson Ave.
313-451-2197

Farmington Hills MI 48333-2951
Dormition Cathedral ROR
<Sterling Heights MI>
P.O. Box 2951
313-939-3490, 313-795-3766

Flint MI 48505
Ss. Peter & Paul UOD
715 E. Parkway

Grand Rapids MI 49504
St. John Chrysostom PER
40 National N.W.
616-454-1166

Redford MI 48239
St. Innocent PER
23300 W. Chicago
313-538-1142

Redford MI 48239-2250
St. Michael the Archangel PER
26355 W. Chicago Rd.
26375 W. Chicago Rd.
313-937-2120

Saginaw MI 48601
Holy Trinity UOD
1987 S. Wabash

Southfield MI 48075
St. Mary Protectress Cathedral UCU
20107 Mada & Evergreen Rd.
313-356-1636

St. Clair Shores MI 49080
St. Spyridon GMA
23410 Greater Mack

Sterling Heights MI
Dormition Cathedral ROR
@Holy Ghost Church -
38500 Ryan Rd.
313-939-3490, 313-795-3766

Sterling Heights MI 48310-2980
Holy Ghost ROR
38500 Ryan Rd.
313-795-3766, 313-268-7444

Warren MI 48092
Mother of God MOC
21740 Ryan Rd.

Westland MI 48185 MAIL
Great Martyr George & St. Nectarios CHR
<Ecorse MI>
34518 Warren Rd. Suite 254
313-451-2197

Minnesota

Fridley MN 55432-5720
Resurrection of Christ ROR
1201 Hathaway Ln. N.E.
612-574-1001

Minneapolis MN 55414 MAIL
Resurrection of Christ ROR
<Fridley MN>
P.O. Box 14607
612-574-1001

Minneapolis MN 55414
St. George UCU
316 S.E. 4th Ave.
612-379-1647

Minneapolis MN 55413
St. Michael UCU
505 4th St. N.E.
612-379-2280

Minneapolis MN 55414-3637
St. Panteleimon ROR
2210 S.E. Franklin Ave.
612-379-7335

St. Paul MN 55104-3548
Prophet Elias AUX
1896 Feronia Ave.
612-646-5505

St. Paul MN 55104
Ss. Volodymyr & Olha UCU
873 Portland Ave.
612-222-0619

Mississippi

Waveland MS 39576
St. Mary Magdalene HOC
125 Hartsie Dr.
601-467-3723

Missouri

House Springs MO 63051-0536
St. John Chrysostom ROR
3774 Gravois Rd.
P.O. Box 536
314-677-4333, FAX 314-376-3223

Kansas City MO 64109
Holy Resurrection VAS
P.O. Box 090492
826-931-0142

St. Ann MO 60374
St. Luke SGP
P.O. Box 735
314-426-2829

St. Louis MO 63110
Christ the Good Shepherd VAS
2309 Thurman Ave.
314-664-8132, 314-772-6609

St. Louis MO 63109
St. Basil GMA
3615 McCausland

St. Louis MO 63109
St. Basil the Great ROR
3615 McCausland Ave.
314-645-1905

St. Louis MO 63123-2553
St. Katherine of Sinai AUX
8400 New Hampshire Ave.
314-352-2564

Nebraska

Lincoln NE 68522
Holy Archangels VAS
1740 W. Burnham
402-423-8070

Lincoln NE 68542-2237
Roman Rite Vicariate DHE
P.O. Box 22237
402-475-6492

Lincoln NE 68502
St. Fanourios - Archdiocesan Chancery VAS
1827 S. 11th St.
402-438-1332, FAX 402-438-2595

Lincoln NE 68503
St. John of Kronstadt VAS
2800 Holdrege St.

Lincoln NE 68542-2237
St. Tikhon DHE
1319 S. 11th St.
P.O. Box 22237
402-476-2676, 402-572-6360

Lincoln NE 68508
Three Hierarchs UCU
450 'E' St.
708-361-5165

Omaha NE 68107
St. Gabriel VAS
3219 R St.
402-423-8070

Omaha NE 68134-0362
St. John of San Francisco DHE
P.O. Box 34362
402-572-6360

New Hampshire

Concord NH 03301-4249
Dormition of the Theotokos AUX
4 Union St.
603-225-4909

Manchester NH 03103-5437
Ss. Peter & Paul PER
306 Beech St.
603-623-1700

New Jersey

Bayonne NJ 07002
St. Nicholas PER
606 Kennedy Blvd.
201-339-7488

Bayonne NJ 07002
St. Sophia UCU
38 W. 23rd St.
201-436-8350

Buena NJ 08310-9633
Protection of the Holy Virgin ROR
East Weymouth Rd.; R.D. 2 - Box 358
609-697-2027

Carteret NJ 07008
St. Demetrius Cathedral UCU
645 Roosevelt Ave.
908-541-1530

Clifton NJ 07013
Holy Ascension UCU
635-655 Broad St.
201-471-8131

Clifton NJ 07011
St. Mary Protectress UCU
71-83 Washington Ave.
908-546-2473

Dorothy NJ 08317
Holy Trinity BAM
P.O. Box 255

Elizabeth NJ 07208
Ss. Peter & Paul PER
159 Stiles St.
908-352-1192

Garfield NJ 07026
Three Saints PER
St. Vladimir's Square; 454 Outwater Ln.
201-772-8973

Hackettstown NJ 07840
Elevation of the Holy Cross PER
909 Rt. 517
P.O. Box 781
908-852-5611

Highland Park NJ 08904
Mother of God of Zyrovicy BAM
9 River Rd.

Howell NJ 07731-8582
St. George ROR
57 E. 3rd St.
201-364-4226

Howell - Lakewood NJ 07731-8684
St. Alexander Nevsky ROR
200 Alexander Ave. @ Rt. 9
908-364-3330, 908-367-9835, FAX 908-364-5625

Irvington NJ 07111
Holy Trinity UCU
836 Lyons Ave.
680 Stuyvesant Ave.

Jackson NJ 08527-0143
St. Vladimir Memorial ROR
Rt. 571
P.O. Box 143
908-928-1248

Little Falls (Singac) NJ 07424
St. John the Baptist PER
29 Weaver St.
201-256-0314

Maplewood NJ 07040
Holy Ascension UCU
652 Irvington Ave.
201-763-7644

Millville NJ 08332
Ss. Peter & Paul UCU
77 Center Grove Rd.
609-825-6720

Millville NJ 08332
St. Nicholas ROR
5th St. & Garrison Ave.
609-825-5952

Montville NJ 07045
Christ the Savior PER
103 Horseneck Rd.
201-316-8145

New Brunswick NJ 08901-2942
Protection of the Holy Virgin ROR
301 Handy St.
201-247-4621

Newark NJ 07104-2214
Our Lady of Kazan ROR
70-78 Heller Pkwy.
201-482-5627

Passaic NJ 07055-6706
Ss. Cosmas & Damian ROR
44 Van Buren St.
201-471-4485

Passaic NJ 07055
Ss. Cyril & Methodius MOC
124 Hamilton Ave.

Passaic NJ 07055
Ss. Peter & Paul PER
3rd & Monroe Sts.
201-778-0826

Paterson NJ 07502-2106
St. Michael's Cathedral ROR
52-56 Sherman Ave.
334 Cumberland Ave.
201-595-5816

Perth Amboy NJ 08861-2808
St. Spiridon ROR
649 Elizabeth St.
648 Charles St.
908-826-4818

Red Bank NJ 07701-1114
St. Nicholas ROR
15-17 Pearl St.
201-747-2247

Somerset NJ 08873
Ss. Fanourios & Haralampos GMA
Victor St.

South Bound Brook NJ 08880
St. Andrew Memorial UCU
P.O. Box 495
908-469-7486, FAX 908-271-8908

South River NJ 08882
St. Euphrosynia BYC
S. Whitehead Avenue
908-888-9328

Trenton NJ 08611-1720
Assumption ROR
106 Jackson St.
609-586-5455

Trenton NJ 08610
Holy Assumption UOD
Broad & Market Sts.

Trenton NJ 08610
Holy Trinity UCU
824 Adeline St.
609-393-5330

Vineland NJ 08360-3492
Holy Trinity ROR
2211 W. Landis Ave.
609-696-1579

Yardville NJ 08620
St. George UCU
839 Yardville-Allentown Rd.
609-585-1935

New Mexico

Alamagordo NM 88311-1432
St. Peter the Aleut CHR
505-434-5277

Albuquerque NM 87102
Holy Royal Martyrs VAS
324 Hazeldine Ave. S.W.
505-242-6186

Farmington NM
St. Nicholas CHR
505-434-5277

Hobbs NM 88240-3146
St. Benedict ROR
1714 E. Rose Ln.
505-393-4630

Las Cruces NM
Ss. Constantine & Helen CHR
505-434-5277

Santa Fe NM 87501-4795
St. Tikhon ROR
11 Calle Medico - Suite #1
505-982-8871, 505-471-1150

New York

Albany NY
Nativity of Our Lady ROR
@ Holy Virgin Protection;
2040 Euclid Ave.
Schenectady NY

Astoria NY 11103-4228
Holy Trinity ROR
25-36 37th St.
718-726-7870

Astoria NY 11105
Holy Trinity MAT
38-10 20th Rd.

Astoria NY 11106 MAIL
St. Andrei the Apostle VAS
<Jamaica NY>
33-20 29th St. 2nd Floor

Astoria NY 11105
St. Dionysios VAS
P.O. Box 9001
212-996-0355

Astoria NY 11105
St. Irene Chrysovalantou Cathedral GMA
36-07 23rd Ave.

Astoria NY 11105
St. Markella Cathedral CHR
22-68 26th St.
718-932-1592, FAX 718-274-2875

Bayside NY 11361
St. George the Great-Martyr PER
211-49 46th Ave.
201-316-8627

Bethpage NY 11714
St. Isidore of Chios CHR
910 Stewart Ave.
516-933-1736

Brooklyn NY 11211
Holy Cross VAS
P.O. Box 110482

Brooklyn NY 11209
St. Cyprian & St. Justina HOC
Chapel of St. Mary Magdalene
P.O. Box 248
718-836-6215

Brooklyn NY 11217
St. Cyril of Tarau Cathedral BAI
401 Atlantic Ave.
908-560-0058

Brooklyn NY 11209
St. Mary Magdalene HOC
P.O. Box 248
718-836-6215

Brooklyn NY 11220
St. Nektarios GMA
340 67th St.

Brooklyn NY 11204
St. Nicholas GMA
1822 65th St.

Buffalo NY 14220
St. George VAS
534 McKinley Pkwy.

Buffalo NY 14212-1560
St. Nicholas ROR
197 Stanislaus St.
716-896-2729

Cheektowaga NY 14227
Holy Trinity UCU
200 Como Park Blvd.
716-684-0738

Eastport NY 11941
St. Mary UCU
Montauk Hwy.
P.O. Box 305
516-878-8240, 516-727-3325

Elmhurst-Maspeth NY 11378
Ss. Paraskevi & Haralambos VAS
73-05 Grand Ave.
718-899-0922

Endicott NY 13760-3938
St. Nicholas ROR
308 N. Page Ave.
607-754-0881

Flushing NY 11355-1731
Holy Annunciation ROR
42-67 147th St.
718-359-5373

Glen Cove NY 11542
Ascension Cathedral ROR
Old Tappan Rd.
516-676-7683

Glen Cove NY 11542-1810
Holy Virgin Protection ROR
14 Alvin St.
516-671-5316

Glen Spey NY 12737-0178
Ss. Peter & Paul UCU
P.O. Box 178
717-343-7165

Glendale NY
St. Toma VAS

Glenham NY 12527
St. Nicholas ROR
13 Maple St.
P.O. Box 800
914-831-2164

Herkimer NY 13350
St. Mary UCU
331 Moore Ave.
315-866-3952

Hudson NY 12534
St. Michael UCU
59 Partition St.
518-828-3121

Jackson Heights NY 11372-7945
St. Alexander Nevsky ROR
94-17 Roosevelt Ave.
718-429-7232

Jamaica NY
St. Andrei the Apostle VAS

Jamaica NY 11432
St. Gerasimos VAS
84-41 164th St.
718-523-1859

Jamesville NY 13078-9745
Entrance of the Holy Virgin into the Temple ROR
607 Tecumseh (at Peak Hill Rd.)
315-446-1781

Johnson City NY 13790
St. John UCU
1 St. John's Pky.
607-797-1584

Lackawanna NY
Ss. Cyril & Methodius MOC
4785 Lake Ave.

Maspeth NY
St. Paraskeve AUX
Grand Ave.

New York City NY 10031-1001
Holy Fathers ROR
524 W 153rd St.
212-281-3992

New York City NY 10013
Holy Trinity Cathedral UCU
359 Broome St.
212-226-4351

New York City NY 10128-1331
Mother of God of the Sign Cathedral ROR
75 E. 93rd St.
212-534-1601

New York City NY 10029
St. Nicholas Patriarchal Russian Cathedral PER
15 E. 97th St.
212-289-1915

New York City NY 10128-1331
St. Sergius of Radonezh Chapel ROR
75 E. 93rd St.
212-534-1601

New York City NY 10024
St. Volodymyr Cathedral UCU
160 W. 82nd St.
212-873-8550

North Tonawanda NY 14120
Holy Protection AUX
530 Oliver St.
716-634-2590

Nyack NY 10960-3744
Protection of the Holy Virgin ROR
51 Prospect St.
38 S. Mill Rd.
914-358-4982

Olivebridge NY 12446-0386
St. Volodymyr UCU
P.O. Box 1386
914-626-2088

Pine Bush NY 12566
All Saints of Russia PER
R.D. #2, Box 251
914-744-3129

Poughkeepsie NY 12601-4801
St. Nicholas ROR
100 Livingston St.
914-454-6822

Richmond Hill NY 11419
Asssumption ROR
119-02 94th Ave.
718-847-0260

Richmond Hill NY 11418-2930
St. Cyril of Turov BYC
104-29 Atlantic Ave.
718-847-4123, 718-441-8053

Rochester NY 14607
Protection of the Mother of God ROR
460 East Ave.
716-473-4568

Rochester NY 14617
St. Mary Protectress UCU
3176 St. Paul Blvd.
716-342-1076

Rome NY 13440
St. Nicholas UCU
512 N. George St.
315-337-9518

Schenectady NY 12306-4102
Protection of the Holy Virgin ROR
2040 Euclid Ave.
518-456-8228

Sea Cliff NY 11579-1332
St. Seraphim ROR
131-A Carpenter Ave.
516-671-2075

Syracuse NY
St. George MOC
5083 Onandaga Rd.

Syracuse NY 13057
St. Sergius & St. Herman VAS
6421 Franklin Park Dr.

Troy NY 12180
St. Nicholas UCU
376 3rd St.
518-274-5482

Uniondale NY 11553
St. Michael UCU
237 Maple Ave.
516-669-7402

Utica NY 13502
Holy Cross UCU
841 Bleecker St.
315-733-9339

Utica NY 13502
Ss. Peter & Paul UCU
815 Hamilton St.
315-732-2895

Utica NY 13501-3131
St. John of Kronstadt ROR
1009 Conkling Ave.
315-797-6539

Valley Cottage NY 10989-0599
St. Sergius of Radonezh ROR
Tolstoy Farm - Lake Rd.
914-268-6551

Van Brunt NY 11215
St. Michael UOD
16 26th St.

Warners NY 13164
St. Luke UCU
3290 Warners Rd.
315-468-3472

West Henrietta NY
St. Demetrius MOC
234 Telephone Rd.

West Islip NY 11795
Ss. Peter & Paul UCU
64 Higbie Ln.
516-422-4453

Williamsville (Buffalo East) NY 14221-6721
St. Theodore ROR
96 Los Robles St.
716-774-0062

Woodbourne NY 12788
Ss. Peter & Paul ROR
Ulster Heights Rd.
914-434-8723

Woodside NY 11377
Ss. Fanourios & Gerasimos Cathedral VAS
44-02 48th Ave.
718-786-4495, FAX 718-786-7887

Woodside NY 11377-6344 MAIL
St. Toma VAS
<Glendale NY>
44-02 48th Ave.

North Carolina

Raleigh NC
Orthodox Mission ROR

St. Helena NC 28425
Ss. Peter & Paul PER
919-259-7336

North Dakota

Wilton ND 58579
Holy Trinity UCU
Rt. 1 Box 98
701-734-6494

Ohio

Barberton OH 44203
Great Martyr George BAM
558 W. Tuscaworas

Blue Ash OH 45242
St. George ROR
4905 Myrtle Ave.

Brunswick OH 44212
St. Stephen Church of Millenium UCU
1905 Pearl Rd.
216-237-6238

Brunswick OH 44212 MAIL
Virgin of All Who Sorrow Icon ROR
<Cleveland OH>
2030 Hathaway Dr.
216-225-5615

Cincinnati OH 45231-3830
St. James ROR
9158 Winton Rd.
513-729-1600

Cleveland OH 44102
Holy Resurrection ROR
6201 Detroit Ave.
216-651-2879

Cleveland OH 44109
Mother of God of Zyrovicy BAM
3517 W. 25th St.

Cleveland OH 44111
St. Panteleimon UCU
3747 W. 135th St.
216-251-1064

Cleveland OH
Virgin of All Who Sorrow Icon ROR
1350 W. 69th St.
216-225-5615

Columbus OH 43213
Dormition MOC
3564 Medway Ave.

Columbus OH 43207
St. Nectarios of Aegina VAS
1618 S. Champion Ave.

Green OH 44232
St. Nikola MOC
5305 Masillon Rd.

Lorain OH 44055
St. Mary UCU
2304 E. 34th St.
216-277-8757, 216-277-6110

North Royalton OH 44133
Holy Trinity UCU
9672 State Rd.
216-237-0104

Parma OH 44134-4802
St. Sergius ROR
6520 Broadview Rd.
216-447-1015

Parma OH 44134
St. Volodymyr Cathedral UCU
5913 State Rd.
216-885-1509

Pickerington OH 43147-1368
Holy Trinity AUX
579 Pickerington Hills Dr.
614-833-1170

Urbana OH 43078-2021
Our Lady of Kazan ROR
218 W. Market St.
513-653-5179

Warren OH 44483
St. Matrona of Chios CHR
425 Kenworth N.E.
718-932-1592

Youngstown OH 44502-2326
Nativity of Christ PER
727 Miller Ave.
216-788-0151, FAX 216-788-9361

Youngstown OH 44509
Ss. Peter & Paul UCU
1025 N. Belle Vista Ave.
216-799-3830

Oklahoma

Oklahoma City OK 73135-2527
St. Benedict ROR
3900 Jones Blvd.
405-672-1441, FAX 405-787-6665

Oregon

Donald OR
Dormition CHU

Eugene OR 97401
St. Paul the Apostle VAS
135 E. 13th

Gervais OR 97026
Holy Transfiguration MOR
12929 Bethlehem Dr. N.E.

Gervais OR
St. Nicholas CHU

Medford OR 97501-2301
St. Innocent ROR
719 Welsh St.
503-772-0851, 503-826-3215

Milwaukie OR 97222
Annunciation VAS
13515 S.E. Rusk Rd.
503-659-3646

Mulino OR 97042-9633
New Martyrs of Russia ROR
13848 S. Union Hall Rd.
503-632-7040

Portland OR 97209
Holy Apostles VAS
2069 N.W. Overton
503-222-3469

Portland OR 97206
Nativity of the Theotokos AUX
5209 S.E. 64th St.
503-285-3881

Portland OR 97202
St. John the Baptist UCU
8014 SE 16th Ave.
408-997-9343

Portland OR
St. Moses the Ethiopian VAS

Portland OR 97209
St. Raphael VAS
2057 N.W. Overton

St. Benedict OR 97373
Our Lady of Tikhvin MAR

Williams OR 97544
Holy Spirit - Paraclete SGP
20012 Williams Hwy.
503-846-6935

Woodburn OR
St. Nicholas CHU

Woodburn OR 97071
Theotokos of Kursk UCU
1250 Hardcastle St.

Pennsylvania

Alden PA 18634 MAIL
Christ the Saviour ROR
<Sugar Notch - Wilkes-Barre>
11 W. Kirmar Ave.
717-822-3358

Ambridge PA 15003-2350
St. Vladimir UCU
313 9th St.
412-266-3530

Arnold PA 15068
Holy Virgin UCU
1701 Kenneth Ave.
412-335-1302

Belle Vernon PA 15012
St. Basil the Great ROR
R.D. #3 (Ridge Rd.) - Box 187
412-929-2878

Blakely PA 18447
St. Andrew UCU
300 Main St.
717-383-0530

California PA 15419-1402
Holy Trinity ROR
630 American St.
412-938-7216

Carnegie PA 15106
Ss. Peter & Paul UCU
200 Walnut St.
412-279-2111

Cheltenham PA 19012 MAIL
St. Michael PER
<Philadelphia PA>
103 Hilldale Rd.
215-627-6148, 215-635-0509

Chester PA 19013
Assumption of the Blessed Virgin Mary UCU
2412 W. 3rd St.
215-494-7853

Chester PA 19013
St. Nicholas PER
2513 W. 4th St.
215-497-3860

Coatesville PA 19320
Holy Ghost UCU
399 Charles St.
P.O. Box 48
215-384-2460

Dixonville PA 15734
St. John the Baptist UCU
St. John's Way, Box 81
412-349-4821, 412-463-0958

Edinboro PA 16412-9619
St. Nicholas PER
8442 Pageville Rd.
814-756-4548

Elmora PA 15737
Ss. Peter & Paul UCU
P.O. Box 147
814-948-6718

Erie PA 16507-1612
Nativity of Christ ROR
152 German St.
814-459-8515, 814-459-8618

Erie PA 16507-1727
Nativity of Our Lady ROR
721 E. 5th St.
814-454-8618

Jeanette PA 15644
St. Michael UCU
112 13th St.
412-523-8849

Johnstown PA 15907
Ss. Peter & Paul UCU
St. Clair Rd.
P.O. Box 1233
814-535-8707

Lyndora PA 16045
Ss. Peter & Paul UCU
21 Evergreen Dr.
412-287-4448

Mayfield PA 18433-2015
St. John the Baptist ROR
706 Hill St.
717-876-0730, FAX 717-876-2534

McKees Rocks PA 15136
St. Mary UCU
116 Ella St.
412-331-2362

McKeesport PA 15132-2917
Holy Dormition ROR
330 Shaw Ave.
412-672-3444, 412-672-0736

Minersville PA 17954
St. George UCU
336 N. Front St.
717-544-4553

Monessen PA 15062
St. Nicholas UCU
17 Reed Ave.
412-684-3614

Mt. Holly Springs PA 17065
Three Pillars of Orthodoxy AUX
Mill St. & Zion Rd.
717-486-5642

Nanti Glo PA 15931
Holy Ascension UCU
980 Caroline St.
412-463-0958, 412-349-4821

New Castle PA 16101
Holy Trinity UCU
940 Rose Ave.

Northampton PA 18067
Assumption of the Virgin Mary UCU
1301 Newport Ave.
215-262-2882

Old Forge PA 18518
St. Stephen Protomartyr ROR
St. Stephen's Ln. & Hickory St.
P.O. Box 181
717-457-3384

Palmerton PA
St. George PER
730 Church St.
215-635-0509

Philadelphia PA 19130-3231
Joy of All Who Sorrow ROR
560 N. 20th St.
215-568-6788

Philadelphia PA 19126
St. Andrew UOD
1070 69th Ave.

Philadelphia PA 19123
St. Andrew's Cathedral PER
709 N. 5th St.
215-627-3338

Philadelphia PA 19137
St. Basil the Great VAS
4526 Mercer St.

Philadelphia PA 19126
St. Mary Protectress UCU
12th St. & Oak Lane Ave.
215-548-4786

Philadelphia PA 19123
St. Michael PER
335-37 Fairmount Ave.
215-627-6148, 215-635-0509

Philadelphia PA 19126
St. Vladimir Cathedral UCU
6740 N. 5th St.
215-927-2287

Pittsburgh PA 15203
St. Volodymyr UCU
1810 Sidney St.
412-431-9758

Reading PA 19602
St. Nicholas PER
241-243 S. 3rd St.
215-375-2946

Scranton PA 18504-2309
Ss. Peter & Paul PER
Washburn St. & Fillmore Ave.
1720 Academy St.
717-343-8128

Scranton PA 18504
St. Michael UCU
540 N. Main Ave.
717-343-7165

Sharon PA 16146
St. John the Baptist UCU
389 Clark St.
412-342-0335

Simpson PA 18407-1245
St. Basil ROR
33 Midland St.
717-282-2314

Slickville PA 15684
Holy Ghost UCU
Westmoreland & Indiana Aves.
Box 3
412-335-1302

Smithmill PA 16680
St. Volodymyr UCU
P.O. Box 106
814-378-5041

Sugar Notch (Wilkes-Barre) PA
Christ the Saviour ROR
558 Main St.
717-822-3358

Wilkes-Barre PA 18702
St. Nicholas PER
58 Seneca St.
717-823-0905

Willow Grove PA 19090
St. Theodore the Tyro VAS
126 Allison Rd.

Puerto Rico - See under "Mexico and the Carribean"

Rhode Island

Woonsocket RI 02895-1843
St. Michael UCU
74 Harris Ave.
401-762-3939

South Carolina

Summerville SC 29484-0932
Ss. Cyril & Methodius ROR
123 W. Richardson Ave.
P.O. Box 932
803-871-1160, 803-873-3718, FAX 803-871-1165

Traveler's Rest SC 29690
Good Samaritan VAS
199 Lang Fort Rd.

South Dakota

Sioux Falls SD 57104-4327
Holy Enlighteners AUX
514 S. Duluth
605-331-4938

Sioux Falls SD 57105-1713
St. Seraphim of Sarov ROR
1606 S. Duluth Ave.
605-338-5922

Tennessee

Brentwood TN 37027-7306
Ss. Peter & Paul AUX
8111 Vaden Dr.
615-377-6477

Liberty TN 37095-9801
Annunciation / Agape Community ROR
1180 Orthodox Way
615-536-5239

Memphis TN 38111
St. Seraphim VAS
3174 Carnes Ave.
901-323-4830

Nashville TN 37211
St. Basil HOC
355 Tusculum Rd.
615-834-1936

Texas

Dallas TX 75211
Orthodox Mission DHE
4690 S. Counts

Dallas TX 75214-3136
St. Nicholas ROR
@All Saints Episcopal Church, 3617 Abrams Rd.
6511 Bob-o-Link Dr.
214-827-0213, 214-467-9304

Houston TX 77064
St. Demitrios VAS
10107 Silver City Dr.

Houston TX 77087-2409
St. John Chrysostom Cathedral HUS
3011 Roe Dr.
713-645-0843

Houston TX 77087
St. Juvenaly of Alaska CYP
6530 Kernel St.

Houston TX 77022-1906
St. Vladimir ROR
24 E. Tidwell Rd.
713-695-3223

Lubbock TX
Orthodox Mission ROR

Odessa TX 79760
Holy Theotokos VAS
P.O. Box 301

Rochelle TX 76872
Holy Trinity ROR
Rt. 1 - Box 115A
915-463-5538

Utah

South Jordan UT 84065
St. Nicholas of Myra ROR
9589 S. Kilmvir Circle
801-569-0881

West Jordan UT 84088-4105
St. George AUX
1538 W. 7800 S.
801-562-4508

Virginia

Catlett VA 22019-9018
Holy Wisdom AUX
4561 Dumfries Rd.
703-788-3074

Mechanicsville VA 23111-3812
St. Seraphim of Sarov AUX
2036 Culley Dr.
804-750-8348

Richmond VA 23227
St. Andrew VAS
1629 Westbrook Rd.
804-266-3364

Washington

Ferndale WA 98248-9431
Prophet Elias AUX
5977 Paradise Rd.
206-380-6238

Kelso WA
Holy Nativity UCU

Port Townsend WA 98368-4834
St. Herman of Alaska VAS
552 Hastings

Riverside WA 98849-9613
New Iveron DHE
HC 65 Box 146a

Seattle WA 98102
Holy Trinity UCU
206-524-3496

Seattle WA 98118
Ss. Sergius & Herman VAS
4619 S. Brandon

Seattle WA 98144-2229
St. Innocent DHE
1838 S. King Hwy.
206-726-7972

Seattle WA 98133-9410
St. Nectarios AUX
10300 Ashworth Ave. N.
206-522-4471, FAX 206-523-0550

Seattle WA 98122-2513
St. Nicholas Cathedral ROR
1714 13th Ave.
206-322-9387

West Virginia

Wayne WV 25570-9755
Entrance into the Temple of the Mother of God ROR
Rt. 2 - Box 2343
304-849-3553

Wisconsin

Baraboo WI 53913-0704
St. Patrick SGP
P.O. Box 704
608-356-2808

Blue River WI 53518
St. John the Baptist CYP
18426 Chezik Rd.
608-537-2978

Granton WI 54436
Holy Trinity UCU
Rt. 2
715-238-7247

Lublin WI 54447 MAIL
Holy Trinity UCU
<Thorp WI>
c/o Frank Knusta; N-683-
7th Ave.
612-789-0456

Madison WI 53714
Madison Orthodox Mission
VAS
157 Farrell St.

Milwaukee WI 53204-2217
Holy Trinity ROR
1136 W. Madison St.
414-383-1477

Milwaukee WI 53204
St. Mary Protectress UCU
1231 W. Scott St.
414-672-9285

Thorp WI
Holy Trinity UCU
612-789-0456

Parishes and Missions in Canada

Alberta

Barrhead AB T0G 0E0
Holy Trinity PCN

Boyle AB T0A 0L0
Holy Resurrection PCN

Calgary AB T2E 0S2
All Saints ROR
905 8th Ave. N.E.
403-230-7015

Calgary AB T2E 0W4
Mother of God Keeper of the Portal AUX
639 9th Ave. N.E.
403-276-4347

Calmar AB T0G 0V0
Holy Ascension PCN

Chipman AB T0B 0W0
Nativity of St. John the Baptist PCN

Edmonton AB T5H 2K3
Holy Trinity ROR
10902 96th St. N.W.
403-429-1925

Edmonton AB T5C 1S7
St. Vladimir Cathedral ROR
6824 128th Ave. N.W.
403-476-2381

Edson AB T7E 1K8
Holy Apostle Andrew ROR
4823 7th Ave.
403-325-2357

Lethbridge AB T1H 1E9
Holy Dormition ROR
906 9th Ave. N.
205-251-6694

Nisku AB T0C 2G0
St. Mary PCN

North Star AB T0H 2T0
Ss. Peter & Paul PCN

Rabbit Hill AB
Nativity of the Theotokos PCN

Redwater AB T0A 2W0
Ss. Peter & Paul PCN

Shishkovci AB
Nativity of the Theotokos PCN

Skaro AB T0B 4E0
Ascension of Christ PCN

Spirit River AB T0H 3G0
Holy Trinity PCN

Therien AB T0A 3H0
Nativity of St. John the Baptist PCN

Thorsby AB T0C 2P0
Holy Trinity PCN

Vegreville AB T0B 4G0
Nativity of St. John the Baptist PCN

Wildwood AB T0E 2M0
Great Martyr George ROR
403-325-2357

Wildwood AB T0E 2M0
MAIL
Holy Apostle Andrew ROR
<Edson AB>
P.O. Box 104
403-325-2357

Wostok AB T0B 4S0
Holy Trinity PCN

British Columbia

Burnaby BC V5C 3E3
MAIL
St. Nicholas ROR
<Vancouver BC>
4764 Parker St.
604-873-8110

Chilliwack BC
St. Tikhon UCU

Dewdney BC V0M 1H0
MAIL
Descent of the Holy Spirit UCU
<Vancouver BC>
37323 Hawkins Rd.
604-826-9336

Dewdney BC V0M 1H0
MAIL
Holy Nativity UCU
<Kelso WA (USA)>
37323 Hawkins Rd.
604-826-9336

Dewdney BC V0M 1H0
MAIL
St. Michael the Archangel UCU
<Vancouver BC>
37323 Hawkins Rd.
604-826-9336

Dewdney BC V0M 1H0
MAIL
St. Symeon UCU
<Nanaimo BC>
37323 Hawkins Rd.
604-826-9336

Dewdney BC V0M 1H0
MAIL
St. Tikhon UCU
<Chilliwack BC>
37323 Hawkins Rd.
604-826-9336

Dewdney BC V0M 1H0
Theotokos 'Joy of Canada' Cathedral UCU
37329 Hawkins Rd.
604-826-9336

Langley BC
St. Nicholas UCU
4828 216A St.

Nanaimo BC
St. Symeon UCU

Vancouver BC
Descent of the Holy Spirit UCU
604-826-9336

Vancouver BC V5M 1E2
Holy Trinity ROR
2733 E. 2nd Ave.
604-254-2571

Vancouver BC V5N 3B6
St. Michael VAS
1736 E. 32nd Ave.

Vancouver BC
St. Michael the Archangel UCU

Vancouver BC V5T 2L5
St. Nicholas ROR
810 East 13th St.
604-873-8110

Victoria BC V8V 3J5
St. Sophia ROR
947 Meares St.

Manitoba

Russell MB R0J 1W0
St. Nicholas the Wonder-worker AUX
P.O. Box 512
204-773-2364

Winnipeg MB R2W 2X5
Holy Ascension CYP
197 Euclid Ave.

Winnipeg MB R2W 1Y9
Holy Resurrection ROR
732 Alfred Ave.
204-586-4152

Nova Scotia

Bear River NS B0S 1B0
Holy Protection GMA
Box 119

Ontario

Hamilton ON L8M 2G7
Holy Veil of the Theotokos ROR
77 Sanford Ave. S.
905-529-7043

Hamilton ON
St. Nahum of Ohrid MOC

Jackson Point ON L0E 1L0
Our Lady of Smolensk ROR
Birch Rd. near Jackson Point
416-763-6822

London ON N6C 4T8
Christ the Saviour ROR
140 Fairview Ave.
519-433-7458

Nepean ON K2H 9R0
St. Xenia of Petersburg ROR
3501 Carling Ave.
P.O. Box 26123
613-726-8123

Niagara Falls ON L2E 1Z5
St. John of Rila ROR
4871 Willmott St.

Ottawa ON K1Y 4R7
Protection of the Holy Virgin ROR
99 Stonehurst Ave.
613-722-6247

Toronto ON M4M 3A7
Agioi Anargyroi GOC
281 Jones Ave.

Toronto ON M6C 3S3
Holy Resurrection ROR
213 Winona Dr.
416-233-1543

Toronto ON M5T 1W9
Holy Trinity ROR
23 Henry St.
416-265-5651

Toronto ON M5A 1R1
Mother of God of Prussa AUX
461 Richmond St. E.
416-364-8918

Toronto ON M4H 1J5
Mother of God the Life-Giving Spring CYP
47 Thorncliffe Park Dr.
1124

Toronto ON M4H 1C5
St. Clement of Ohrid MOC
76 Overlea Blvd.

Toronto ON M6H 2X8
St. Euphrosynia BYC
1008 Dovercourt Rd.
416-536-4449

Toronto ON M6H 2Y1
St. Joseph of Arimathea AUX
1223 Dovercourt Rd.
416-537-8300

Toronto ON M4B 1N3
St. Kosmas Aitolos GMA
2817 St. Clair Ave. E.

Toronto ON M6H 3W7
St. Kyrilla of Turov BAM
524 St. Clarens Ave.

Toronto ON M6H 2Y1
St. Nectarios Cathedral AUX
1223 Dovercourt Rd.
416-537-7283

Windsor ON N8Y 2R9
Holy Trinity ROR
1410 Drouillard Rd.
519-945-2862

Windsor ON
St. Nicholas MOC

Quebec

Chamedy PQ H2E 1A7
St. Irene Chrysovalantou GOC
1474 Chamedy

Lachine PQ H8S 2Y3
Saint-Jean le Martyr ROR
660 Ave. 6iem
514-637-4189

Montreal PQ H2M 2K8
American Orthodox Mission HOC
8893 St.-Hubert
514-384-6391

Montreal PQ H2V 4A1
Evangelismos/St. Nektarios GOC
4520 Hutchinson

Montreal PQ P0B 3M7
Hagia Sophia AUX
898 St. Roch

Montreal PQ H3N 2K4
Saint-Seraphim de Sarov ROR
8011 Champagneur Ave.
514-271-5823

Montreal PQ H3N 2T5
St. Anna CHR
7870 Birnam
514-276-8408

Outremont PQ H2V 2P5
Cathedrale de Saint-Nicholas ROR
422 Boul. Saint-Joseph O.
514-276-8322

Rawdon PQ J0K 1S0
Notre Dame de Kazan ROR
3836 Sunshine Ave.
C.P. 1277

Saskatchewan

Foam Lake SK S0A 1A0
St. Onufry PCN

Insinger SK S0A 1L0
Ss. Peter & Paul PCN

MacNutt SK S0A 2K0
Assumption of the Theotokos PCN

Parishes and Missions in Mexico and the Carribean

Barbados

Bridgetown
Mission Congregation OCC
c/o Michael Mansour
809-429-7818

Cuba

Havana 2
Ss. Constantine & Helena OCC
Paseo Marti 20

Dominican Republic

Ensanche Luperon Santo Domingo
San Antonio OCC
Calle Federico Bermudez 85
809-681-7465, 809-541-4156

Haiti

Petion Ville
Holy Resurrection OCC
Meltivier

Petion Ville
Maison Orthodoxe (Central Office) OCC
Morne Calvaire
509-57-48-05, FAX 509-57-06-72

Petion Ville
St. George OCC
Coin Rue Metelleus et Oge
509-57-04-10, 509-57-48-05

Petion Ville
St. Nectarios OCC
Morne Calvaire
509-57-48-05

Petion-Ville
St. John the Baptist OCC
Lamothe

Jamaica

Kingston
St. Nicholas OCC
2 Cherry Garden Ave.
809-924-2550

Mexico

Atizapan de Zaragoza Mexico
Ss. Cosmas & Damian VAS
#36 Condado de Sayavedra

Merida Mexico
Orthodox Church AMC

Mexico City 01900 Mexico MAIL
Orthodox Church AMC
c/o Pirules 110 Jardinas del Pedregal de San Andre
525-652-7772

Mexico City 01900 Mexico
St. George Cathedral AMC
Pirules 110 Jardinas del Pedregal de San Andreas
525-652-7772

Trinidad

Maraval Trinidad
St. Elias OCC
c/o Elias Aboud; 25 Eagle Crescent; Fairways

United States (Puerto Rico)

Arroyo PR
San Miguel VAS

Rio Piedras PR 00932
Our Lady of Peace OCC
Calle Albacete #509
809-250-0647, 809-769-3471

Rio Piedras PR 00928
St. Mark of Ephesus OCC
P.O. Box 21195 65th Inf. Sta.
809-752-1374

Monastic Communities in North America

Monasteries in SCOBA Jurisdictions

All-Merciful Saviour Monastery OCA
26621 99th Ave. S.W.
P.O. Box 1047
Vashon Island, WA 98070-1047
USA
206-463-5918, FAX 206-463-3461

Canadian Serbian Monastery SOC
7470 McNiven Rd.
Milton, ON
CANADA
416-878-1909

Community of the Holy Cross OCA
135 Balboa Ave.
P.O. Box 563
Pt. Reyes Station, CA 94956-0563
USA
415-663-1705

Community of the Holy Myrrhbearers OCA
R.D. 2; Box 188
Otego, NY 13825-9650
USA
607-432-3179

Dormition of the Mother of God Monastery OCA
3389 Rives Eaton Rd.
Rives Junction, MI 49277-9739
USA
517-569-2873

Emmaus House OCA
Box 189
Cambridge, NY 12816-9704
USA
518-677-8863

Glorious Ascension Monastery OCA
5052 S. Dixie Hwy.
P.O. Box 397
Resaca, GA 30735-0397
USA
706-277-9442, FAX 706-277-9443

Holy Assumption Monastery OCA
1519 Washington St.
Calistoga, CA 94515
USA
707-942-6244

Holy Cross Monastery CRC
19520 Darnestown Rd.
P.O. Box 152
Beallesville, MD 20839-0152
USA
301-349-5835, FAX 202-526-3316

Holy Mother of God 'The Life-Giving Fountain' Monastery CRC
1484 Star Route 171
Woodstock Valley, CT 06282
USA
203-974-2133

Holy Nativity Convent GOA
121 St. Elias Ln.
Saxonburg, PA 16056
USA
412-352-1533

Holy Transfiguration Monastery OCA
R.D. 1; Box 184X
Ellwood City, PA 16117
USA
412-758-4002

Holy Transfiguration Skete OCA
Fitch Bay, PQ
CANADA

Holy Transfiguration Skete OCA MAIL
<Fitch Bay PQ>
240 Chemin Noel; R.R. 3
Magog, PQ J1X 2W4
CANADA

Marcha Monastery SOC
5095 Broadview Rd.
Richfield, OH 44286
USA
216-659-4027

Most Holy Mother of God Monastery NGM
P.O. Box 496
Grayslake, IL 60030-0496
USA

Most Holy Mother of God Monastery SOC
Shadeland Farms; R.D. 1
Box 247
Shadeland, PA 16435
USA
814-587-6209

Nativity of the Mother of God Monastery SOC
32787 Early Rd.
New Carlisle, IN 46552
USA
219-652-7994

Monasteries in SCOBA Jurisdictions

New Skete Monastery OCA
Cambridge, NY 12816-9704
USA
518-677-3928

New Valaam Monastery OCA
414 Maison Rd.
Kodiak, AK 99615
USA

Our Lady of the Sign Monastery OCA
R.D. 1 Box 34
Cambridge, NY 12816-9704
USA
518-677-3810

Protection of the Holy Virgin Monastery OCA
444 Boulder St.
Calhan, CO 80808
USA
714-347-2426

Skete of the Holy Virgin of Kazan OCA
2735 Victoria Dr.
Santa Rosa, CA 95407-7847
USA
707-542-7798

St. Barbara Monastery GOA
P.O. Box 582
Middletown, NJ 07748
USA
908-671-5932

St. Gregory Palamas Monastery GOA MAIL
<Perrysville OH>
P.O. Box 206
Hayesville, OH 44838-0206
USA
419-368-5335

St. Gregory Palamas Monastery GOA
934 County Rd. 2256
Perrysville, OH 44864
USA
419-368-5335

St. Gregory Palamas Skete / St. Gregory of Sinai Monastery OCA MAIL
<Richmond CA>
P.O. Box 11672
Burnt Ranch, CA 94701
USA
510-215-0301

St. Gregory Palamas Skete / St. Gregory of Sinai Monastery OCA
5717 Clinton Ave.
Richmond, CA 94805
USA
510-215-0301

St. Herman Monastery UOA
4410 Franklin Blvd.
Cleveland, OH 44103
USA
216-961-3806

St. John the Theologian Monastery OCA
5862 Allyn Rd.
Hiram, OH 44234
USA
Phone/FAX 216-274-2052

St. Mark Monastery NGM
P.O. Box 2093
Sheffield Lake, OH 44054
USA

St. Michael's Skete OCA
P.O. Box 38
Canones, NM 87516
USA

St. Sava Monastery SOC
P.O. Box 519
Libertyville, IL 60048
USA
708-362-2440, 708-362-2441

St. Tikhon of Zadonsk Monastery OCA
South Canaan, PA 18459
USA
717-937-4067

St. Tikhon's Monastery OCA
South Canaan, PA 18459
USA
717-937-4067

Theotokos 'The Living Spring' Convent GOA
38562 Dunlap Rd.
P.O. Box 400
Dunlap, CA 93621-0400
USA
209-338-3110

Women's Monastery of Martha & Mary CRC
19520 Darnestown Rd.
P.O. Box 152
Beallesville, MD 20839-0152
USA
301-349-5834

Monasteries in Non-SCOBA Jurisdictions

Agioi Panton Monastery GOC
ON
CANADA

Auxiliary Convent of Our Lady of Vladimir ROR
1550 Fell St.
San Francisco, CA 94117-2146
USA
415-824-3475, 415-931-8850

Bethany Skete VAS
25 Ocean St.
Dorchester, MA 02124
USA

Blessed Pasha and Pelagia Monastery ROR
County Rd. 103
P.O. Box 1049
Blanco, TX 78606-1049
USA
210-833-5860

Canadian Orthodox Monastery of All Saints of North America UCU
37323 Hawkins Rd.
Dewdney, BC V0M 1H0
CANADA
604-826-9336

Christ of the Hills Monastery ROR
New Sarov, County Rd. 103
P.O. Box 1049
Blanco, TX 78606-1049
USA
210-833-5363, FAX 210-833-5813

Christ the Saviour Monastery ROR
27 Whitman St.
P.O. Box 1272
Pawtucket, RI 02860
USA
401-725-1692

Community of St. Elizabeth ROR
Jordanville, NY
USA
315-858-2208

Community of St. Elizabeth ROR MAIL
<Jordanville NY>
R.D. #2; Box 382C
Mohawk, NY 13407-9548
USA
315-858-2208

Convent of Our Lady of Vladimir ROR
3365 19th St.
San Francisco, CA 94110-1816
USA
415-824-3475

Convent of St. Elizabeth the Grand Duchess of Russia CYP
Hwy. 3
P.O. Box 398
Etna, CA 96027-0398
USA

Convent of the Holy Myrrbearers HUS
3011 Roe Dr.
Houston, TX 77087-2409
USA
713-645-0104

Convent of the Nativity of the Virgin Mary ROR
3766 Gravois Rd.
P.O. Box 536
House Springs, MO 63051-0536
USA
314-677-1131, FAX 314-376-3223

Coop City UIU
Hunter Ave.
Bronx, NY 10475
USA

Dormition Skete ROR
P.O. Box 104
Wildwood, AB T0E 2M0
CANADA
403-325-2357

Dormition Skete ROR
29020 County Rd. 187
P.O. Box 3177
Buena Vista, CO 81211
USA
719-395-6395, 717-395-8898

Four Evangelists Monastery HUS
3011 Roe Dr.
Houston, TX 77087-2409
USA
713-645-0843

Greek Orthodox Convent GMA
42-11 Ditmars Blvd.
Astoria, NY 11105
USA

Monasteries in Non-SCOBA Jurisdictions

Hermitage of St. Mary Magdalene AUX
4559 Dumfries Rd.
Catlett, VA 22019-9018
USA
703-788-3053

Hermitage of St. Paisius ROR
R.D. 2 Box 213-A
Troy, PA 16947-9541
USA

Holy Annunciation Monastery VAS
211 Bay State Rd.
Melrose, MA 02176
USA

Holy Apostles Convent ROR
29001 County Rd. 187
P.O. Box 3118
Buena Vista, CO 81211
USA
719-395-8898, 717-395-6395

Holy Cross Skete VAS
184 Dent St.
West Roxbury, MA 02132
USA

Holy Cross hermitage ROR
3774 Gravois Rd.
P.O. Box 363
House Springs, MO 63051-0363
USA
314-677-2345

Holy Nativity Convent AUX
70 Codman Rd.
Brookline, MA 02146-7555
USA
617-566-0156, 617-566-1786

Holy Spirit Community UIU
47 W. Portal Ave.
San Framcisco, CA 94127
USA

Holy Transfiguration Monastery ROR
R.R. 1
Mansonville, PQ J0E 1X0
CANADA
514-292-3102

Holy Transfiguration Monastery AUX
278 Warren St.
Brookline, MA 02146-5997
USA
617-734-0608, 617-232-2326, FAX 617-730-5783

Holy Trinity Monastery ROR
Robinson Rd. & Rt. 167
P.O. Box 36
Jordanville, NY 13361-0036
USA
315-858-0940, FAX 315-858-0505

Holy Virgin Protection Hermitage PRC
407 157th St.
Calumet City, IL 60409-4703
USA
708-862-0868

Kursk Mother of God Hermitage/ Nativity of the Most Holy Mother of God ROR
Rt. 6 - Box 1050
Mahopac, NY 10541-3403
USA
914-628-4975

New Valaam Monastery VAS
Monk's Lagoon, AK
USA
907-248-9659, 907-486-6526

New Valaam Monastery VAS MAIL
<Monks' Lagoon AK>
P.O. Box 90
Ouzinke, AK 99644
USA
907-248-9659, 907-486-6526

Novo Diveevo Convent ROR
Smith Rd.
Spring Valley, NY 10977
USA
914-356-0425

Our Lady of Kazan Monastery VAS
324 Hazeldine Ave. S.W.
Albuquerque, NM 87102
USA
505-242-6186

Paradise Hermitage - Palestinian Martyrs Chapel ROR
Rt. 3 Box 158
Ellisville, MS 39437
USA
601-584-8128

Monasteries in Non-SCOBA Jurisdictions

Resurrection of Christ Hermitage ROR
1201 Hathaway Ln. N.E.
Fridley, MN 55432-5720
USA
612-574-1001

Skete of St. Andrew the Apostle CYP
18465 Chezik Rd.
Blue River, WI 53518
USA

St. Andrew's Monastery UIU
2237 Hunter Ave.
Bronx, NY 10475
USA

St. Anna Convent CHR
7870 Birnam
Montreal, PQ H3N 2T5
CANADA
514-276-8408

St. Anthony Monastery UOD
R.R. 2 Box 259
Knox, IN 46534
USA

St. Anthony the Great Monastery CHR
Alamagordo, NM 88311-1432
USA
505-434-5277, 602-957-3054

St. Barbara's Monastery GMA
P.O. Box 582
New Monmouth, NJ 07748
USA

St. Blaise House UIU
230 Acme Rd.
White Salmon, WA 98672
USA

St. Gregory Palamas Monastery CYP
1307 Sawyers Bar Rd.
P.O. Box 398
Etna, CA 96027-0398
USA

St. Herman of Alaska Monastery VAS
P.O. Box 70
Platina, CA 96076
USA

St. Isaac of Syria Skete ROR
Rt. 1 - Box 168
Boscobel, WI 53805-9619
USA
608-375-5500, FAX 608-375-5555

St. Katherine Skete DHE
1317 S. 11th St.
Lincoln, NE 68542
USA
402-476-2676

St. Mark's Monastery ROR
429 E. 117th St.
New York City, NY 10035
USA
212-289-3071

St. Mary of Egypt Skete VAS
1901 N. Pennsylvania
Indianapolis, IN 46202
USA

St. Mary's Convent ROR
P.O. Box Bluffton
Bluffton, AB T0C 0M0
CANADA
403-843-6434

St. Michael's Monastery GMA
800 S. Euclid St.
Fullerton, CA 92634
USA

St. Michael's Skete VAS
Monk's Lagoon, AK
USA
907-248-9659, 907-486-6526

St. Michael's Skete VAS MAIL
<Monks' Lagoon AK>
P.O. Box 90
Ouzinke, AK 99644
USA
907-248-9659, 907-486-6526

St. Nicholas Monastery ROR
13 Maple St.
P.O. Box 800
Glenham, NY 12527
USA
914-831-2164

St. Paisius Abbey VAS
7777 Martinelli Rd.
P.O. Box 130
Forestville, CA 95436
USA
707-887-9740, FAX 707-887-9023

St. Seraphim of Sarov (Monastic House Chapel) ROR
Moss Beach, CA 94038
USA

St. Siglitiki Convent CHR
Farmingdale, NY
USA
516-293-2641, 718-952-1592

St. Xenia Skete VAS
Wildwood Rural Branch
Redding, CA 96001
USA

St. Xenia Skete VAS
P.O. Box 260
Wildwood, CA 96076-0260
USA
77-887-9740, FAX 707-887-9023

St. Xenia Skete Metochion VAS
1901 N. Pennsylvania Ave.
Indianapolis, IN 46202
USA
317-925-3034

Theophany Skete VAS
824 Chestnut St.
Chico, CA 95928
USA
916-893-1814

Educational Institutions
Publications
Resources and Social Services (including Pan-Orthodox Groups)
Military Chaplains
Campus Fellowships
Youth Camps and Shrines
Alphabetical Index
Addendum

Agape Community Orthodox School ROR
1180 Orthodox Way
Liberty, TN 37095-9801
USA
615-536-5239

Annunciation Orthodox School GOA
3511 Yoakum Blvd.
Houston, TX 77006
USA
713-524-1227

Antiochian House of Studies, Theological Studies Program ANT
Rt. 711 N.
P.O. Box 638
Ligonier, PA 15658
USA

Argyrios Fantis Parochial School GOA
195 State St.
Brooklyn, NY 11201
USA
718-624-0501

C. Goulandris-T. Tsolainos Greek Orthodox Parochial School of St. Spyridon GOA
120 Wadsworth Ave.
New York City, NY 10033
USA
212-795-6870

Catechetical School of St. Anna CHR
7870 Birnam
Montreal, PQ H3N 2T5
CANADA
514-276-8408

Cathedral School (Holy Trinity Cathedral) GOA
319 E. 74th St.
New York City, NY 10021
USA
212-249-2840

Center for Traditionalist Orthodox Studies, St. Gregory Palamas Monastery CYP
P.O. Box 398
Etna, CA 96027-0398
USA

Christ the Saviour Seminary / Mount Christ the Saviour CRC
225 Chandler Ave.
Johnstown, PA 15906
USA
814-539-0116

Demosthenes Ecole Primaire GOA
3730 boul. Levesque
Chomedey-Laval, PQ H7V 1E8
CANADA
514-686-1800

Ecole Primaire Socrates GOA
5777 Wilderton Ave.
Montreal, PQ H3S 2V7
CANADA
514-738-2421 ext. 306

Ecole Primaire Socrates, Socrates I GOA
275 Houde St
Ville St. Laurent, PQ H4N 3J3
CANADA
514-340-3562

Ecole Primaire Socrates, Socrates II GOA
5757 Wilderton Ave.
Montreal, PQ H3S 2K8
CANADA
514-738-2421 ext. 212

Ecole Primaire Socrates, Socrates III GOA
11 Eleventh St.
Roxboro, PQ H8Y 1K6
CANADA
514-685-1833

Ecole Primaire Socrates, Socrates IV GOA
5220 Grande Allee
St. Hubert, PQ J3Y 1A1
CANADA
514-656-4832

Ecole Primaire Socrates, Socrates V GOA
938 Emerson Dr.
Chomedey-Laval, PQ H7W 3Y5
CANADA
514-681-5142

Greek-American Institute GOA
3573 Bruckner Blvd.
Bronx, NY 10461
USA
718-823-2393

Hellenic American School of Holy Trinity GOA
41 Broadway
Lowell, MA 01854
USA
508-453-5422

Educational Institutions

Hellenic College / Holy Cross Orthodox School of Theology GOA
50 Goddard Ave.
Brookline, MA 02146
USA
617-731-3500

Hellenic Orthodox School of St. Nectarios CHR
3044 N. 27th St.
Phoenix, AZ 85016-7926
USA
602-957-3054

Hellenic School of Holy Dormition Church CHR
1910 Douglas Ave.
Clearwater, FL 34615
USA
813-443-3999

Hellenic School of St. Isiodore Church CHR
910 Stewart Ave.
Bethpage, NY 11714
USA
516-933-1726, 718-274-5579

Hellenic School of St. Markella Cathedral CHR
22-68 26th St.
Astoria, NY 11105
USA
718-932-1592, FAX 718-274-2875

Holy Cherubim & Seraphim Orthodox Education Center VAS
R.R. 1, Box 54
Eagle, NE 68347
USA

Holy Cross Parochial School GOA
8502 Ridge Blvd.
Brooklyn, NY 11209
USA
718-836-8096

Holy Trinity Orthodox Seminary ROR
P.O. Box 36
Jordanville, NY 13361-0036
USA
315-858-0940

Holy Virgin Protection Church School ROR
Prospect St. & Cedar Hill Ave.
Nyack, NY 10960
USA
914-358-4982

Institute for Byzantine and Modern Greek Studies PAN
115 Gilbert Rd.
Belmont, MA 02178
USA
617-484-6595

Institute for Eastern Orthodox Studies HUS
3011 Roe Dr.
Houston, TX 77087-2409
USA
713-645-0843

Jamaica Day School of St. Demetrios / Archbishop Iakovos High School GOA
84-35 152nd St.
Jamaica, NY 11432
USA
718-526-2622

Koreas Greek-American School GOA
11025-45 S. Roberts Rd.
Palos Hills, IL 60465
USA
708-974-3402

Nemanjic Institute for Serbo-Byzantine Studies UCU
37323 Hawkins Rd.
Dewdney, BC V0M 1H0
CANADA
604-826-9336, FAX 604-820-9758

Orthodox Christian Schools, Inc. PAN
Dr. Mary Ford, St. Tikhon's Seminary
South Canaan, PA 18459
USA
717-937-4309

Orthodox Christian Tutorial Program CHR
St. Nectarios; 3044 N. 27th St.
Phoenix, AZ 85016-7926
USA
602-957-3054

Orthodox Home-School Network ROR
P.O. Box 45
Beltsville, MD 20705-0045
USA
301-890-3552

Patriarch Athenagoras Orthodox Graduate Theological Union GOA
2400 Ridge Rd.
Berkeley, CA 94709
USA
415-593-4093

Plato Greek-American School GOA
601 S. Central Ave.
Chicago, IL 60644
USA
312-626-1728

School of the Transfiguration GOA
98-07 38th Ave.
Corona, NY 11368
USA
718-478-8181

Serbian Seminary NGM
Grayslake, IL 60030-0496
USA
708-223-4305

Socrates Greek-American School GOA
6041 W. Diversey Ave.
Chicago, IL 60639
USA
312-622-5979

Soterios Ellenas Parochial School GOA
224 18th St.
Brooklyn, NY 11215
USA
718-499-5900

Ss. Cyril & Methodius High School ROR
6200 Geary Blvd.
San Francisco, CA 94121
USA
415-752-5122

St. Alexander Nevsky School ROR
200 Alexander Ave.
Howell - Lakewood, NJ 07731-8684
USA
908-370-1881, FAX 908-364-5625

St. Andrew's College UOC
475 Dysart Rd.
Winnipeg, MB R3T 2M7
Canada
204-474-8901, FAX 204-275-0803

St. Anthony the Great Orthodox College CHR
Alamagordo, NM 88311-1432
USA
718-932-1592, 505-434-5277

St. Athanasius Academy ANT
6778 Pasado Rd.
P.O. Box 1325
Goleta, CA 93116
USA
805-685-3111

St. Basil Academy GOA
Rt. 2; Box 8A
Garrison, NY 10524-9742
USA
914-424-3500

St. Catherine (St. Demetrios Annex) GOA
30-11 30th Dr.
Astoria, NY 11105
USA
718-728-1100

St. Catherine Iconography School VAS
1901 N. Pennsylvania Ave.
Indianapolis, IN 46202
USA
317-925-3034

St. Demetrios Greek-American School of Astoria GOA
30-03 30th Dr.
Astoria, NY 11102
USA
718-728-1754, 718-726-6734

St. Elias School of Orthodox Theology DHE
740 S. 11th St.
P.O. Box 22237
Lincoln, NE 68542-2237
USA
402-475-6492

St. Fanourios Cathedral School VAS
44-02 48th Ave.
Woodside, NY 11377-6344
USA

St. Herman of Alaska Parochial School VAS
64 Harvard Ave.
Allston, MA 02134
USA

St. Herman's Orthodox Theological Seminary OCA
414 Mission Rd.
Kodiak, AK 99615
USA
907-486-3524, FAX 907-486-5935

St. John of Damascus Sacred Arts Academy ANT
Rte. 711 N. Box 638
Ligonier, PA 15658-0638
USA

St. John's Greek Orthodox Day School GOA
2418 Swann Ave.
Tampa, FL 33609
USA
813-876-4569

St. Nicholas Day School GOA
9501 Balboa Blvd.
Northridge, CA 91325
USA
818-886-6751

St. Sophia Ukrainian Orthodox Seminary UCU
P.O. Box 240
South Bound Brook, NJ 08880
USA
908-469-7555

St. Stephen's Course of Studies in Orthodox Theology ANT
358 Mountain Rd.
Englewood, NJ 07631
USA
201-871-1355, 201-871-1356, FAX 201-871-7954

St. Tikhon's Orthodox Theological Seminary OCA
South Canaan, PA 18459
USA
717-937-4411, FAX 717-937-4939

St. Vincent College Program for Orthodox ANT
Latrobe, PA
USA

St. Vladimir's Orthodox Theological Seminary OCA
575 Scarsdale Rd.
Crestwood, NY 10707-1699
USA
914-961-8313, FAX 914-961-4507

Three Hierarchs Parochial School GOA
1724 Ave. P
Brooklyn, NY 11229
USA
718-375-1885

Valaam Academy VAS
7777 Martinelli Rd.
Forestville, CA 95436
USA
707-887-9740

Wm. Spyropoulos Greek American Day School of St. Nicholas GOA
43-15 196th St.
Flushing, NY 11358
USA
718-357-5583

Publications

A.C.O.R.N. - Antiochian Christian Orthodox Radio Network ANT
P.O. Box 12377
Beaumont, TX 77726
USA
409-898-1922

AGAIN Magazine ANT
10090 'A' Hwy. 9
P.O. Box 76
Ben Lomond, CA 95005-0076
USA
408-336-5118, FAX 408-336-8882

Alive in Christ OCA
Diocesan Center
South Canaan, PA 18459
USA

Bee CHR
St. Anthony Orthodox Publications, 3044 N. 27th St.
Phoenix, AZ 85016-7926
USA
602-957-3054, FAX 602-956-4203

Canadian Orthodox Messenger OCA
43 Newcourt Pl.
Kingston, ON K7M 6Y1
CANADA

Canadian Orthodox Messenger OCA MAIL
<Kingston ON>
P.O. Box 179
Spencerville, ON K0E 1X0
CANADA

Canadian Orthodox Missionary PAN
P.O. Box 689
Lynden, WA 98264
USA

Christian Activist
P.O. Box 740
Mt. Hermon, CA 95041
USA

Church Messenger CRC
312 Garfield St.
Johnstown, PA 15748-1518
USA
814-539-9143, FAX 814-536-4699

Church Messenger (editorial office) CRC
280 Clinton St.
Binghamton, NY 13905
USA
814-539-9143, FAX 814-536-4699

Credinta RMA
19959 Riopelle St.
Detroit, MI 48203
USA

Credo ANT
Box 84
Stanton, NJ 08885
USA

DOXA OCA
P.O. Box 38
Canones, NM 87516
USA

Dawn OCA
P.O. Box 191109
Dallas, TX 75219-8109
USA

Desert Voice CHR
St. Anthony Orthodox Publications, 3044 N. 27th St.
Phoenix, AZ 85016-7926
USA
602-957-3054, FAX 602-956-4203

Diocesan Voice GOA
372 Santa Clara Ave.
San Francisco, CA 94127
USA
415-753-3075

Enlightener VAS
1827 S. 11th St.
Lincoln, NE 68502
USA

Epiphany Journal VAS
16 Channel Rd.
P.O. Box 2250
South Portland, ME 04116-2250
USA
207-767-1889

First Hour PAN
206 Sarles Ln.
Pleasantville, NY 10570
USA

GOTELCOM (Greek Orthodox Telecommunication) GOA
59 Schermerhorn St.
Brooklyn, NY 11201
USA
718-243-9300, FAX 718-243-0288

Greek Orthodox Theological Review GOA
50 Goddard Ave.
Brookline, MA 02146
USA
617-232-4544

H Parakatathiki GOA
162 Goddard Ave.
Brookline, MA 02146
USA
617-277-4742

Harvest OCA
P.O. Box 397
Resaca, GA 30735
USA
706-277-9442

Herald UOC
9 St. John's Ave.
Winnipeg, MB R2W 1G8
Canada

Heraldo de la Orthodoxia OCA
Cancelleria de la Iglesia
Orthodoxa Catolica en Mexico
Apartado Postal M-8576
Centro Mexico, D.F. 06000
Mexico

Illuminator GOA
5201 Ellsworth Ave.
Pittsburgh, PA 15232
USA
412-621-5529, FAX 412-621-1522

Jacob's Well OCA
24 Colmar Rd.
Cherry Hill, NJ 08002
USA

Joyous Light OCA MAIL
<Jackson MI>
P.O. Box 185
Grass Lake, MI 49240-0185
USA
517-522-3656, FAX 517-522-5907

Joyous Light OCA
2522 Grey Tower Rd.
Jackson, MI 49201-9120
USA
517-522-3656, FAX 517-522-5907

Kathedra OCA
825 Harrington Rd.
Rockville, MD 20852
USA

Light of Christ PAN
3027 Foxhall Rd. N.W.
Washington, DC 20016
USA

Living Orthodoxy ROR
1180 Orthodox Way
Liberty, TN 37095-9801
USA
615-536-5239

Lumina Lina OCA MAIL
<Jackson MI>
P.O. Box 185
Grass Lake, MI 49240-0185
USA
517-522-3656, FAX 517-522-5907

Lumina Lina OCA
2522 Grey Tower Rd.
Jackson, MI 49201-9120
USA
517-522-3656, FAX 517-522-5907

Nemanjic Institute for Serbo-Byzantine Studies Journal UCU
37323 Hawkins Rd.
Dewdney, BC V0M 1H0
Canada
604-826-9336, FAX 604-820-9758

ONE - Orthodox New England OCA
95 Butterworth Ln.
Southington, CT 06489
USA

One Church PER
158 Stiles St.
Elizabeth, NJ 07208
USA
216-788-0151

One Church PER
727 Miller Ave.
Youngstown, OH 44502
USA
216-788-0151

Orthodox America ROR
P.O. Box 992132
Redding, CA 96099-2132
USA

Orthodox Apologist DHE
HC 65 Box 146a
Riverside, WA 98849-9613
USA

Orthodox Christian Witness AUX
10300 Ashworth Ave. N.
Seattle, WA 98133-9410
USA
206-522-4471, FAX 206-523-0550

Orthodox Church OCA
Route 25A
P.O. Box 675
Syosset, NY 11791
USA
516-922-0550, FAX 516-922-0954

Orthodox Family ROR
P.O. Box 45
Beltsville, MD 20705
USA
301-890-3552

Orthodox Herald PAN
P.O. Box 9
Hunlock Center, PA 18621
USA

Orthodox Home School ROR
P.O. Box 45
Beltsville, MD 20705
USA
301-890-3552

Orthodox Life (English) ROR
P.O. Box 36
Jordanville, NY 13361-0036
USA
315-858-0940, FAX 315-858-0505

Orthodox Light AUX
28 Flintwood Ct.
Willowdale, ON M2J 3P2
CANADA

Orthodox Messenger ROR
75 E. 93rd St.
New York City, NY 10128-1331
USA
212-410-4258

Orthodox North Star OCA
414 Mission Rd.
Kodiak, AK 99615
USA

Orthodox Observer GOA
8 E. 79th St.
New York City, NY 10021
USA
212-628-2590, FAX 212-570-4005

Orthodox Outreach HUS
3011 Roe Dr.
Houston, TX 77087-2409
USA
713-645-0843

Orthodox Path PAN
P.O. Box 2833
Garden Grove, CA 94114
USA

Orthodox People Together Newsletter OPT
P.O. Box 1128
Torrance, CA 90505
USA
310-378-9245

Orthodox Russia ROR
P.O. Box 36
Jordanville, NY 13361-0036
USA
315-858-0940, FAX 315-858-0505

Orthodox Telecommunications PAN
Box 1100
Youngstown, OH 44501-1100
USA
216-750-0505

Orthodox Tradition CYP
P.O. Box 398
Etna, CA 96027-0398
USA

Orthodox Unity PAN
17600 Detroit Ave. #508
Lakewood, OH 44107
USA

Orthodox Voice DHE
P.O. Box 34362
Omaha, NE 68134-0362
USA

Orthodox Voices ROR
P.O. Box 23644
Lexington, KY 40523
USA
606-271-3877

Orthodox Way GOA
27 Teddington Park Ave.
Toronto, ON M4N 2C4
CANADA
416-462-0833; FAX 416-485-5919

Orthodox West OCA
141 E. Foster Rd.
Santa Maria, CA 93456
USA

Orthodox Word VAS
P.O. Box 70
Platina, CA 96076
USA

Othigitria-Guide GOA
4317 Watt
Waco, TX 76710
USA
817-752-4087

Path of Orthodoxy SOC
P.O. Box 36
Leetsdale, PA 15056
USA
412-741-3660, FAX 412-741-9235

Patony PAN
P.O. Box 1269
Johnstown, PA 15907
USA

Pilgrim DHE
P.O. Box 22237
Lincoln, NE 68542-2237
USA
402-476-2676

Pravoslavnaya Put ROR
P.O. Box 36
Jordanville, NY 13361-0036
USA
315-858-0940, FAX 315-858-0505

Pravoslavnaya Rus ROR
P.O. Box 36
Jordanville, NY 13361-0036
USA
315-858-0940, FAX 315-858-0505

Pravoslavnaya Zhizn ROR
P.O. Box 36
Jordanville, NY 13361-0036
USA
315-858-0940, FAX 315-858-0505

Russian Orthodox Journal PAN
10 Downs Dr.
Wilkes-Barre, PA 18705
USA

Russkiy Pastyr ROR
738 27th Ave.
San Francisco, CA 94121
USA

Russky Palomnyk / Russian Pilgrim VAS
P.O. Box 70
Platina, CA 96076
USA

Sacred Art Journal PAN
1157 Crescent Dr.
Painesville, OH 44077
USA

Samaritan PAN
422 E. Penn Run Box 432
Indiana, PA 15701
USA

Solia - The Herald OCA MAIL
<Jackson MI>
P.O. Box 185
Grass Lake, MI 49240-0185
USA
517-522-3656, FAX 517-522-5907

Solia - The Herald OCA
2522 Grey Tower Rd.
Jackson, MI 49201-9120
USA
517-522-3656, FAX 517-522-5907

St. Herman Seminary Star OCA
414 Mission Rd. - Pouch 1
Kodiak, AK 99615
USA

St. Vlaimir's Theological Quarterly OCA
575 Scarsdale Rd.
Crestwood, NY 10707
USA

Struggler AUX
8111 Vaden Dr.
Brentwood, TN 37027-7306
USA
615-377-6477

Torch of Orthodoxy CHR
St. Anthony Orthodox Publications, 3044 N. 27th St.
Phoenix, AZ 85016-7926
USA
602-957-3054, FAX 602-956-4203

Tree of Life VAS
543 Cherokee Ave.
Atlanta, GA 30312
USA

True Vine AUX
P.O. Box 129
Roslindale, MA 02131-0129
USA

Truth PAN
225 Hause Ave.
Pottstown, PA 19464
USA

Ukrainian Orthodox Herald UOA
90-34 139th St.
Jamaica, NY 11435
USA

Vigil OCA MAIL
<Palos Park IL>
605 W. Iowa St.
Oak Park, IL 60302
USA
708-361-1684, FAX 708-923-1706

Vineyard OCA
523 E. Broadway
South Boston, MA 02127
USA

Way GOA
601 S. Central Ave.
Chicago, IL 60644
USA
312-626-5400, FAX 312-626-4814

Word Magazine (Editorial Office) ANT
52 78th St.
Brooklyn, NY 11209
USA
718-748-7940, 201-871-1355 FAX 718-855-3608

Word Magazine (Subscription Office) ANT
358 Mountain Rd.
Englewood, NJ 04631
USA
718-748-7940, 201-871-1355 FAX 718-855-3608

Social Services / Pan-Orthodox Groups

All Saints Center GOA
Raft Island, WA
USA

All Saints Center GOA MAIL
<Raft Island WA>
2402 Belvedere Ave. S.W.
Seattle, WA 98126
USA
206-323-8557

American Orthodox Mission to Russia PAN
c/o K. McCaffery; 1065 Sutter St.
San Francisco, CA 94109
USA
415-931-0866

Archbishop Averky Memorial Fund ROR
P.O. Box 36
Jordanville, NY 13361-0036
USA
315-858-0940

Bilateral Commission of the Antiochian Archdiocese & the OCA PAN
358 Mountain Rd.
Englewood, NJ 07631
USA

Blessed Xenia Memorial Fund ROR
75 E, 93rd St.
New York City, NY 10128
USA
212-662-6472

Central Florida Council of Orthodox Churches PAN
Orlando, FL
USA
407-331-4687

Colorado Clergy Brotherhood PAN
9641 S. Ulster Ct.
Engelwood, CO 80112
USA

Committee of Concerned Orthodox PAN
3 Prestwood Pl.
Winnipeg, MB R3T 4Y9
CANADA

Council of Eastern Orthodox Churches of Central Massachusetts PAN
P.O. Box 604
Maynard, MA 01754
USA
508-877-2989

Council of Eastern Orthodox Youth Leaders of America PAN
,
USA

Council of Orthodox Churches PAN
119 Peachtree Rd.
Cheektowaga, NY 14225
USA

Eastern Orthodox Clergy Association of Youngstown OH PAN
Box 1100
Youngstown, OH 44501-1100
USA
216-750-0505

Eastern Orthodox Foundation PAN
422 E. Penn Run Box 432
Indiana, PA 15701
USA

Education Commission Ukrainian Orthodox League PAN
899 S. Plymouth Ct. #303
Chicago, IL 60605
USA

FROC Mission HOTLINE OCA
6610 Cypress Point Rd.
Alexandria, VA 22312-3126
USA
703-354-3242

Fellowship of Orthodox Churches of Connecticut (FORCC) PAN
39 Pemberton Rd.
Turnbull, CT 06611
USA
203-261-7461, FAX 203-374-5770

Fellowship of St. Philip PAN
P.O. Box 5455
San Diego, CA 92105-5455
USA

Fellowship of the Apostle Silas ANT
Box 1949
Hollywood, CA 90078
USA
818-896-0177

Fr. Dn. Keith Powley, Prison Chaplain ANT
Federal Prison, Stafford AZ
1224 5th Ave.
Stafford, AZ 85546
USA
602-428-5988

Fund for Assistance to the Russian Orthodox Church Outside of Russia ROR
75 E. 93rd St.
New York City, NY 10128-1331
USA
212-534-1601

Fund of St. John of Kronstadt, Inc. ROR
P.O. Box 56
Utica, NY 13502
USA
315-724-2093

Greek Orthodox Counseling and Social Services, Inc. GOA
24 W. Preston St.
Baltimore, MD 21201
USA
301-727-1831

Guadalupe Homes for Children PAN
1470 Cooley Dr.
P.O. Box 848
Colton, CA 92324
USA
909-825-5588, FAX 909-825-8004

HANAC / Archbishop Iakovos Senior Citizen's Center GOA
New York City, NY
USA

Heritage and Learning Center ANT
Rt. 711 N.
P.O. Box 638
Ligonier, PA 15658
USA
412-238-3677, 412-238-9565

Holy Archangels Orthodox Christian Broadcasting Center PAN
3027 Foxhall Rd. N.W.
Washington, DC 20016
USA
202-362-5524

Holy Ascension Cemetery OCA
Rhein, SK S0A 3K0
CANADA
306-783-2153

Holy Ascension Monastery Cemetery OCA MAIL
<Sifton MB>
34 3rd Ave. N.W. #1
Dauphin, MB
CANADA

Holy Ascension Monastery Cemetery OCA
Sifton, MB R0L 1X0
CANADA

Holy Meeting of Joachim & Anne Apostolia GOA
1819 Sealy St.
Galveston, TX 77550
USA
409-762-3283

Holy Mother of God Odigitria of Smolensk BYC
Religious Recreation Center Belair-Miensk
P.O. Box 250
Glen Spey, NY 12737-0250
USA

Holy Resurrection Cemetery OCA
@Ascension Monastery,
5052 S. Dixie Hwy.
Resaca, GA
USA
706-277-9442, FAX 706-277-9443

Holy Trinity Nursing Home PAN
P.O. Box 195
Worcester, MA 01614-0195
USA
508-754-8000

Holy Trinity Russian Orthodox Retreat Center ROR
29110 Holy Trinity Rd.
Round Mountain, CA 96084
USA

House of Mercy PAN
812 N. Alvarado St.
Los Angeles, CA 90026
USA
213-483-6952

Inter-Orthodox Christian Fellowship of New York PAN
175 Lexington Ave.
New York City, NY 10016
USA
212-686-3730

Social Services / Pan-Orthodox Groups

Inter-Orthodox Council of Greater Cleveland PAN
8409 Wainstead Rd.
Parma, OH 44129-4848
USA
216-884-1303

International Orthodox Christian Charities (SCOBA) PAN
711 W. 40th St. Suite 306
Baltimore, MD 21211
USA

Minneapolis Inter-Orthodox Group PAN
4445 Portland Ave. S.
Minneapolis, MN 55407
USA

Moscow Patriarchate Social Sevices PER
8630 Fenton St. #910
Silver Spring, MD 20910
USA

Novo Diveevo Convent ROR
Smith Rd.
Spring Valley, NY 10977
USA
914-356-0425

OCAMPR Ethics Institute PAN
Holy Cross Center, 105 Summit Ct.
Westfield, NJ 07090-2834
USA

OCHAG ROR
451 27th Ave.
San Francisco, CA 94121
USA
415-751-4623

Oklahoma Orthodox Christians for Life PAN
3900 Jones Blvd.
Oklahoma City, OK 73135-2527
USA
405-672-1441, FAX 405-787-6665

Orthodox ActionLine PAN
1-800-225-0235
COLLECT 617-731-3505

Orthodox Benevolent Fund & Society ROR
Box 743
Rye, NH 03870
USA
603-964-5114, Voice/FAX 603-964-5472

Orthodox Broadcasting Commission (SCOBA) PAN
575 Scarsdale Rd.
Crestwood, NY 10707
USA

Orthodox Brotherhood of the Virgin Mary PAN
P.O. Box 1
Elkhorn, WV 24831-0001
USA
304-862-3313

Orthodox Charities Department PAN
Box 1100
Youngstown, OH 44501-1100
USA
216-750-0505

Orthodox Christian Adoption Referral Service OCA
P.O. Box 675
Syosset, NY 11791-0675
USA
516-922-0550

Orthodox Christian Association of Medicine, Psychology, & Religion PAN
P.O. Box 958
Cambridge, MA 02238
USA
617-868-6557

Orthodox Christian Center & Mission PAN
280 New Braintree Rd.
West Brookfield, MA 01585-0287
USA
508-867-7039

Orthodox Christian Centre, Inc. OCA
Box 3512
Ft. Qu'Appelle, SK
CANADA

Orthodox Christian Education Commission (SCOBA) PAN
P.O. Box 174 Centuck Sta.
Yonkers, NY 10710
USA
201-768-7966, 201-768-3146

Orthodox Christian Foundation PAN
P.O. Box 727
Mt. Hermon, CA 95041
USA
408-335-9668, FAX 408-336-8882

Orthodox Christian Laity PAN
4815 N. Lindbergh
St. Louis, MO 63044
USA

Orthodox Christian Library Outreach PAN
285 Alden Ave.
New Haven, CT 06515
USA
203-387-3882

Orthodox Christian Prayer Network PAN
P.O. Box 1165 FDR Station
New York City, NY 10150
USA
212-969-0724, 914-961-6582

Orthodox Christian Women of America PAN
4000 Cleveland Ave.
St. Louis, MO 63110
USA
314-772-6609

Orthodox Christian Women of Montreal PAN
Montreal, PQ
CANADA
514-481-5093

Orthodox Christians for Life PAN
Box 805
Melville, NY 11747
USA

Orthodox Community Outreach Center PAN
574 Pennsylvania St.
Denver, CO 80203
USA
303-871-8060

Orthodox Community Services DHE
217 S. Maple St.
Centralia, IL 62801
USA
618-532-4456

Orthodox Counselling Center PAN
Box 1100
Youngstown, OH 44501-1100
USA
216-750-0505

Orthodox Fellowship of St. Cyprian PAN
#706 - 2350 Dundas St. W.
Toronto, ON M6P 4B1
CANADA

Orthodox Food Center PAN
14 Hammond St.
Worcester, MA 01610-1513
USA
508-799-0040

Orthodox Home for the Aged ROR
14 Alvin St.
Glen Cove, NY 11542
USA
516-671-5316

Orthodox Liturgical Arts Association, Inc. PAN
840 Cabot Ct.
Winter Park, FL 32792-2904
USA
407-677-1360

Orthodox Missions Board & Center (SCOBA) PAN
Box 4319
St. Augustine, FL 32085
USA
904-829-5132

Orthodox Palestine Society ROR
75 E. 93rd St.
New York City, NY 10128-1331
USA
201-325-1442

Orthodox Pastoral Counseling Institute PAN
P.O. Box 10354
Pittsburgh, PA 15234
USA
412-335-9988, 412-381-5522

Orthodox People Together PAN
5045 Eldridge St.
Golden, CO 80403
USA
303-830-0306

Orthodox Social Services CHR
3044 N. 27th St.
Phoenix, AZ 85016-7926
USA
602-957-3054

Orthodox Society of America PAN
429 Forbes Ave. Suite 1616
Pittsburgh, PA 15219
USA

Pan-Orthodox Alliance Romiosini PAN
8012 Querbes
Montreal, PQ H3N 2C1
CANADA
514-273-3954

Pastoral Counseling Associates PAN
Writers' Two
1805 S. Bellaire, Suite 109
Denver, CO 80222
USA
303-692-8006

Patristic Society PAN
206 Sarles Ln.
Pleasantville, NY 10570
USA

Prison Ministry ANT
Arizona State Prison Complex
P.O. Box 629
Florence, AZ 85232
USA
602-868-4011 ext. 5011

Prisoner's Fund - St. Athansius Academy of Orthodox Theology ANT
P.O. Box 606
Ben Lomond, CA 95005
USA

Project Mexico PAN
Tijuana,
MEXICO
714-559-5838

Project Mexico PAN MAIL
<Tijuana MEXICO>
4949 Alton Pkwy.
Irvine, CA 92071
USA
714-559-5838

Raphael House Family Shelter VAS
1065 Sutter St.
San Francisco, CA 94109
USA
415-474-4621, FAX 415-771-4251

Religious Books for Russia, Inc. PAN MAIL
<Sea Cliff NY>
P.O. Box 522
Glen Cove, NY 11542
USA
516-671-7716, 516-671-1011, FAX 516-671-1012

Religious Books for Russia, Inc. PAN
Wentways, Littleworth Ln.
Sea Cliff, NY 11579
USA
516-671-7716, 516-671-1011, FAX 516-671-1012

Resurrection Orthodox Counseling Center GOA
20104 Center St.
Castro Valley, CA 94546
USA
510-653-8220

Russia for Jesus PAN
159-34 Riverside Dr. W. Apt. 2K
New York City, NY 10032-1020
USA
212-927-1015

Russian Orthodox Theological Fund OCA
P.O. Box 36 Bowling Green Sta.
New York City, NY 10274
USA

Russian Womens Home of Mercy of the Holy Virgin's Protection OCA
1232 15th Ave.
San Francisco, CA 94122
USA
415-664-5551, 415-566-5429

SYNDESMOS Youth Group - North American Region PAN
5 Alandale
Norwood, PA 02062
USA
617-769-2443

SYNERGY - Chicago Clergy / Laity PAN
32 Lynn Dr.
Hawthorne Woods, IL 60047
USA

Sclater Cemetery OCA
Minitonas, MB
CANADA

Sclater Cemetery OCA MAIL
<Minitonas MB>
Box 1093
Swan River, MB R0L 1Z0
CANADA

Southern California Orthodox Clergy Council PAN
966 Maryhurst Dr.
Claremont, CA 91711
USA

Spiritual Famine Relief Fund ROR
P.O. Box 992132
Redding, CA 96099-2132
USA

Ss. Cosmas & Damian Adult Home OCA
2099 Forest Ave.
Staten Island, NY 10303-2239
USA
718-720-8800, FAX 718-447-8095

Ss. Peter & Paul Cemetery OCA
Washtao, AB
CANADA

St. Basil Workers Hospital/Food Program PAN
255 Poland Ave.
Struthers, OH 44471
USA
216-755-6959

St. Bridget Youth House & Mission VAS
20 Steiner St.
San Francisco, CA 94117
USA

St. Demetrios the Physician & Healer Hospital Ministry VAS
P.O. Box 919 Lenox Hill Sta.
New York City, NY 10021
USA
212-996-0355

St. Dismas the Penitent Prison Ministry & Mission VAS
543 Cherokee Ave. S.E.
Atlanta, GA 30312
USA

St. Elias Cemetery OCA
Rhein, SK S0A 3K0
CANADA
306-783-2153

St. Elias Retreat Center GOA
121 St. Elias Ln.
Saxonburg, PA 16056
USA
412-352-1533

St. Eugene's Retreat Ctr. OCA
135 Balboa Ave.
P.O. Box 563
Pt. Reyes Station, CA 94956-0563
USA
415-663-1705

St. Herman's House of Hospitality UOA
4410 Franklin Blvd.
Cleveland, OH 44113
USA
216-961-3806

St. Innocent Orphanage PAN
Calle Rocio, Lomas de San Antonio
Rosarito,
MEXICO
714-559-5838

St. Innocent Orphanage PAN MAIL
<Rosarito MEXICO>
4949 Alton Pkwy.
Irvine, CA 92071
USA
714-559-5838

St. John of Damascus Association of Iconographers Iconologists & Architects PAN
1157 Crescent Dr.
Painesville, OH 44077
USA
216-352-0194

St. John of Kronstadt Convalescent Center ROR
4432 James Ave.
P.O. Box 2794
Castro Valley, CA 94546-0794
USA
510-889-7000

St. Macarius the Roman Orthodox Reference Library ROR
1180 Orthodox Way
Liberty, TN 37095-9801
USA

St. Mary Magdalene Retreat House HOC
125 Hartsie Dr.
Waveland, MS 39576
USA
601-467-3723

St. Michael's Home for the Aged / Taxiarchai Chapel GOA
3 Lehman Terrace
Yonkers, NY 10705
USA
914-476-3374

St. Nicholas Memorial Cemetery OCA
Seattle, WA
USA

St. Paisius Velichkofsky Study & Retreat Center VAS
7777 Martinelli Rd.
Forestville, CA 95436
USA

St. Vladimir's Russian Senior Residence ROR
89 Stonehurst Ave.
Ottawa, ON K1Y 4R6
Canada
613-729-0159

Teleios Ministries ANT
P.O. Box 1267
Tavares, FL 32778-1267
USA
904-343-3866

Theotokos House Retreat Center ROR
Rt. 1 - Box 115A
Rochelle, TX 76872
USA
915-463-5538

Tolstoy Foundation ROR
200 Park Ave. S.
New York City, NY 10003
USA
212-677-7770

Tolstoy Foundation Nursing Home ROR
Valley Cottage, NY 10989-0599
USA
914-268-6551

Triple Cities Orthodox Clergy Association PAN
Binghamton, NY
USA

Triple Cities Orthodox Clergy Association PAN
New York City, NY
USA

Ukrainian Orthodox Library UCU
P.O. Box 495
South Bound Brook, NJ 08880
USA
908-356-3017

Ventura / Santa Barbara Orthodox Clergy Association PAN
6778 Pasado Rd.
Goleta, CA 93117
USA

Washington Council of Churches PAN
9370 Mercerwood Dr.
Mercer Island, WA 98040
USA

Washington Inter-Orthodox Group PAN
11523 Gainsborough Rd.
Potomac, MD 20854
USA

Women's Orthodox Ministries & Education Network PAN
1805 S. Bellaire St. Suite 109
Denver, CO 80222
USA
303-692-8006

Yvonne S. Lysack, M.A., Counseling & Education PAN
7-297 Sunnyside Ave.
Ottawa, ON K1S 0R9
Canada
613-730-0242

Military Chaplains

1st Lt. Angelo J. Michaels GOA
419 TFW SS/HC, Hill A.F.B
Ogden, UT 84056-5000
USA

1st Lt. Dean C. Hountalas GOA
76th Div. Training
125 Cottage
Portsmouth, NH 03801-4108
USA

1st Lt. John E. Anderson OCA
Att: ATSC-TD-AC
Ft. Monmouth, NJ 07703
USA

2nd Lt. Paul Schellbach OCA
U.S. Army Chaplain Candidate, Ft. Monmouth NJ
575 Scarsdale Rd.
Crestwood, NY 10707
USA

CDR James D. Moulketis GOA
360 Williams Way
Wyckoff, NJ 07481
USA

CDR Michael Simerick OCA
Office of Chaplain, Frazier Hall, Naval Station
Norfolk, VA 23551
USA
804-444-7361, 804-721-7869

CDR Paul Pyrch OCA
Chaplain Dept. NTS (Code 05)
Great Lakes, IL 60088
USA
708-688-2288, 708-688-2402

CDR Sam J. Kalamaras GOA
9426 Little Rd.
New Port Richey, FL 34654
USA

CDR Theofanis J. Degaltas GOA
PCD (Code 90) Naval Hospital
San Diego, CA 92134
USA
619-725-1223

CPT-P John A. Capariosos GOA
HQ Btty. 2/214 FA, GA Army National Guard
P.O. Box 447
Statesboro, GA 30458-0667
USA

Captain Adam Yonitch, Jr. SOC
3700 LTC-HCSC, Lackland A.F.B.
San Antonio, TX 78236-5000
USA

Captain Edward Michael Macura OCA
Off. of Chaplain DISCOM, 25th ID
Scoffield Brks., HI 96758
USA
808-624-4636

Captain Joseph Gallick OCA
210 N.E. 46th St.
Lawton, OK 73503
USA
405-442-3915, 405-355-7859

Captain Peter A. Baktis OCA
21D/DISCOM 2D Frwd. Supt. Btl. Hovey
APO AP, NY 96224
USA

Captain Theodore J. Shomsky OCA
R.D. 3 Box 31
DuBois, PA 15801
USA
814-371-4416

Col. Gregory H. Pelesh OCA
Personnel / Mate Off. of A.F. Chief of Chaplains
Washington, DC 20332
USA
202-767-1482, 410-672-3229

Fr. Andrew Harrison OCA
24113 Hartland St.
West Hills, CA 91307
USA
818-703-7368

Fr. Anthony Moschonas GOA
Davis-Monthan A.F.B.
1145 E. Ft. Lowell Rd.
Tucson, AZ 85719
USA

Military Chaplains

Fr. Daniel Rohan ANT
910th Airlift Group
Vienna, OH 44473
USA
216-392-1393, 216-750-0505

Fr. David E. Pratt OCA
Off. of the Chaplain 1st Mar. Div. Det.
Twenty-Nine Palms, CA 92278
USA
619-368-5521

Fr. James M. Jadick OCA
R.D. 1 Box 259
Herkimer, NY 13350
USA
315-866-3272

Fr. John Tkachuk OCA
4381 Harvard Ave.
Montreal, PQ
CANADA
514-481-5093

Fr. Mark Karl Kish OCA
Off. of Chaplain Marine Div. FMF
Camp Pendleton, CA 92055
USA

Fr. Milan Sturgis SOC
CHC, USN OCS, Chaplains Office, Mar. Corps Base
Quantico, VA 22134
USA
703-640-2904

Fr. Paul Pantelis GOA
Loring A.F.B.
90 Sanford St.
Bangor, ME 04401
USA

Fr. Peter Carmichael OCA
18 Hunter Dr.
Derry, NH 03038
USA
603-434-8177

Fr. Stephen Ziton ANT
7515 E. 13th @ Broadmoor
Wichita, KS
USA
316-636-4676

LCDR John A. Shaloub ANT
727 Barn St.
Jacksonville, NC 28540
USA

LCDR William J. Bartz GOA
Graduate Theological Union
2400 Ridge Rd.
Berkeley, CA 94709
USA

LTJG Andrew Nelko OCA
Off. of Com. Chap. Marine Corps Base
Camp Lejeune, NC 28542
USA
919-451-2113

Lt. Adam Linton OCA
Rel. Min. Dept. NAS
Memphis (Cd00C00)
Millington, TN 38054
USA
901-873-5341

Lt. Jerome Cwiklinski OCA
17th CGD (DWL)
P.O. Box 25517
Juneau, AK 99802
USA
907-463-2131

Lt. John E. Constantine GOA
604 Village Dr.
Newark, NJ 08873
USA

Lt. Mark Koczak OCA
10787-A Jeanne Ter.
Santee, CA 92071
USA
619-448-5299

Lt. Milan Sturgis OCA
Office of the Chaplain 3rd Mar. Div. FMF
FPO, NY 96602
USA

Lt. Milton Gianulis GOA
573 N. Highland
Millington, TN 38122
USA

Lt. Theodore Boback, Jr. OCA
Chief Resource Mng. Br.
Off. of the Chaplain
Ft. Knox, KY 40121
USA
502-624-5255, 502-942-3408

Major F. Paul Mayernick OCA
50 Spacewing
Falcoln A.F.B., CO 80914
USA

Major Gregory E. Roth OCA
HQ 60AW/HC
Travis A.F.B., CA 94535
USA
707-424-2651

Major H. Gregory Dudash OCA
85 FW/HC
Luke A.F.B., AZ 85390-5000
USA
602-856-6211, 602-412-0567

Major John N. Kondratick OCA
LTC-HCFC Chapel 8
1950 Barnes Rd.
Lackland A.F.B., TX 78236
USA
210-655-5638

Major John W. Stefero OCA
CPD/HCX Bldg. 1404
525 Chenault Cir.
Maxwell A.F.B., AL 36112
USA
205-953-2821

Major Ken James Stavresky OCA
55 WG/HC
301 Lincoln Hwy.
Offutt A.F.B., NE 68113
USA

Major Nicholas A. Czaruk OCA
2205 Stride Ln.
Fayetteville, NC 28304
USA
910-433-2429

Major Peter Telencio OCA
HQ Berlin Brigade Off. of Chap. #1000
APO, NY 09742
USA

Campus Fellowships

Auburn University
Orthodox Campus Fellowship
Auburn, AL
USA
205-263-1366

BOSTON AREA
Fellowship of Orthodox Christian University Students
Boston, MA
USA
617-547-1234

Boston College
Orthodox Campus Fellowship
Chestnut Hill, MA
USA
617-277-4742, 617-630-9606

Boston University
Orthodox Campus Fellowship
Boston, MA
USA
617-277-4742, 617-730-9515

Bradley University
Orthodox Campus Fellowship
Peoria, IL
USA
309-682-5824

Columbia University
Orthodox Campus Fellowship
New York City, NY
USA
212-927-0596, 212-854-1744

Duke University
Orthodox Campus Fellowship
Durham, NC
USA
919-682-1414, 919-493-7403

Harvard University
Orthodox Campus Fellowship
Cambridge, MA
USA
617-547-1234, 617-493-2359

Idaho State University
Orthodox Campus Fellowship
Pocatello, ID
USA
208-232-5519, 208-236-2663

Indiana University of Pennsylvania
Orthodox Campus Fellowship
Indiana, PA
USA

Kansas State University
Orthodox Campus Fellowship
1133 Village Dr.
Manhattan, KS 66502
USA
913-776-6797

Kent State University
Orthodox Campus Fellowship
Kent, OH
USA
216-434-4521

Massachusetts Institute of Technology
Orthodox Campus Fellowship
Cambridge, MA
USA
617-547-1234, 617-225-7569

North Texas State University
Orthodox Campus Fellowship
Denten, TX
USA
214-991-1166

Northeastern University
Orthodox Campus Fellowship
Boston, MA
USA
617-277-4742, 617-729-9535

Ohio State University
Orthodox Campus Fellowship
Columbus, OH
USA
614-224-9020, 614-421-2355

Pennsylvania State University
Orthodox Campus Fellowship
State College, PA
USA

Princeton University
Orthodox Campus Fellowship / Transfiguration Chapel
Murray Dodge Hall
Princeton, NJ 08540
USA
609-924-7368, 609-258-7537

Slippery Rock University
Orthodox Campus Fellowship
Slippery Rock, PA
USA
412-282-6868, 412-287-8597

Southern Methodist University
Orthodox Campus Fellowship
Dallas, TX
USA
214-991-1166

Texas A & M
Orthodox Campus Fellowship
College Station, TX
USA
713-526-5377

Tufts University
Orthodox Campus Fellowship
Medford, MA
USA
617-277-4742, 617-629-3920

University of Berkeley
Orthodox Campus Fellowship
Berkeley, CA
USA
510-649-2450

University of Chicago
Orthodox Campus Fellowship
Chicago, IL
USA
708-974-3400, 312-667-0038

University of Georgia
Eastern Orthodox Christian Fellowship
475 Baldwin St. #48
Athens, GA 30605
USA
813-724-9140

University of Illinois
Eastern Orthodox Christian Fellowship
2010 Three Hierarchs Ct.
Champaign-Urbana, IL 61820
USA
217-352-3452

University of Iowa
Orthodox Campus Fellowship
Iowa City, IA
USA
319-363-1559, 319-363-8361, 319-364-5460

University of Kansas
Orthodox Campus Fellowship
1318 Louisiana
Lawrence, KS 66044
USA
913-271-6411

University of Maryland
Orthodox Campus Fellowship
College Park, MD
USA
410-263-2550

University of Michigan
Orthodox Campus Fellowship
Ann Arbor, MI
USA
313-459-8473, 313-781-9341

University of Minnesota
Orthodox Campus Fellowship
Minneapolis, MN
USA
612-781-7667

University of Minnesota - Duluth
Orthodox Campus Fellowship
Duluth, MN
USA

University of Oklahoma
Orthodox Campus Fellowship
Norman, OK
USA
918-584-7300, 918-252-2477, 405-372-1422

University of Oregon
Orthodox Campus Fellowship
Eugene, OR
USA
503-683-3519

University of Ottawa
Orthodox Campus Ministry
P.O. Box 450, Station A
Ottawa, ON K1N 6N5
CANADA
613-564-5741, FAX 613-564-5683

University of Toronto
Orthodox Campus Fellowship
#706 - 2350 Dundas St. W.
Toronto, ON M6P 4B1
CANADA

University of Wisconsin - Madison
Orthodox Campus Fellowship
Madison, OR
USA
414-544-6661, 608-251-6484

Vanderbilt University
Orthodox Campus Fellowship
Nashville, TN
USA
615-333-1047

Virginia Tech
Orthodox Campus Fellowship
Blacksburg, VA
USA
703-362-3601

Washburn University
Orthodox Campus Fellowship
Topeka, KS
USA
913-271-6441

Washington & Jefferson College
Orthodox Campus Fellowship
Washington, PA
USA
412-745-5205

Yale University
Orthodox Campus Fellowship
New Haven, CT
USA
203-387-3882

Youth Camps and Shrines

Annunciation Cathedral Camp GOA
Yosemite, CA
USA
415-861-1296

Antiochian Village ANT
R.D. # 1 Box 307
Bolivar, PA 15923-9664
USA
412-238-3677

Archangels Pan-Orthodox Camp GOA
Prescott, AZ
USA
602-991-3009

Ascension Cathedral Camp GOA
Ravencliff, CA
USA
510-531-0057

Burial Site of St. Herman of Alaska OCA
Spruce Island - Monk's Lagoon, AK
USA

Camp Angelos GOA
Portland, OR
USA
503-234-0468

Camp Fenari GOA MAIL
<Williamsby WI>
2501 S. Wolf Rd.
Westchester, IL 60154
USA
708-562-2744

Camp Fenari GOA
Williamsbay, WI
USA

Camp Nazareth CRC
339 Pew Rd.
Mercer, PA 16137
USA
412-662-4840, FAX 412-662-4840

Camp St. Nicholas ANT
11770 Frontier Rd.
HC 2 Box 9994
Frazier Park, CA 93225
USA
805-245-3571, FAX 805-245-0710

Camp Vatra OCA
Jackson, MI
USA
313-562-1521

Chesapeake Youth Camp GOA
Glyndon, MD
USA
410-995-0353

Diocese of Boston Summer Camp GOA
162 Goddard Ave.
Brookline, MA 02146
USA
617-277-4742

Diocese of Detroit Summer Camp GOA MAIL
<Rose City MI>
17400 2nd Blvd.
Detroit, MI 48203
USA
313-868-1844

Diocese of Detroit Summer Camp GOA
Rose City, MI
USA

Diocese of Pittsburg Summer Camp GOA MAIL
<Mercer / Ligonier PA>
5201 Ellsworth Ave.
Pittsburgh, PA 15232
USA
412-621-5529

Eastern Orthodox Youth Camp GOA
12001 Wornall Rd.
Kansas City, MO 64145
USA
816-942-9100

Ft. Ross Shrine / Holy Trinity Chapel OCA
Ft. Ross, CA
USA

Good Shepherd Camp GOA
St. Basil Academy
Garrison, NY
USA
908-233-8533

Holy Trinity Camp GOA
4070 Park Ave.
Bridgeport, CT 06604
USA
203-374-5561

Holy Trinity Camp GOA
Henlopen Lewes, DE
USA

Holy Trinity Camp GOA MAIL
<Henlopen Lewes DE>
808 N. Broom St.
Wilmington, DE 19806
USA
302-654-4446

Youth Camps and Shrines

Minnesota Eastern Orthodox Camp GOA
Finland, MN
USA
612-825-9595

Minnesota Eastern Orthodox Camp GOA MAIL
<Finland MN>
3450 Irving Ave. S.
Minneapolis, MN 55408
USA
612-825-9595

Orthodox Christian Summer Camp GOA
Yorktown, TX
USA
713-526-5377

Patriarch Athenagoras Center GOA
Cheyenne, WY
USA
307-638-3322

Raft Island Camp GOA
Raft Island, WA
USA
206-244-8511

Relics of St. Herman of Alaska OCA
Holy Resurrection Church;
410 Mission Rd.
Kodiak, AK 99615
USA

Russian Bishop's House PAN
Sitka, AK
USA

St. Andrew's Camp OCA
Jewell, NY 13042
USA
315-675-8409

St. Basil Camp GOA
Garrison, NY
USA
212-570-3534

St. George Great Martyr (summer camp) ROR MAIL
<New Pavlosk NY>
95 Elm St.
Elmwood Park, NJ 07407
USA
518-883-8585

St. George Great Martyr (summer camp) ROR
New Pavlovsk, NY
USA
518-883-8585

St. Herman's Camp OCA
Woody Island, AK
USA
907-486-3524

St. Mary Camp GOA
McGregor, MN
USA
612-825-9595

St. Nicholas Ranch & Retreat Ctr. GOA
38526 Dunlap Rd.
P.O. Box 400
Dunlap, CA 93621-0400
USA
209-338-2103

St. Photios National Shrine GOA
41 St. George St.
P.O. Box 1960
St. Augustine, FL 32085-1960
USA
904-829-8205

St. Sava Children's Camp SOC
R.D. 1 Box 247
Shadeland, PA 16435
USA
814-587-2627

St. Sava Monastery Camp SOC
32400 N. Milwaukee Ave.
P.O. Box 519
Libertyville, IL 60048
USA
708-362-1760, 708-367-9801

St. Silas Camp GOA
7220 Granby St.
Norfolk, VA 23505
USA
804-355-3687

St. Sophia Camp GOA
1324 S. Normandie Ave.
Los Angeles, CA 90006
USA
213-737-2424

St. Stephen Camp GOA
Aiken, SC
USA
404-633-5870

St. Tikhon's Camp OCA
South Canaan, PA 18459
USA
717-937-4411

St. Vladimir Chapel &
Youth Camp OCA
Ohagamuit, AK
USA

Alphabetical Index of Parishes & Institutions

Alphabetical Index of Institutions

Alphabetical Index of Institutions

Holy Cross, GOA, Macon, GA, USA
Holy Cross, RMA, Malin, AB, Canada
Holy Cross, OCA, Medford, NJ, USA
Holy Cross, RMA, Omaha, NE, USA
Holy Cross, ANT, Palmdale, CA, USA
Holy Cross, ANT, Pittsburg, CA, USA
Holy Cross, GOA, Pittsburgh, PA, USA
Holy Cross, ANT, Pleasant Hills, CA, USA
Holy Cross, UIU, Post Falls, ID, USA
Holy Cross, UOD, Richmond, ME, USA
Holy Cross, GOA, Stroudsburg, PA, USA
Holy Cross, UCU, Utica, NY, USA
Holy Cross, GOA, Whitestone, NY, USA
Holy Cross, GOA, Wichita Falls, TX, USA
Holy Cross, GOA, Windsor, ON, Canada
Holy Cross, UOC, Winnepegosis, MB, Canada
Holy Cross, ANT, Yakima, WA, USA
Holy Cross Monastery, CRC, Beallesville, MD, USA
Holy Cross Parochial School, GOA, Brooklyn, NY, USA
Holy Cross Skete, VAS, West Roxbury, MA, USA
Holy Cross hermitage, ROR, House Springs, MO, USA
Holy Cross-Ss. Constantine & Helen, GOA, Huntsville, AL, USA
Holy Cross-St. Nektarios, GOA, Orillia, ON, Canada
Holy Dormition, PER, Benld, IL, USA
Holy Dormition, ROR, Lethbridge, AB, Canada
Holy Dormition, ROR, McKeesport, PA, USA
Holy Dormition of the Theotokos, CHR, Clearwater, FL, USA
Holy Enlighteners, AUX, Sioux Falls, SD, USA
Holy Epiphany, VAS, Pawcatuck, CT, USA
Holy Epiphany, ROR, Roslindale, MA, USA
Holy Fathers, ROR, New York City, NY, USA
Holy Fathers, UOC, Wildwood, AB, Canada
Holy Ghost, OCA, Ambridge, PA, USA
Holy Ghost, UOC, Boyle, AB, Canada
Holy Ghost, UOC, Brandon, MB, Canada
Holy Ghost, OCA, Bridgeport, CT, USA
Holy Ghost, BEC, Cincinnati, OH, USA
Holy Ghost, UCU, Coatesville, PA, USA
Holy Ghost, CRC, East Chicago, IN, USA
Holy Ghost, UOC, Glendon, AB, Canada
Holy Ghost, UOC, Goodeve, SK, Canada
Holy Ghost, UOC, Insinger, SK, Canada
Holy Ghost, UOC, Ituna, SK, Canada
Holy Ghost, UOC, Kindersley, SK, Canada
Holy Ghost, CRC, Manville, NJ, USA
Holy Ghost, UOC, Mazeppa, SK, Canada
Holy Ghost, UOC, Petlura, MB, Canada
Holy Ghost, CRC, Phoenixville, PA, USA
Holy Ghost, UOC, Red Water, AB, Canada
Holy Ghost, UOC, Regina, SK, Canada
Holy Ghost, UOC, Saskatoon, SK, Canada
Holy Ghost, UOC, Shortdale, MB, Canada
Holy Ghost, UCU, Slickville, PA, USA
Holy Ghost, UOC, Smoky Lake, AB, Canada
Holy Ghost, UOC, Smuts, SK, Canada
Holy Ghost, ROR, Sterling Heights, MI, USA
Holy Ghost, UOC, Stry, AB, Canada
Holy Ghost, UOC, Tolstoi, MB, Canada
Holy Ghost, UOC, Whitebeach, SK, Canada
Holy Ghost, UOC, Whitkow, SK, Canada
Holy Ghost, OCA, Youngstown, OH, USA
Holy Innocents, HOC, Harahan, LA, USA
Holy Meeting of Joachim & Anne Apostolia, GOA, Galveston, TX, USA
Holy Mother of God, GOA, Tallahassee, FL, USA
Holy Mother of God 'The Life-Giving Fountain' Monastery, CRC, Woodstock Valley, CT, USA
Holy Mother of God Odigitria of Smolensk, BYC, Glen Spey, NY, USA
Holy Myrrhbearing Women, OCA, West Sacramento, CA, USA
Holy Nativity, OCA, Chicago, IL, USA
Holy Nativity, UCU, Dewdney, BC, Canada
Holy Nativity, UCU, Kelso, WA, USA
Holy Nativity, VAS, South Portland, ME, USA
Holy Nativity Convent, AUX, Brookline, MA, USA
Holy Nativity Convent, GOA, Saxonburg, PA, USA
Holy Protection, GMA, Bear River, NS, Canada
Holy Protection, AUX, North Tonawanda, NY, USA
Holy Protection, GMA, Roslindale, MA, USA
Holy Protection Cathedral, ROR, Des Plaines, IL, USA
Holy Resurrection, OCA, Alden Station, PA, USA
Holy Resurrection, OCA, Aleknagik, AK, USA
Holy Resurrection, VAS, Allston, MA, USA
Holy Resurrection, OCA, Belkofsky, AK, USA
Holy Resurrection, OCA, Belle Vernon, PA, USA
Holy Resurrection, OCA, Berlin, NH, USA
Holy Resurrection, PCN, Boyle, AB, Canada
Holy Resurrection, NGM, Chicago, IL, USA
Holy Resurrection, SOC, Chicago, IL, USA
Holy Resurrection, OCA, Claremont, NH, USA
Holy Resurrection, ROR, Cleveland, OH, USA
Holy Resurrection, OCA, Clinton, MS, USA
Holy Resurrection, OCA, Forest Hills, PA, USA
Holy Resurrection, ANT, Gary, IN, USA
Holy Resurrection, RMA, Hamilton, ON, Canada
Holy Resurrection, GOA, Hilton Head, SC, USA
Holy Resurrection, ANT, Hobart, IN, USA
Holy Resurrection, VAS, Kansas City, MO, USA
Holy Resurrection, OCA, Kodiak, AK, USA
Holy Resurrection, NGM, Lebanon, PA, USA
Holy Resurrection, AUX, Norcross, GA, USA
Holy Resurrection, OCA, Oakland, CA, USA
Holy Resurrection, OCA, Palatine, IL, USA
Holy Resurrection, OCC, Petion Ville, , Haiti
Holy Resurrection, CRC, Potomac, MD, USA
Holy Resurrection, ROR, Santa Barbara, CA, USA
Holy Resurrection, OCA, Saskatoon, SK, Canada
Holy Resurrection, OCA, Sifton, MB, Canada
Holy Resurrection, SOC, Steubenville, OH, USA
Holy Resurrection, ROR, Toronto, ON, Canada
Holy Resurrection, ANT, Tucson, AZ, USA
Holy Resurrection, OCA, Vancouver, BC, Canada
Holy Resurrection, OCA, Warren, OH, USA
Holy Resurrection, OCA, Wayne, NJ, USA
Holy Resurrection, OCA, West Brownsville, PA, USA
Holy Resurrection, ROR, Winnipeg, MB, Canada
Holy Resurrection, AUX, Worcester, MA, USA
Holy Resurrection Cathedral, OCA, Wilkes-Barre, PA, USA
Holy Resurrection Cemetery, OCA, Resaca, GA, USA
Holy Royal Martyrs, VAS, Albuquerque, NM, USA
Holy Sepulchre, VAS, Palm Harbor, FL, USA
Holy Spirit, BAM, East Detroit, MI, USA
Holy Spirit, ANT, Huntington, WV, USA
Holy Spirit, OCA, Venice, FL, USA
Holy Spirit, OCA, Vernon, NJ, USA
Holy Spirit - Paraclete, SGP, Williams, OR, USA
Holy Spirit Chapel, OCA, Massilon, OH, USA
Holy Spirit Community, UIU, San Framcisco, CA, USA
Holy Taxiarchai-St Haralambos, GOA, Niles, IL, USA
Holy Theotokos, VAS, Odessa, TX, USA
Holy Theotokos, VAS, San Francisco, CA, USA
Holy Theotokos of Vladimir, ROR, St. Petersburg, FL, USA
Holy Transfiguartion, UOC, Agassiz, BC, Canada
Holy Transfiguration, GOA, Anchorage, AK, USA

Alphabetical Index of Institutions

Changes/Corrections

Willits CA 95490
St. John the Almsgiver ROR
Box 302 (Mailing Address)
24200 Redwood Highway North
(707) 459-5424

Southhampton NJ 08088
Orthodox Church of the Carribean AMC
c/o 23 Dorchester Dr.

Southhampton NJ 08088
Orthodox Church of Cuba AMC
Sts. Constantine & Helena Church
c/o 23 Dorchester Dr.
Southampton NJ 08088

Additions

Autonomous Metropolitanate of Western Europe and Canada of the Ukrainian Orthodox Patriarchate of Kiev UOP J
His Beatitude Metropolitan Evloghios
Via San Gregorio, 5
Milan, Italy
Tel: 2046996

CANADA
Archdiocese of Canada UOP
37323 Hawkins Rd.
Dewdney BC V0M 1H0
Archbishop Lazar (Puhalo)

Langley BC
St. Nicholas UOP

Chilliwack BC
St. Tikhon UOP

Vancouver BC
St. Michael the Archang
UOP

Dewdney BC
Theotokos 'Joy of Cana
UOP

Edmonton BC
St. Michael the Archang
UOP

Vancouver BC
Descent of the Holy Spi
Mission UOP

Calgary AL
All Saints Mission UOP

USA
Portland OR
Kurkaya Parish UOP

Fresno CA
St. Moses the Black UC

Bellingham WA
Holy Spirit UOP

Kelso WA
Nativity of Christ UOP

Billings MT
St. Basil of Ostrog UOP

Lakewood OH 44107
St. Panteleimon UOP
2018 Dowd Ave.

eek Orthodox Patriarchate of Jerusalem
R J
). Box 19632
rusalem 91190
RAEL
2-2-280683

n Francisco CA 94127
George JER
9 San Fernando Way
Ocean Avenue
15) 334-2234

hnert Park CA
. George JER
87 Snyder Lane
15) 334-2234

urch of the True (Old Calendar) Orthodox
ristians of Greece & the Diaspora
ynod of Archbishop Joachim) JOA J
ellenic Orthodox Exarchate of
rth & South America)
merican Exarchate) His Eminence
etropolitan Germanos
44 Howard Ave.
eveland OH 44113 USA
16) 771-8027

rishes & Missions in the USA

chigan
azer 48026
. Phanourios Cathedral JOA
Mile & Utica Rd.
13) 294-4060

y City 48706
. Nectarios Chapel JOA
1117 Fraser St.
(517) 892-2835

Ohio
Cleveland 44113
St. Nectarios & St. Spyridon
Chapel JOA
1544 Howard Ave.
(216) 7781-8027

Toledo 43613
St. Michael the Archangel
1828 Talbot
(419) 474-7484

Tennessee
Bartlett 38133
St. George JOA
6984 Hwy. 70
Barlett TN 38133
(901) 388-5910

United American Orthodox
Church UAO G
Bishop David
Rt 3 Box 31
Lake Maurer Rd.
Excelsior Springs MO 64024

Excelsior Springs 64024
MO
St. Innocent UAO
552 S. Kansas City Ave.
(816) 630-1503

Monasteries
Saints Mary and Martha
House OCA
931 N. Lucas St.

West Columbia SC 29169
(803) 926-8744; (803) 926-7176

Holy Monastery & Shrine of St. Nectarios JOA
1544 Howard Ave.
Cleveland OH 44113
(216) 771-8027

Monastery of the Dormition of the
Holy Theotokos ROR
RR 1 Box 192
Preston Hollow NY 12469
(518) 239-4650

Monastery of All Saints of North America UOP
37323 Hawkins Rd.
Vancouver BC V0M 1H0
CANADA

Holy Transfiguration Skete UOP
North Edmonton Alberta
CANADA

Monastery of St. Anthony UAO
Rt. 3 Box 31 Lake Maurer Rd.
Excelsior Springs MO 64024

Others

St. Antony of Kiev Seminary UOP
37323 Hawkins Rd.
Vancouver BC V0M 1H0
CANADA

St. Theophan the Recluse Society
of America PAN
Box 1573
Forestville CA 95436

St. George Mission-BAM
830 West Bonita Ave.
Clairmont CA. 91711

Deletions
St. James ROR
Cincinatti OH

Change
St. Ignatius of Antioch
Virginia Beach VA to
St. Ignatius of Antioch RO

ORDER FORM

DIRECTORY OF ORTHODOX PARISHES & INSTITUTIONS IN NORTH AMERICA, 1994 EDITION (ISBN NO. 1-879038-16-1)

Complete the order form below to assure you are one of the first to obtain this rich and unique resource. SEND $8.95 NOW to save shipping costs (20% Discount for orders of 5 or more). Otherwise, you can be billed (shipping/handling charges of $1.00 for 1st copy and .50 each additional copy in same order).

This 1994 edition is dedicated to the Mission to Alaska in 1794, exactly 200 years ago, which presented the Holy *Orthodox* Catholic and Apostolic Church to the North American Continent. Today, over 3000 parishes and institutions exist, all part of the legacy of the eight missionaries who sailed into Kodiak Harbor in September, 1794. ALL are included in this Directory.

The Directory will continue to be a most valuable resource for years. Contact us for library, trade and store discounts. Also for computer disc of complete directory, address labels, etc.

****

Name______________________________________

Address____________________________________

City/State(Province)/ZIP(Code)_________________

Phone/FAX_________________________________

Quantity__________ Check Enclosed__________(made out to OPT) Bill Us______________

Mail order to: OPT, Box 1128, Torrance, California 90505-0128. Tel./FAX: (800) 747-9245.

Supporters and Advertisers

Orthodox Peace Fellowship

of the Protection of the Mother of God

Kanisstraat 5
1811 GJ Alkmaar
Holland

tel (+31.72) 11.25.45
fax (+31.72) 15.41.80

It is certainly a finer and more wonderful thing to change the mind of enemies to another way of thinking than to kill them . . . The mystery [of the Eucharist] requires that we should be innocent not only of violence but of all enmity, however slight, for it is the mystery of peace.

—Saint John Chrysostom

Occasional Paper is sent to members and supporters of the Orthodox Peace Fellowship.

Editors: Jim and Nancy Forest

Membership is open to any Orthodox Christian who accepts the principles of the Orthodox Peace Fellowship. A membership folder is available on request.

Contributions can be sent to the Orthodox Peace Fellowship account with the ABN Bank in the Netherlands (56.35.21.260) or directly to the OPF. US supporters can send checks to the Fellowship of Reconciliation (Box 271, Nyack, NY 10960), indicating the gift is for the Orthodox Peace Fellowship.

The OPF is affiliated with the Fellowship of Reconciliation/ USA (Box 271, Nyack, NY 10960) and the International Fellowship of Reconciliation, (Spoorstraat 38, 1815 BK Alkmaar, The Netherlands).

OPF/USA address:
Mariquita Platov, Rt 1, Box 4, Tannersville, NY 12485 USA

HOLY GOSPEL
Gospel with partial enamel, icons and stones
10½" X 13½"
CHALICE SETS - 5 pieces
Consist of Chalice with Sterling Silver cup, matching Paten, star cover, lance, spoon and are goldplated
B. Ht. 10½", Cup dia. 3¾"
C. Ht. 12¼", Cup dia. 3¾"
C
oly Bread Bowl -
oldplated with liner Ht.
0", dia. 15"
D. Holy Mystery Table
Size 33" Ht. X 34" lgt. X 23½" wd.
spital Communion Kit
dplated 1½" X 3" X 7"
B. Icon Stand - Open 17" X 17" X 54

ST. LUKE'S
ORTHODOX CHURCH

35 ANNIVERSARY

Celebrating 35 Years as a Pan-Orthodox Parish
of the
Antiochian Orthodox Christian Archdiocese

1959 - 1994

SAINT LUKE'S ORTHODOX CHURCH

Archpriest Gabriel M. Ashie, Pastor
13261 Dunklee Avenue
Garden Grove California 92640
(714) 971-2244 / FAX (714) 971-2245

THE EXPLANATION OF THE HOLY GOSPEL ACCORDING TO ST. MATTHEW

Blessed Theophylact

Translated by Fr. Christopher Stade

0-9635183-1-3 259 pages Paper $12.00

THE EXPLANATION OF THE HOLY GOSPEL ACCORDING TO ST. MARK

0-9635183-3-X 144 pages Paper $12.00

For the first time in English! Bl. Theophylact's Explanation of the New Testament has been standard among European Orthodox for 900 years. It is a digest of all the Holy Fathers' teaching on the Gospels. The comprehensiveness, patristic authority, and the simplicity of this great work makes it valuable to any Christian in understanding the meaning of the Gospels.

These are much needed for Orthodox Christians in New Testament studies. **Bishop Hilarion, Manhattan NY**

An invaluable contribution to English-speaking Orthodox...The material is superb, inspiring and lofty, and the translator has rendered the original in English which does it creditt. **Bishop Chrysostomos, Etna CA**

PREFERRING CHRIST: *A DEVOTIONAL COMMENTARY ON THE RULE OF ST. BENEDICT*

Norvene Vest, OBLATE OSB

0-940147-14-9 190 pages Paper $15.95

The Rule has influenced Christianity and Civilization for 1500 years. Here is the monastic spirit in its intricacy and simplicity, for all who journey to God. The 73 sections of the book include Fr. Luke's new and complete translation of the Rule, authoritative and accessible Commentary, and Reflections on how the Rule may be applied to contemporary living: "Every element of our ordinary day is potentially holy." *Preferring Christ* is used in formation programs at many convents and monasteries.

I much appreciate the sense of the presence of the sacramental in the midst of the ordinary. I look forward to recommending the book to others. **Rt. Rev. Fred Borsch, Episcopal Bishop of Los Angeles**

THESE AND MANY OTHER FINE RELIGIOUS BOOKS ARE AVAILABLE FROM SOURCE BOOKS P.O. Box 794 Trabuco Canyon CA 92678 Phone/Fax (714) 858-1420

THEOTOKOS HOUSE

Theotokos House
Route 1 Box 115A
Rochelle, Texas 76872
Voice or FAX 915 - 463-5538

We are an Apostolate dedicated to the Mother of God. We are pilgrims who have answered her call to prayer, fasting and a deeper devotion to Christ, and a return to God-centered lives. We are a family in the Orthodox Church dedicated to loving and serving Christ in one another and in all men and women. Theotokos House is available for anyone who wants to live the gospel of love in community in response to God's call - for whatever time. Weekend visitors are most welcome. We mount and sell icons and do custom icon mounting at reasonable prices. Call or write for information.

We are located in the village of Mercury, Texas, one mile off Hwy. 377 and five miles south of the Colorado River, between Brownwood and Brady. Mercury is the geographic center of Texas, deep in the heart of Texas, and deep in the heart of God.

Nikodemos Orthodox Publication Society

ORTHODOX AMERICA

"Unless a man be born again . . ."

A newspaper-format journal

FEATURES: ***Spiritual Heroes of the 20th century, Orthodox missions, ancient and contemporary texts on spiritual life, Lives of Saints, contemporary issues, scriptural commentary, book reviews, and more!***

Send for FREE sample copy, or subscribe today —for yourself, your church or local library

Subscriptions: $8/yr (8 issues)
Churches, clergy, students, libraries: $6
30% discount on 5 or more copies to one address
Outside US, please inquire.

BOOKS

New!

Saint John of Shanghai & San Francisco —Apostle, Ascetic, Archpastor and Wonderworker of the Latter Times. 250 pp., illus. (available July 1994)

New!

Listen, Prison! by Zoya Khrahmalnikova. An Orthodox convert and former prisoner of conscience shares her reflections on her spiritual journey and the dangers Christianity faces from those who reject its maximalism and seek to adapt it to the world. 133 pp., paper—$6.95.

Grand Duchess Elizabeth of Russia by Lubov Millar. The most extensive biography to date of an extraordinary spiritual heroine and convert to Orthodoxy. 288 pp., illus., hdcv—$15.00

P. O. Box 992132-F, Redding, California 96099-2132

Holy Trinity-Holy Cross
Greek Orthodox Cathedral
307 South 19th Street
Birmingham, Alabama 35233
(205)716-3080
